**Refiguring**

**ENGLISH STUDIES**

Refiguring English Studies provides a forum for scholarship on English Studies as a discipline, a profession, and a vocation. To that end, the series publishes historical work that considers the ways in which English Studies has constructed itself and its objects of study; investigations of the relationships among its constituent parts as conceived in both disciplinary and institutional terms; and examinations of the role the discipline has played or should play in the larger society and public policy. In addition, the series seeks to feature studies that, by their form or focus, challenge our notions about how the written "work" of English can or should be done and to feature writings that represent the professional lives of the discipline's members in both traditional and nontraditional settings. The series also includes scholarship that considers the discipline's possible futures or that draws upon work in other disciplines to shed light on developments in English Studies.

**Volumes in the Series**

David B. Downing, editor, *Changing Classroom Practices: Resources for Literary and Cultural Studies* (1994)

Jed Rasula, *The American Poetry Wax Museum: Reality Effects, 1940–1990* (1995)

James A. Berlin, *Rhetorics, Poetics, and Cultures: Refiguring College English Studies* (1996)

Robin Varnum, *Fencing with Words: A History of Writing Instruction at Amherst College during the Era of Theodore Baird, 1938–1966* (1996)

Jane Maher, *Mina P. Shaughnessy: Her Life and Work* (1997)

Michael Blitz and C. Mark Hurlbert, *Letters for the Living: Teaching Writing in a Violent Age* (1998)

Bruce Horner and Min-Zhan Lu, *Representing the "Other": Basic Writers and the Teaching of Basic Writing* (1999)

# Refiguring the Ph.D. in English Studies

## Writing, Doctoral Education, and the Fusion-Based Curriculum

### STEPHEN M. NORTH
*University at Albany, State University of New York*

with Barbara A. Chepaitis, David Coogan, Lâle Davidson,
Ron MacLean, Cindy L. Parrish, Jonathan Post, and Beth Weatherby

National Council of Teachers of English
1111 W. Kenyon Road, Urbana, Illinois 61801-1096

Manuscript Editor: Bonny Graham
Production Editor: Kurt Austin
Interior Design: Jenny Jensen Greenleaf
Cover Design: Evelyn C. Shapiro

NCTE Stock Number: 39779-3050

It is the policy of NCTE in its journals and other publications to provide a forum for the open discussion of ideas concerning the content and the teaching of English and the language arts. Publicity accorded to any particular point of view does not imply endorsement by the Executive Committee, the Board of Directors, or the membership at large, except in announcements of policy, where such endorsement is clearly specified.

**Library of Congress Cataloging-in-Publication Data**

North, Stephen M.
    Refiguring the Ph.D. in English studies: writing, doctoral education, and the fusion-based curriculum/Stephen M. North; with Barbara Chepaitis . . . [et al.].
        p.  cm.—(Refiguring English studies)
    Includes bibliographical references and index.
    ISBN 0-8141-3977-9 (pbk.: alk. paper)
    1. English philology—Study and teaching (Graduate)—New York (State)—Albany. 2. State University of New York at Albany—Graduate work. I. Chepaitis, Barbara. II. Title. III. Series.
PE69.A47.N67  1999
820'.71'174743—dc21
                                                                99-051595

*To SUNY–Albany's graduate students, past and present: thanks for showing the way.*

# CONTENTS

Contents

# PREFACE

The idea for this book dates back to the summer of 1992. At the time, all eight of the people listed on the title page were involved with the English Department at SUNY Albany—one as a faculty member, and the other seven as graduate students at various stages in the program. All of us were also excited by our experience with the department's new doctoral curriculum, and in particular by the possibilities it seemed to present to us as writers. So we began a series of meetings aimed at determining how best to go public, as it were: how to explain those possibilities, and convey that excitement, to the larger field.

As things turned out—and despite some promising early drafts—the project we envisioned never fully got off the ground. This was partly a conceptual problem, in that we were unable at the time to explain that curricular promise in any sustained, systematic way. But it was also, and rather more simply, a logistical matter: all of us had other obligations, the graduate students in particular facing the far more immediate demands of coursework, examinations, and dissertations. In short, we all found ourselves with more than enough to do either in mounting or surviving the new curriculum, let alone completing a book that sought to explain it.

In the years since, however, I have found myself both unable and unwilling to let go of the spirit of that group or, as this book testifies, of the task we set for ourselves. Thus, while the others have gone on to all sorts of other projects—and have done so, I think it fair to say, in ways that make Albany proud to number them among its alumni—I have returned to this project again and again, sustained by our original commitment to one another, but also driven by the sense of a debt unpaid.

I mention all this to explain the role played by the seven people whose names appear after the "with" on the title page—Barbara

Chepaitis, David Coogan, Lâle Davidson, Ron MacLean, Cindy Parrish, Jonathan Post, and Beth Weatherby—for while identifiable school writings by Chepaitis and MacLean figure prominently in certain chapters, this is not true for the others. I also mention it, however, to explain the book's slightly unconventional pattern of narration. Sections I and III feature the same "I" that is narrating this Preface; the chapters therein evolved long after our original group had disbanded and therefore are—for better or worse—my responsibility.

Section II, however, is a direct extension of our original collaborative effort. Indeed, through all the years I have continued to work on this project—and continued to make use, I should add, of those early drafts—I have understood this section in particular to be making not my case so much as *our* case, the one we all set out to make in the summer of 1992. With the group's blessing, then, Chapters 5 through 9 are narrated by an appropriately collaborative "we," and this "I" finally makes good on his end of the bargain. Barbara, David, Lâle, Ron, Cindy, Jonathan, and Beth: here's to you.

STEPHEN M. NORTH
*Albany, New York*

# ACKNOWLEDGMENTS

Special thanks, first, to all the graduate students whose work informed this project, and in particular to those who granted permission for the use of their writings here: Jennifer Beck, Lois Dellert-Raskin, Christiane Farnan, Chris Gallagher, Wilma Kahn, Deb Kelsh, Laura Lane, John Latta, Brenda-Lee Rabine, Jan Ramjerdi, Claudia Ricci, Catherine Sustana, Joanne Tangorra, and Jeff Van Schaick. Thanks also to a number of generous commentators: Lori Anderson and Amy Schoch, who were there at the beginning, and, at various later stages, Wendy Bishop, Ron Bosco, Don Byrd, Sharon Crowley, Gene Garber, Judith Fetterley, Amy Lee, Hans Ostrom, Derek Owens, Martha Rozett, and Bob Yagelski. Thanks to Michael Greer, NCTE's Senior Editor, for his energy and insight, and to NCTE's outside reviewers and Editorial Board for their thoughtful responses. Finally, thanks to Liz, Matt, Patricia, and David North, without whose endless support—and considerable patience—there would have been no book at all.

# INTRODUCTION

In the fall semester of 1990, the English Department at the University at Albany, State University of New York launched a doctoral curriculum entitled "Writing, Teaching, and Criticism." New doctoral curricula in English are rarely considered major news, even by the educational press; and, fairly or not, this is even more likely to be the case when the venue is a midsized, public Research II university like Albany. Nevertheless, this particular program received a fair amount of public notice. For example, David Simpson, who had been a key consultant in its design, announced its arrival in MLA's *ADE Bulletin* in an essay titled "Teaching English: What and Where Is the Cutting Edge?" which was followed by a response from C. H. Knoblauch—"The Albany Graduate English Curriculum"—written from Knoblauch's perspective as the English Department's acting director of graduate studies. Warren Ginsberg, who chaired the department for most of the program's first five years, offered another essay-length account of the enterprise, "Institutional Identity at the State University of New York at Albany: The New Ph.D. in English," in a 1994 collection titled *English Studies/Culture Studies: Institutionalizing Dissent*. And James Berlin, describing innovative graduate programs in Chapter 8 of his *Rhetorics, Poetics, and Cultures* (1996), compares "Writing, Teaching, and Criticism" quite favorably to analogous efforts at such institutions as Carnegie Mellon and the University of Pittsburgh.

As this level of commentary might suggest, Albany's curricular experiment has a number of interesting features, and my collaborators and I will say a good deal about its overall conception and structure in Section II. For our purposes, though, by far the most significant and exciting element of the program, and the one that led us to undertake this project, is the way it situates *writing*. A doctoral program in English obviously involves disciplinary training in a number of activities: reading, research of various kinds, course design, speaking (as teacher and scholar), and so on. Ultimately, however—and the field's legion of ABDs (All But Dissertation) serves as perhaps the most powerful testimony to the accuracy of this claim—none of these activities plays as important a role as writing: doctoral students must write their way into English Studies. Any serious effort to alter graduate education in the discipline, my contributors and I therefore contend, must account for—must be *grounded* in—a refiguring of the role that writing plays in such education. And in terms of both conception and performance, no program we know of has taken that challenge more seriously than Albany's "Writing, Teaching, and Criticism."

In making such an assertion, of course, we are also declaring both our interest and our considerable investment in the program and its founding principles. All of us have been involved with this curriculum over a substantial period of time, one as a member of the faculty and the others as students during the crucial early years of its development and implementation—years during which, for reasons that will become clear in Chapter 5, students were perhaps even more crucial to its realization than the faculty. The chapters that follow, therefore, are not offered as a disinterested or dispassionate analysis of the writing this program has sponsored, with samples chosen at random or with an eye toward claiming comprehensiveness or even local consensus. They constitute, rather, an argument: our account of the writings we believe to be among the program's most interesting and important realizations to date, chosen for their power to illustrate what we believe are its most promising possibilities.

We also believe, however, that there is more at stake in this argument than the role that writing ought to play in this particular graduate program, or even the role that writing ought to play in English doctoral education overall. This will become clear very quickly in a curricular sense. That is, precisely because writing is so central to the English doctoral curriculum, these accounts of its refigured role inevitably involve accounts of changes in other components of that curriculum, too, so that the book's argument is to an extent about the nature of English doctoral education in general. Even more, though, the book makes an argument about the discipline as a whole: about what English Studies might be, or indeed ought to be. Doctoral education, after all, has always been the conservative linchpin of English as a discipline, a profession, a set of institutional practices: the means by which the graduate faculty disciplines the doctoral students who become the professors who discipline the undergraduates who become the high school and elementary teachers who discipline the students who go on to become English majors, and so on in a cycle that, like most such cycles in our culture, has enormous powers of self-perpetuation. And since, as we previously suggested, writing is at the heart of doctoral education, it also turns out to be at the heart of this cycle of disciplinary perpetuation. In other words, while writing is the primary means by which doctoral students make their way into English Studies, it is also the primary means by which, through what is always a complex set of negotiations, the discipline is written into the students. To follow current parlance: while doctoral students are working to make English Studies their subject, English Studies (however we understand the agency of such entities) is at work making doctoral students its subjects, too. Insofar, therefore, as the writing practices described here alter those negotiations—in particular, as will become evident, by allowing students greater latitude in the disciplinary positions they might assume and the disciplinary agencies they might exercise—they represent possibilities for rewriting, refiguring English Studies itself.

My collaborators and I recognize, of course, that these are ambitious claims to be making about a book grounded most directly in the writings of a dozen or so doctoral students. And, indeed, we acknowledge the peculiarity—not to say the utter hubris—of the project undertaken here. Even family and friends have long since asked the obvious question: "You're going to devote most of a book to the writing practices of a single doctoral program, and so you've chosen to focus on . . . Albany?!" Let us therefore be clear: we have no illusions about either Albany's status as a graduate institution or our own as its products and apologists. The current program itself is in fact still too new to appear in any national rankings, and it is unlikely to debut high up when it does. As measured by such schemes, and despite the aforementioned bits of positive press, it will almost certainly be rated as too new, too small, and too idiosyncratic; and, if history is any indicator, it will have a hard time ever escaping such labels.[1] Albany is not Harvard or Yale, Stanford or Wisconsin, Columbia or Princeton; it does not, in other words, bring to the table a century or more of Ph.D.-granting tradition nor the cumulative institutional momentum and resources that, in U.S. higher education, tend to accrue thereto.

Moreover, similar kinds of judgments can and probably will be extended to us as graduate degree holders who have done our work at such an institution. In any previous era—indeed, until as recently as 1960 or so—only a few of us could have anticipated attending a college or university at all, let alone aspiring to a doctorate in English. For the latter purpose, especially, most of us would have had the wrong demographic profile: wrong sex, wrong class, wrong (or, quite likely, no) undergraduate degree, wrong disciplinary interests (in such areas, e.g., as rhetoric and composition, creative writing, feminist theory, or, what is perhaps even worse, various combinations thereof).

But all this is precisely to the point. Tradition and cumulative institutional momentum and resources obviously have their advantages, not the least of which in this case has been to provide a good deal of insulation from the forces—political, economic, intellectual, and, that most concrete of adjectives in this context, demographic—that have transformed higher education in general, and English Studies in particular, since the end of World War II. However, such insulation just as obviously has its disadvantages: insulation can come to function as insularity, protection as constraint, a sense of security as complacency. And it can do so all the more readily in a discipline concerned primarily with the rapidly changing mosaic of the nation's language and literacy practices.

This is not to say, of course, that English doctoral education at places such as Harvard and Yale, Stanford and Wisconsin, Columbia and Princeton has gone unchanged over the past fifty years. That would be both unfair and patently untrue. It *is* to say, however, that the pace and pattern and substance of such change has been very different in those places from what it has been at the substantial majority of doctoral programs founded since 1946—some 80 of the 140 or so currently in operation—and also that by no means has all of that difference accrued to the disadvantage of the newer programs. Indeed, precisely because these newer programs have been so much less insulated—because, that is, they have not only been shaped but to a considerable extent *created* by those very forces from which the older programs have been protected—they have a significantly different, and in certain ways more immediate and vital, connection with American language, literacy, and letters than their more established counterparts. Thus, while there might be good reasons to examine curricular practices in English doctoral education at those older programs, there are also reasons—as good and in some ways better—to study them in the newer ones, as well.

And in those terms, the doctoral program in English at Albany is not merely a reasonably good representative: it could be, if you will excuse the expression, the poster child for what we will describe in Chapter 4 as the postwar transformation of English doctoral education. The department's host institution, founded in 1844 as the New York State Normal School, had been dedicated for all of its first century exclusively to the education of teachers, rarely granting a doctoral degree in anything, and certainly not in English. However, a rapid series of changes—fueled especially, as one historian puts it, by "'demographics' and 'Rockefeller,'" (the latter a reference to Nelson A. Rockefeller, New York's big-spending governor from 1959 to 1973) (Birr 119)—produced both a new name and a new mission.[2] Thus, by 1962 the State University of New York at Albany was "commissioned to become a university" (Birr 119), or, more precisely, one of four university centers in what would eventually become the largest state university system in the country, the State University of New York (SUNY). The English Department was among Albany's first units to be transformed in aid of this new mission, admitting its first Ph.D. students in 1963–64. They were followed in short order—1971—by its first Doctor of Arts (D.A.) students, a degree program the university developed with the help of a Carnegie Corporation grant.

However, even a quick outline of the department's subsequent history illustrates what it means to call these post–World War II institutions and their programs uninsulated. The darkest stretch began in 1975, when the State Education Department, having completed a review of all doctoral programs in New York state, recommended a suspension of admissions to Albany's English Ph.D.—one of only two programs in the state thus targeted, and this after just over a decade of operation. In 1976, 1977 (twice), and 1978, high profile challenges to this recommendation—including three court challenges—were unsuccessful, each failure generating a new round of negative publicity.

After bottoming out in 1978, however, the department's doctoral fortunes took a somewhat more favorable turn. Boosted in part by resources invested in the efforts to save the Ph.D., the D.A. program—which by this time had developed particular emphases in writing and teaching—was beginning to prosper, and it continued to do so throughout the 1980s, with strong applicant pools, good placement rates, and graduates who were notably successful both in the academy and elsewhere. Encouraged by this success, in 1988 the department hired consultant David Simpson to help it further bolster its doctoral offerings. This process ultimately led to a proposal for a new Ph.D., one based on the D.A.'s proven strengths but also incorporating more effectively the resources of all the available faculty: hence "Writing, Teaching, and Criticism." By 1992 this new Ph.D. program had been fully approved, the plan being to offer it in parallel with the D.A. In 1994, however, the university made an internal decision to suspend admissions to the D.A. program, thus bringing the department as a doctorate-granting enterprise pretty much back to where it had begun in 1963: launching a new Ph.D.

Even without the details, this obviously is not an entirely pleasant recitation: not the history anyone would have wished on the English Department; not one we would wish on any other institution; nor, finally, one which, though it is obviously a matter of public record, we are ordinarily all that eager to rehearse. We offer it here, however, because it represents as thorough and intensive a set of lessons in building English doctoral programs as any U.S. institution has ever had: a painfully earned license, if ever there was one. Above all, perhaps, this cycle of building and loss and rebuilding at Albany has taught us how very special such programs are; made us acutely aware of how vulnerable they can be; and impressed upon us, therefore, how crucial it is to keep alive the disciplinary and professional inquiry, the hard-edged conversations, that bring them into being in the first place. We believe these are lessons of relevance to English Studies as a whole, and it is in that spirit that my collaborators and I offer the study that follows here.

# THE PH.D. IN ENGLISH, DOCTORAL EDUCATION, AND WRITING: A HISTORICAL PERSPECTIVE

The purpose of the first four chapters of this book is to provide context for the claims that Albany's program in "Writing, Teaching, and Criticism" marks a substantial departure in English doctoral education. In other words, I want to present enough background information about English doctoral education in general, and the role of writing in such education in particular, to make the significance of the practices my contributors and I describe in Section II clearly visible. Under ordinary circumstances—or at least the circumstances I would prefer—this would be a fairly straightforward task, and might not even require an entirely separate chapter, let alone a full section. I would begin by drawing on the key published histories of English doctoral education for an outline of the social, political, and institutional forces most relevant to the emergence of contemporary programs; move expeditiously to an overview of the leading curricular models as they have been described in the professional literature; and then close my considerations by narrowing the focus still further, reviewing those studies which, like this one, emphasized the role of writing in such curricula. And I would do all this essentially as a reminder for our audience; that is, I would assume that while readers might not know all the details of the materials reviewed, they would at least have a strong shared sense of the historical trajectories and curricular trends.

Unfortunately, such an approach is not practicable for two major reasons. First, despite its otherwise inordinate level of disciplinary self-consciousness, especially over the past twenty years or so, English appears to have very little historical sense, shared or otherwise, of its efforts at doctoral education. Certainly it can claim no published work—no book, no monograph, no article— that even approaches the status of a standard history of those efforts. Thus, Gerald Graff's *Professing Literature*, widely (albeit somewhat problematically) regarded as the discipline's most comprehensive institutional history to date, has little to say about graduate education of any sort. The same is largely true for those histories that take what is usually regarded (again, somewhat problematically) as a more specialized focus. So, for example, while Kermit Vanderbilt's *American Literature and the Academy: The Roots, Growth, and Maturity of a Profession* at least devotes perhaps twenty-five of its six hundred pages to the emergence of graduate studies in that field (see especially Chapter 20, "American Literature in the University: Curriculum, Graduate Research, and Controversy in the Thirties"), neither James Berlin's various accounts of rhetoric and composition nor D. G. Myers's *The Elephants Teach* (on creative writing) offer any extended account of doctoral education as such. In fact, the fullest sustained account of the history of English doctoral education in the United States is probably still to be found in Don Cameron Allen's *The Ph.D. in English and American Literature: A Report to the Profession and the Public* (1968), now over thirty years old; and even there, the bulk of what can be construed as the historical commentary comes to less than thirty pages.

Second, English has no significant tradition of dealing with doctoral education *as* education: neither from a historical perspective nor from any contemporary perspective. To be sure, there is a tradition of commentary on the overall shape of doctoral training, a concern for what might be called the programmatic as opposed to the curricular. The first Ph.D. in the United States was granted at Yale in 1861 and the first that might be claimed for English at Harvard in 1876. And almost from these beginnings, publications and reports have appeared dealing with what has been termed perhaps most often the "problem" of the Ph.D., early on in general terms (see, e.g., William James's oft-cited 1903 "The Ph.D. Octopus") but also, gradually, with specific reference to English—and they have never stopped. Some titles might help to suggest the pattern: Stuart P. Sherman's 1913 "Professor Kittredge and the Teaching of English"; Howard Mumford Jones's 1931 essay on "Graduate English Study: Its Rationale" in *Sewanee Review*; Wellek and Warren's 1949 "The Study of Literature in the Graduate School" (Chapter 20 of *Theory of Literature*); Warner G. Rice's 1962 "Teachers of College English: Preparation, Supply, and Demand"; Allen's aforementioned *The Ph.D. in English and American Literature* (1968); and MLA's 1989 *The Future of Doctoral Studies in English* (edited by Lunsford, Moglen, and Slevin). Despite this reasonably steady stream of programmatic commentary, however, the details of such training—what actually *happens* during the seventy or more credit hours most programs have long since required—may have been discussed in faculty lounges or teaching assistant offices but rarely in the pages of *PMLA* or *College English*. And this has been, if anything, even more adamantly the case for the role that writing, especially writing prior to the dissertation, might have played in such training; almost no one says anything about who might have written what, to or for whom, and why.[1]

The upshot is that the chapters in this first section represent not so much an effort to remind readers of the broad outlines of a history of English doctoral education but rather to introduce them to it, and to do so with at least some concern for such education *as* education. Chapter 1 traces the institutional origins of English Ph.D. programs in this country over their first seventy-five years or so, from 1876 to 1950: the influence of the German university model, the relationship between the Ph.D. and careers in college teaching, and the part that demographics appear to have played in shaping this emerging discipline-cum-profession. Chapter 2 tries to reconstruct the general set of curricular practices to which these institutional arrangements gave rise—practices I have labeled the Magisterial curriculum. In Chapter 3, I turn to the dramatic institutional changes that took place in English doctoral education between the end of World War II and 1990, an era of extraordinary expansion followed by an equally dramatic but good deal more painful era of contraction. And, finally, Chapter 4 considers the legacy of those postwar years: the professional and disciplinary crisis of identity that brought about the demise of the Magisterial tradition and, to take its place, a range of new curricular models, including, of course, Albany's "Writing, Teaching, and Criticism."

## CHAPTER ONE

# Establishing the Tradition: 1876–1950

As with so many features of U.S. higher education, our system of doctoral education can be traced in large part to the formative influence of the German university. Accounts of that influence in general have come to be a commonplace in histories of how the United States' small collection of private, religiously affiliated colleges was transformed into one of the world's most prominent university systems between roughly 1850 and 1910, and details of its specific influence on English programs can be found in a number of sources (see, for example, Berlin, *Rhetorics, Poetics, and Cultures*; Connors; and Graff, *Professing Literature*). As such accounts explain, universities at places such as Berlin and Heidelberg were primarily graduate institutions. Their heaviest emphasis was on research, and they had little direct concern for anything we currently understand as undergraduate education. Their basic mission was the making of knowledge, and their primary credentialing function—a matter, really, of self-perpetuation—was to produce more researchers, holders of what had come to be called the *Philosophiae Doctor*.[1]

## The German Professor: Not Born, but Made

Most often, this German influence has been invoked—almost by way of lament—from the undergraduate side of the U.S. system's perennial research-versus-teaching debates: that is, to explain in terms of disciplinary and institutional formation why undergraduate teaching has always had such a problematic status in the Ph.D.-driven research university. For my purposes, though, the German system's more significant legacy has to do with those students it actually *did* serve. For while its heavy emphasis on research may have done little to account for either undergraduate students or undergraduate education, it did offer a rather compelling image of their graduate counterparts. To be sure, the system's central attraction—the full embodiment of the ideal that so attracted those who would eventually call upon it in reshaping the U.S. system—was not the German graduate student, but the German professor.[2] Gerald Graff makes this case as compellingly as anyone in Chapter 4 of *Professing Literature,* which features this emblematic passage from James Morgan Hart as its epigraph:

> The German professor is not a teacher in the English sense of the term; he is a specialist. He is not responsible for the success of his hearers. He is responsible only for the quality of his instruction. His duty begins and ends with himself. (55)

Indeed, it is worth noting here that, at least according to Friedrich Paulsen, it was the German philologists—the forebears and in some cases the founders of what became U.S. English departments—who led the way toward institutionalizing this ideal, their ambition "not being to turn out teachers but scholars. Teaching as such they did not consider at all as an art which could itself be taught, but rather took it for granted that any one who was himself proficient in a science ought to be able to teach others" (189).

Obviously, however, such professors did not come out of nowhere—were not born, but made—and Hart, like so many of his contemporaries, was also a great admirer of what he understood to be the German university's mode of reproducing its professoriate, the way the "entire *personnel* of the faculty is a close corporation, a spiritual order perpetuating itself after the fashion of the Roman Catholic hierarchy" (19). Hart continues:

> The professor has but one aim in life: scholarly renown. To effect this, he must have the liberty of selecting his studies and pushing them to their extreme limits. The student has but one desire: to assimilate his instructor's learning, and, if possible, to add to it. He must, therefore, be his own master. He must be free to accept and reject, to judge and prove all things for himself, to train himself step by step for grappling with the great problems of nature and history. Accountable only to himself

for his opinions and mode of living, he shakes off spiritual bondage and becomes an independent thinker. He *must* think for himself, for there is no one set over him as spiritual adviser and guide, prescribing the work for each day and each hour, telling him what to believe and what to disbelieve, and marking him up or down accordingly. (21–22; emphasis in original)

The pedagogical mainstays of this system consisted of the lecture, the seminar (or, following an older usage, the seminary), and the lab (an instructional setting that has had limited relevance for English). At their best, the lectures were public presentations of work-in-progress, Hart's "specialist" speaking, sometimes entrancingly, sometimes not. Bliss Perry recounts seeing Kuno Fischer give a performance closer to the former at Heidelberg in 1886:

> The hundreds of young men ceased their chattering as the Professor entered, at precisely a quarter past the hour, and they stamped their applause. . . . For forty-five minutes, without notes, he poured forth a torrential stream of eloquence about the character development of Shakespeare's *Richard Third*. I must have missed a good deal of it, for he spoke as rapidly as Phillips Brooks, but the lecture was printed afterward and I still think it a masterly piece of Shakespearean criticism. He stopped in the middle of a sentence, as the hour struck, and stalked out amid a tumult of cheering. (91–92)[3]

The seminar was, as its etymology might suggest, at least in principle a more interactive, even nurturing setting (in an admittedly generous sense of the term, given the competitive spirit that may often have prevailed). Comprised of a select group of advanced students engaged in a focused exploration of an area of the professor's expertise, the course could proceed by discussion and interrogation, student or teacher presentation, or by writing, but the ultimate emphasis was on each student's pursuit of some specific project, with dissertations, "as a rule, produced in this way as first specimens of more or less original research" (Paulsen 189).[4]

It is crucial to note, however, that in keeping with what Hart understood as the imperative that the graduate student "be his own master," these official instructional venues were not part of any tightly regulated system. There was no required curriculum, nor even any strict version of what we now would regard as a residency requirement. As Perry explains, students were therefore both free and forced to generate whatever coherence and sense of progress toward a degree their course of study would assume:

> It must be remembered that in such courses as were then offered by the Philosophical Faculty there were no tests whatever of a student's progress—save for the discussions and reports of a few advanced students in the Seminars—until the final oral examination and thesis for the Ph.D. We did not have to attend lectures unless we wished: the professor signed each student's registration book at the beginning of a course and again at the end, and that was presumptive evidence of his attendance. He might actually be at some other university for that semester, taking a particular course which he coveted. The system was excellent for the strong man who knew what he wanted, but fatal to many a weakling. (97–98)

Indeed, Perry—who enjoyed a successful career that included stints at Williams, Princeton, and, for the bulk of his career, Harvard—ultimately chose not to seek the Ph.D. even though he had qualified to do so and though his principal advisor, a Chaucer scholar named Bernhard ten Brink, urged him to. For "though I knew that a 'Ph.D.' was a pleasant ornament to one's name in a college catalogue," Perry writes,

> I wanted other things very much more. None of us dreamed [in 1887] . . . that within the next thirty years American colleges would insist upon a Ph.D. degree as a requisite for promotion, that its commercial value would consequently be reckoned with all the precision of an actuarial table, and that all academic 'go-getters' would take it in their stride. (113)

## The American Model: College English Teaching, Inc.

As Perry's bemused and perhaps slightly acid retrospective comment suggests, American efforts to embrace and establish the Ph.D.—including, of course, the Ph.D. in English—were both enthusiastic and for the most part quite successful (although to give Perry's comments their due, I should probably add, for better or for worse). By the second half of the nineteenth century, U.S. institutions were feeling the economic and (it is usually argued) patriotic pinch caused by having what gradually had come to be thousands of the United States' best—and best-off—students go abroad to do graduate study, and the leading institutions finally began in earnest to establish this country's first graduate programs, modeling them quite self-consciously on the much ballyhooed German ideal. To some extent, the borrowings were a matter of structures and personnel. Thus the key programmatic elements of German doctoral study—the lectures, seminars, and labs, leading ultimately to the qualifying examinations and the dissertation (understood as original and hence publishable work)—became the key elements of doctoral education in the United States as well. And of course they did so to no small extent because the fledgling U.S. institutions followed the same strategy Thomas Edison (to name one kindred entrepreneur) would pursue in building General Electric during roughly the same era, namely, importing talent: they hired a steady stream of German or German-trained professors to help them get the new programs underway. In his venerable *The American and the German University: One Hundred Years History,* for instance, Charles Franklin Thwing estimates that the number of such people hired "exceeds three hundred" (103). The first of the six he profiles by way of illustration, Francis Lieber, arrived in the United States in 1827 and taught, among other places, at South Carolina and Columbia. The last, Kuno Francke, began teaching at Harvard in 1884.

Most important, though, along with these structures and personnel the U.S. universities imported the informing spirit of the German enterprise. In the strictest structural sense, U.S. higher education never did succeed in duplicating a Berlin or a Heidelberg. Despite some early efforts to establish exclusively graduate universities—most notably at Johns Hopkins and Clark[5]—graduate education in this country has always found its fate to be much more intimately connected with undergraduates and the undergraduate curriculum than was the case in Germany. Early on this connection was a legacy of the "classical" college onto which the university was grafted, as Robert Connors has put it; the new (or perhaps more aptly, hybrid) institution inherited from that system at least some responsibility for "disciplining" students in the older moral and mental senses (see, for example, Russell 36–37). Later, during the first decades of this century, this residual tie was further strengthened by what might be called the professionalization of the Ph.D. as a teaching certificate for higher education. Charles Grigg characterized this process as

> the continual and ever accelerating trend toward the idea that a college teacher should have a Ph.D. The influence of the philanthropic foundations played a vital part in this trend. As Hollis described it, this influence came about in a rather circuitous way:
>> In order to be sure that they were pensioning college professors and making grants to *bona fide* colleges rather than to secondary schools, the philanthropic foundations—especially the General Education Board and the Carnegie Foundation for the Advancement of Teaching—began to require, among other standards, that institutions employ six (later eight) professors who held an earned doctor's degree.
> This requirement by the foundations added to the mounting pressure by regional and national accrediting associations for a larger and larger proportion of college and university faculty to have a Ph.D. degree. (9–10)

And of course this connection to teaching undergraduates has proven to be particularly strong for English. Like so many of its compatriots in the humanities, the pattern of the field's development has tended to limit the value of its doctorates outside the academy. In contrast to those other humanities fields, however, English has proven to be remarkably—indeed, singularly—successful at adapting to America's scheme of undergraduate instruction. Thanks especially to first-year composition, but also to various schemes for general education and distribution requirements, U.S. undergraduates have been required to take English courses with a universality unmatched by any other discipline in the academy (with the possible and interesting exception, during certain periods, of physical education). The net result: from fairly early on, a person who earns a Ph.D. in English has for all practical purposes earned a license to teach at the college level.[6]

However, while this gradual association with college teaching—one that might be called, to elaborate on Hart's "close corporation" metaphor, its *incorporation*—obviously constituted a departure from the traditional career trajectory of the Ph.D.-holding German philologist, it should nevertheless be understood as carrying on very much in the *spirit* of that tradition. Indeed, from certain perspectives, especially that of the graduate professor (which after all was the position that captured the U.S. imagination in the first place), this adaptation can be regarded as an improved systemic expression of the spirit Hart admired so enthusiastically. It made possible an enterprise that would become not only more extensive and arguably more powerful than anything the German system produced, but one that was also as much or more a "close corporation" and an order—"spiritual" and otherwise—extraordinarily able at "perpetuating itself after the fashion of the Roman Catholic hierarchy" (19).

Certainly, the German professor did wield a good deal of discipline-based power; in his sphere, he (and all professors would have been men) was likely to have been more individually powerful than those who would come to hold the top positions in U.S. universities. In a sense, however, this concentration of power in a small number of relatively independent individuals came at the expense of both the institutional range over which that power could be exercised and also the extent to which it could be amplified by being exercised collectively. Graduate study in the nineteenth-century German university could lead in any number of directions other than the doctorate and an academic career: to civil service, teaching, the various professions, and so on. No doubt individual professors enjoyed both varying kinds and varying degrees of influence in these arenas; some were called on by the state, for instance, to construct the *Staatsexamen* by which teachers at lower levels won certification.[7] In nearly all such cases, though—and essentially by definition—each professor operated on his own and in a consultative capacity, the individual expert from one institution being called on by another institution. His sphere of direct influence, in other words, was a good deal smaller, relatively fixed, and to a considerable extent maintained through competition with other professors; it was based, that is, on his research program, support for which he negotiated with the state, and it was exercised in human terms primarily over the limited cadre of graduate students and research assistants who harbored ambitions of eventually seeking a professorial position themselves.

In the United States, by contrast, the incorporation of college teaching provided a field like English with the means of establishing a sphere of direct institutional influence—albeit one featuring somewhat more collective than individual power—that could and did expand as the U.S. system of higher education in general expanded. Thus, as the Ph.D. became more and more the accepted certificate for teaching in a college English department, and as the size, number, and ambitions (or, as some critics have said, pretensions) of those departments increased, the Ph.D.-granting universities were able to hire more graduate faculty, enroll more students, and grant more degrees, confident of their standing in and indeed substantial control over the market for those degree holders. And English was able to carry out this campaign despite the fact that few of the inquiries the field has sponsored over its U.S. history—whatever their merits in other contexts—have helped fuel the rise of the universities as research centers. Thus, while doctoral production in English during this time was never spectacular in any absolute sense, it nevertheless sustained a rate of growth that was both steady and, in its cumulative effects, impressive. The number of doctorates granted climbed through double figures in the first twenty years of this century, reached triple figures in the 1930s, and, after an understandable dip back below the one hundred mark during World War II, crossed the two hundred barrier in 1950 (Harmon and Soldz 10).

Even more striking, however, is the way that English was able to carry out this steady expansion while maintaining an impressive degree of what might be called corporate integrity, its own version of the top-to-bottom closeness Hart so admired in Germany. The key to this effort—one which, given the era, can certainly be characterized as prototypically American, and which also has tended to be the model for much professional training in this country—was the familiar pyramidal corporate structure. The corporation's top prizes, of course, were the graduate professorships at doctorate-granting institutions. As noted previously, such positions have never been entirely divorced from undergraduate instruction. Then as now, some of those who held them taught undergraduate as well as graduate students, sometimes as a matter of obligation, sometimes by choice. But make no mistake: these were *research* positions, valued for their prestige, their salaries, and, most important, for the latitude they provided in terms of what Evan Watkins (1989) has called worktime—this last including, of course, considerable say in terms of how much to teach, to whom, and when.[8] Thus, while the U.S. system may not have been configured so as to duplicate exactly the situation enjoyed by Kuno Fischer and his colleagues, its analogous luminaries have nevertheless held positions of considerable professional autonomy and material comfort: from Francis James Child to George Lyman Kittredge, from R. S. Crane to Cleanth Brooks, and so on.

From a systemic perspective, however, the benefits enjoyed by any given individual occupying one of these top posts were nowhere near as impressive as the way the *idea* of such posts functioned to organize and control the pyramid's lower levels. In his 1994 *Token Professionals and Master Critics: A Critique of Orthodoxy in Literary Studies*—a book devoted, as its title suggests, to exploring the nature of English as a profession—James Sosnoski explores at considerable length a figure he calls "the *Magister Implicatus.*" The *Magister,* he says, represents "the sum of the ways [English] academics portray themselves officially. . . . a personification of the institution's ideally orthodox professor" (73–4). One of his central analogies is especially apt here:

> The *Magister Implicatus* parallels the figure of Christ as an ideal self institutionalized as "the way" to behave. Sometimes called "Master" by his disciples, he is the key figure in maintaining a "corporate identity" in the religious institution we call Christianity. To maintain this identity Christians "incorporate" Christ through the experience of "communion" or internalization. The internalization of the ideal figure of Christ is an imperative for any Christian—*imitatio Christi*. To be a Christian is to be Christlike. The *Magister,* in a parallel fashion, configures an academic conscience that regulates professional conduct. His is the voice in the background that says, you "ought to." His voice resonates within us because its pronouncements are prescribed by the institution of criticism we profess. (81–82)

Sosnoski is primarily concerned with the operations of this *Magister* at the top levels of English's professionalized structure—that is, with the way the token professionals of his title, the vast majority of full, associate, and assistant professors, lead what are often troubled working lives in the shadow of (imagined) master critics; and he invokes the concept in a figurative as much as a historical sense. Still, in a slightly expanded sense the *Magister* can easily serve as an emblem for what, given Sosnoski's choice of analogy (itself so clearly resonant with Hart's) might be reasonably characterized as the propagation of the faith of English in the U.S. academy.

From a historical perspective, the enterprise can be described as growing from the top down and the center out. It begins with the small cluster of graduate professors—a good many of whom would not have been Ph.D.'s themselves—working with the first generations of doctoral candidates, recruiting them to careers in scholarship with the quintessentially *Magisterial* promise: "If you prove worthy, you may become one of us." According to Cameron Allen, in 1893 such professors were hosting fourteen programs, a number that had grown to twenty-four by the turn of the century, at which time there were some 547 students enrolled at such places as Harvard, Yale, Johns Hopkins, Columbia, Chicago, NYU, and Princeton (14).

Year by year, these early Ph.D.'s (along with what would gradually become a regular corps of ABDs) went out to positions in the steadily growing number of, and steadily growing, English departments, both those with and those without doctoral programs, where they began the work they hoped would eventually lead to graduate professorships of their own. One part of that work, albeit traditionally not the most important part, was to teach the undergraduates from among whom they would recruit the next generation of graduate students. It was in this interaction that the *Magister*—conceived, if you will excuse the inevitable wordplay, in graduate seminars—would have been born as the disciplinary Word, the *Magisterial* way, to be revealed both to the undifferentiated populations who made up lower-division and general education courses; but also, and no doubt more fervently, to that subset of undergraduates who, for various reasons, chose to major in English. The basic system can be said to have been in place, then, when the first batch of interested and properly certified seniors—those deemed most suitable to follow the *Magister*—was sent off to graduate school, there to take their own place in the cycle.

As this sketch also suggests, however, once *in* place such a system allowed for remarkably tight control over the corporation's mode of self-perpetuation. The *Magister*, like the Christ in Sosnoski's comparison, turns out to be relentlessly exclusive: many are called, but few indeed are chosen. As aspirants making their way up the corporate hierarchy would discover again and again— the brute numerical fact of this sort of pyramid—attrition rates are substantial at every level. Thus, while we do not have much in the way of detailed statistics for this era, it is safe enough to assert that only a small fraction of those undergraduates who took first-year composition or introduction to literature courses during these years chose or were chosen to be English majors. Of those who completed the major, only some smaller fraction ever chose—or, again, were chosen—to apply to graduate school. Of these, fewer still were accepted, and not all of these would have been awarded the funding which, whatever its practical importance in individual cases, marked a further sign of favor. Among those who actually showed up (presumably not all who were admitted did so) some dropped out with no degree, while a good many others were satisfied to leave with the M.A. degree. Those who did stay on to seek the terminal degree still faced what were, given the challenges they had already survived, rather harsh odds: the best estimate suggests that about half of those who have ever enrolled for the Ph.D. in English have gone on to earn it.[9]

And then, of course, having the degree in hand marked not the *end* of this corporate process of selection, but only a shift in venue. Granted, most of the people awarded English Ph.D.'s during those seventy-five years found themselves in a more promising academic job market than have many graduates of the past twenty-five.[10] Still, there were definitely some lean times and, as a more regular concern, a fairly clear hierarchy among the positions that might be sought: the career path to a graduate professorship was likely to be longer and harder from Parsons, say, than from Oberlin, and longer and harder from Oberlin than from Ohio State, and longer and harder from Ohio State than from Harvard. Moreover, once on the job at whatever campus, the day-to-day demands of scholarship, teaching, and service—woven, as they came to be, with variously configured tenure processes—provided further occasions for selection and self-selection.[11] For, in the end, the field of aspirants clearly had to be narrowed still further: the number of top positions, the graduate professorships, was always—and necessarily—quite small. Thus, at the turn of the century the twenty-four programs granting the Ph.D. in English collectively produced perhaps twenty graduates per year.[12] By 1950, while Ph.D. production had multiplied some tenfold to two hundred, the number of genuinely active doctoral programs had at most doubled. That is, while the cumulative total of all the programs launched between 1875 and 1950 might have been as high as sixty, no more than thirty-five or so were viable in any given year—i.e., would actually have awarded degrees—and the vast majority of those degrees were always awarded by the top fifteen or so institutions. Therefore, while the number of graduate faculty positions definitely increased over the fifty years—indeed, while they increased at a somewhat artificially high rate as a result of efforts to create and staff new, small, and frequently underactive doctoral programs—they never did so at a rate that substantially improved the odds that the new Ph.D.'s of any given year could hope to hold one before the end of their careers.

## Demographics as Doctrine

In organizational terms, this selection process tended from the very beginning to be highly conservative, a promoter of homogeneity. At each of these stages, those who moved ahead (and the temptation to make comparisons with *proselyte, altar server, acolyte, seminarian,* and so on is understandable) tended to be much like those who taught and recruited them. In principle, this need not have been the case. At some point along the way, it might conceivably have become corporate policy to favor demographic heterogeneity of one kind or another, but there is no evidence whatever to suggest that any such shift in policy took place. Moreover, while this homogeneity, like that of the German faculty and the Roman Catholic hierarchy before it, might be said to have had a spiritual, or at least doctrinal, dimension—and indeed, the evolving nature of that dimension is what preoccupies studies such as *Professing Literature* or *American Literature and the Academy*—it would appear to have had a far firmer grounding in the corporeal, social, and institutional. That is, the *Magister,* in concert with prevailing U.S. corporate and higher educational practices, tended to locate whatever it was that constituted doctrinal suitability most often and most intensely in those of a certain race, citizenship, class, gender, age, and educational background.

And this homogeneity reached its systemic peak in the crucible of doctoral education, where the system's most stringently selected students came together with its most stringently selected faculty. On the student side of the desk, I can say with considerable authority—and little risk of surprising anyone—that for these first seventy-five years English doctoral students were nearly all white U.S. citizens. Granted, no study I can find overtly says as much.[13] For instance, Berelson's landmark 1960 book about graduate study in general discusses such things as social background and motivation, and even comments that graduate school is especially valuable for "an ethnic minority traditionally devoted to learning, like the Jews, who are strongly over-represented in the graduate population" (134). But he offers no other observations or information on race or ethnicity, and none at all on citizenship. Cameron Allen, writing at about the same time specifically about the Ph.D. in English, never mentions any of the three.

Nevertheless, it is possible to make strong inferences about the general pattern—which in any case is hardly counterintuitive. Thus, Bowen and Rudenstine report in *In Pursuit of the PhD* (1992) that the total number of English doctorates granted to non-U.S. residents in 1958 was 11 (of 333, or 3 percent), in 1972 was 54 (of 1,370, or 4 percent), and in 1988 was 91 (of 717, or 13 percent) (378). In a related analysis of the Doctorate Records File for 1988 alone, they find that of 615 English doctorates granted to U.S. residents, 26 were awarded to Blacks, 6 to Hispanics, and 12 to Asians (379).[14] It seems eminently reasonable to assume that both 1988 percentages—13 percent for non-U.S.

residents and about 7 percent for resident members of nonwhite racial/ethnic groups—represent about as much diversity in either category as English has ever featured. And however low the latter figure in particular might be as a function of ratios in the general population, both still mark a substantial increase over pre-1950 levels.[15]

We can also assume that the vast majority of these white U.S. doctoral students came from at least middle- to upper-middle-class backgrounds; were in their early to mid-twenties, more or less fresh from undergraduate studies; and were far more often male than female. Of the three markers—class, age, and sex—the last is easiest to trace. Thus we know that although the percentage of women earning doctorates in English has traditionally been somewhat higher than in many other fields, in no year prior to 1960 was it likely to have topped 20 percent, and in many years was more likely to have been in the 10 to 15 percent range.[16] We can also assume, that this figure masks total enrollments somewhat. That is, we know that as a general rule completion rates among female students have been lower—often strikingly lower—than among male students.[17] Still, it is safe to say that before 1950 most English graduate courses would have enrolled at least twice and often three times as many men as women, with that imbalance increasing with more advanced work as differential attrition rates played out.

Similarly, it is likely that the vast majority of these students—men and women both—came from reasonably well-off families. This is not to say that the graduate students themselves were financially secure. In this country, doctoral study in English (as indeed in most fields) often seems to involve penury. Bliss Perry, writing about his graduate teaching at Harvard from about 1910 to 1930, notes that the "case of these graduate students was often pitiable. Most of them were poor in purse—though perhaps a true scholar ought to be poor" (250). Still, such deprivation would for the most part have been elective, one feature of a vocational initiation for those both accustomed to and expecting again to live otherwise.

To be sure, there were also students from other socioeconomic groups. A range of institutional changes, from the formation of land grant and state colleges and universities to the federal aid programs of the New Deal (e.g., the Federal Emergency Relief Administration and later the National Youth Administration), had long since begun to alter the undergraduate mix, and some of these students found their way to graduate school as well. By 1960 Berelson could enthuse about

> the importance of the graduate school as a giant step in the career mobility of young people from what can fairly be described as lower-middle class homes. Well over half the recent recipients [of the Ph.D.] come from families where the father had only a high school education or less—and more often less— or held a job low in the occupational hierarchy. (134)

Still, this kind of mobility was a predominantly post–World War II development. Moreover, given the relatively class-sensitive nature of English as a discipline (a matter which, despite its frequent scholarly explorations of class issues, the field has rarely faced squarely in terms of its own membership), the sort of social-mobility-through-graduate-study Berelson describes seems likely to have come about somewhat more slowly than in many other fields.

The matter of age is hardest of all to track in any systematic way. However, Howard Mumford Jones (1930) offers a profile that has the ring of authenticity for much of the era. Writing about both men and women ("if I speak with the masculine pronoun, every one will grant, I think, that his sister student will present very similar traits and possess very similar backgrounds [*sic*]"), Jones argues that when he (or she) "enters the graduate school for the first time, our student has just ceased being an undergraduate. . . . He is about twenty-one or twenty-two years old, perhaps a little older" (469–70). In an uneven and seasonal way, the mix might include some slightly older and somewhat differently motivated candidates:

> Perhaps, however, our student has taught a year or two in some high school or small college and, alarmed at his obvious deficiencies, he has come to graduate work in order to fill up the gaps in his education. In that event he is likely to be a little more mature than his brother who has just been given his A.B.; and it is very likely in any case that his years of graduate school will be interrupted by the necessity of leaving school to earn

money that he may continue his studies. In many cases the result is that he piles up courses during the summer sessions, or, perhaps, has to allow a lapse of several years between successive periods of attendance at a university. (471)

Overall, though—and especially before the post–World War II GI Bill—doctoral education clearly was not primarily the domain of what we have since come to call the returning student.[18] Ultimately, however, the single most dramatic evidence regarding the demographic homogeneity of the doctoral student body of this era—and a measure that to a considerable degree capsulizes all these others—comes from educational background. The key document is a 1956 report compiled by the National Academy of Sciences tracing the connection between the institutions that awarded baccalaureate degrees and those that subsequently produced students earning doctorates for the period 1936 to 1950. In the category "Language, Literature, and Philology (English)," the rankings for the institutions that produced the most baccalaureate earners who subsequently went on to earn doctorates are remarkably similar to the rankings for the institutions that also eventually granted the most Ph.D.'s:

| B.A. Origin of Ph.D. Earners, 1936–1950 | Ph.D. Granters, 1936–1950 |
| --- | --- |
| 1. Harvard | 1. Yale |
| 2. Yale | 2. Harvard |
| Columbia | 3. Columbia |
| 4. Chicago | 4. Chicago |
| 5. Oberlin | 5. Iowa |
| 6. Princeton | 6. Wisconsin |
| 7. Michigan | 7. Illinois |
| 8. Illinois | 8. Cornell |
| 9. Wisconsin | 9. Michigan |
| Washington | 10. Princeton |

As you can see, Harvard, Yale, Columbia, and Chicago lead in both rankings, with Princeton, Michigan, Wisconsin, and Illinois also appearing on both lists. There are a few variations, to be sure, most notably Oberlin, which obviously sent an unusually high number of its graduates on to the doctorate in English.[19] Still, the overall pattern is clear. For these fifteen years in particular—but also, surely, in a pattern that was characteristic of the entire era—the few institutions that produced the vast majority of Ph.D.'s were also the institutions that produced most of the B.A.'s who went on to doctoral study in the first place.

On the professorial side of the desk in doctoral classrooms, meanwhile, the demographic profile was—to a large extent inevitably—similar to that on the student side. As I have suggested, some of the earliest professors would not have been U.S. citizens nor likely, therefore, have held undergraduate degrees from U.S. institutions. Once the system they helped create was up and running, however, it appears to have become an essentially closed one quite rapidly; those who inherited the top positions were most likely to be products of it. Indeed, allowing for the early imported talent and for a gradually decreasing number of members who, like Perry, did not themselves hold a doctorate,[20] the graduate professors for this era were probably an even more homogeneous group than the student body out of which they emerged, especially on two important counts. First, they appear to have been even more predominantly male. I have been unable to turn up any comprehensive direct evidence to support this assertion, but in addition to the sense of the period that can be gleaned from biographies, bibliographies, university histories, and the like, the figures provided by Cameron Allen's 1965 survey offer considerable evidence of its accuracy. Table 3.28, a census of professors engaged in graduate teaching, reports that of the 1170 graduate professors responding, 94 percent (1,100) were men and 6 percent (70) were women (Allen 140). Considering that World War II and the subsequent rapid expansion in higher education provided U.S. women with greater access to the academy than they had ever had before, it is unlikely that any earlier version of such a survey would have produced either a higher percentage or a larger raw number. And it also suggests that the same systemic trends that affected the rate at which women earned Ph.D.'s during this era continued to operate on those who did in fact move on to academic careers, with the result that a somewhat smaller percentage of the women earning the Ph.D. became graduate professors than was the case among their male counterparts.

Second, my sense is that the dominance exercised by certain institutions over the B.A.-to-Ph.D. pipeline not only continued but was likely amplified, as the Ph.D.'s were sorted out on their way toward the rank of graduate professor. In part, of course, this would simply have been a quantitative matter. Since the market in general was dominated by B.A./Ph.D. holders from some combination of Harvard and/or Yale and/or Columbia and/or Chicago and/or Wisconsin and so on, they would also most often have dominated candidate pools for graduate professorships. And this effect would have been magnified because of the way the system developed. That is, these universities enjoyed their positions of dominance not least because they had had what amounted to a head start, being among the first to put successful doctoral programs in place. This early entry would have provided their Ph.D. graduates with an advantage in the professional marketplace as well: early on, simply by making them available for openings, and then later by putting them in positions of seniority regarding both newly created graduate professorships and any openings in existing ones. At these upper reaches, in short, where decisions were made about who would and who would not be granted membership, the corporation was very closely held indeed; it was for all practical purposes a brotherhood based on race, citizenship, and class, bound together by what might be called, in a play on both its literal and figurative senses, the old school tie.

## CHAPTER TWO

# Lehrfreiheit, Lernfreiheit, *and the* Magisterial Curriculum

G iven the factors that shaped the U.S. system of English doctoral education—the German influence, the adaptation of the pyramidal corporate structure, and the powerfully homogeneous demographics—it only makes sense that the curricular practices to which it gave rise would, like most of its other features, favor the graduate faculty. The German tradition, of course, had its own ideal of curricular balance: on the faculty side, *Lehrfreiheit,* the freedom to teach what and as one chose that so excited the likes of Hart; and on the student side, *Lernfreiheit,* the freedom to learn which, while by no means a complete counterweight— the faculty obviously retained most of the authority—did move students out of the tight confines of the recitation tradition and gave them, moreover, the sort of programmatic flexibility and institutional mobility Perry found so invigorating, whatever its attendant risks. It was in this sense that Hart could plausibly call the German doctoral student his own master. Ultimately, the faculty awarded the degrees, so it was the faculty who set whatever standards needed to be met; but the individual student had a good deal of latitude in terms of how he went about preparing to meet them.

## Shifting the Balance

In the developing U.S. system, however, even this limited degree of balance shifted further toward the side of the professors early on. True, the very first candidates for the Ph.D. in English at U.S. institutions would have found themselves in a situation not all that dissimilar to what they would have faced in Germany, at least in terms of formal institutional requirements. With doctoral education sponsored by a graduate school or a graduate faculty—rather, that is, than by the as-yet-to-emerge discipline-based departments—students would likely have had to fulfill a one- (or at most two-) year residency requirement, examinations in the areas of expertise they claimed, and the subsequent presentation of a dissertation for inspection by the faculty (or some designated subset thereof). By the early decades of this century, however, doctoral education in English, as in most disciplines, was well on its way to being established in departments, and—of primary importance here—by that means becoming integrated into the field's corporate economy. For it was the English department that became that economy's central engine: the primary institutional means by which tuition-generating classroom teaching could be exchanged, through the medium of the credit hour and its various equivalents, for the U.S. graduate professor's flexibility in terms of instructional and research time—flexibility that a German professor would have negotiated from the state, or that a U.S. professor in, say, the physical sciences, would come to purchase through research grants.

Situating English graduate education in this context thus constituted a fundamental shift in the relationship between faculty and graduate students. For whatever other purposes doctoral programs in English might subsequently be designed to serve—and of course there have been others—their primary *systemic* tendency would always be to maximize the students' contributions to this economy while maintaining, or better yet enhancing, the graduate faculty's profits from it. As it turned out, those student contributions came to take two main forms, and the drive to maximize the value of each clearly constrained the development of any version of *Lernfreiheit* for English in the United States.

First and most obviously, graduate students contributed to the corporate economy *as* students, enrolling for coursework, providing employment for the graduate faculty, and (one way or another) paying tuition. Getting the most from them in this capacity was thus a matter of making sure they enrolled for as many credit hours as was feasible—as much, in effect, as the market would bear—on the way to their degrees. One mechanism for doing so, residency requirements, was in place essentially from the beginning. And though such requirements do not appear to have been officially extended on any widespread basis—many programs even today require only a single year in residence—they came to be supplemented and complemented in a number of ways: by requirements for a certain number of credit hours as a necessary preliminary to presenting oneself for qualifying examinations; by specifically required courses; by required *types* of courses (seminars, e.g., or methods courses); and by such "hidden" requirements as prerequisite courses and strongly recommended courses(anyone who has been a graduate student will recognize the euphemism here). Moreover, a given program's hold over its students was reinforced by the development of what might be called institutional impermeability, the practice of limiting the number and type of graduate credits one institution would accept from others. Among other things, these limits made it difficult for students to feel able, as Perry claims he did in Germany, to attend lectures at Columbia, say, while enrolled at Yale or NYU. In sum, whatever educational arguments might be made in favor of this whole range of practices—and surely such arguments were made—they indisputably had the effect of limiting graduate students' ability to chart their own educational course.

We also know, however, that departments determined in fairly short order that the students' contribution to this corporate economy could be substantially increased—further maximized—if they were also engaged as something like junior staff members. That is, if graduate students devoted some portion of their time to working as teaching fellows, teaching assistants, and the like, they could generate (or help the faculty generate) credit hours, and—the key advantage—do so at a fraction of what it cost the institution to pay faculty for the same work. There was some German precedent for such a practice. In that system (as even now in some U.S. disciplines, including—albeit not all that commonly—English), a small number of graduate students would assist the professor in his research while, and in many cases *by*, carrying out their own. It is not clear precisely which U.S. institution first shifted these assistantship duties from research to teaching, but the move obviously made terrific sense for the emerging corporate English departments, all the more so because such duties did not need to be afforded any official curricular or disciplinary value. This was a form of labor, in other words, that in contrast to at least the optimum practice of the German system, did nothing to advance the students' formal progress toward their degrees: it kept them in the system as both paying customers *and* a cheap, tractable, labor pool. It was certainly possible to earn a Ph.D. in English without ever performing such duties; lots of students managed this, and indeed the kind of wholesale reliance on TAs characteristic of contemporary universities did not emerge until the 1970s and 1980s, when something on the order of 60 to 70 percent of those receiving Ph.D.'s in the humanities reported having held assistantships while in graduate school.[1] Nevertheless, the advantages of the TA system have been apparent for a long time, and departments in at least some institutions—perhaps most notably the large public institutions—would have encouraged a good many of their students to take them on.[2]

The impact of such labor on students' freedom to learn was considerable and undeniable. At the most basic level, these duties imposed constraints that can be described as logistical, affecting such things as scheduling, in that graduate students could not take courses at the same time they were teaching them, and both completion rates and time to degree, in that even outside of actual teaching time students could not be "doing their own work" when they were doing the department's (preparing for class, reading and grading papers, and so forth). At another level, though, as my use of the term tractable suggests, membership in this kind of a labor pool could also impose more complex and subtle constraints. For while the duties graduate students performed in such capacities never formally entered the curriculum—never generated credits toward the degree or satisfied curricular requirements, at least on any appreciably wide scale—they nevertheless came to constitute an apprenticeship of sorts, particularly as the Ph.D. in English came to function so extensively as a college teaching certificate. In some instances, the status of this apprenticeship was acknowledged by the establishment of a course or a series of meetings—*practicum* is probably the closest thing to a trade name for such activities—very often required for those with teaching assignments and rarely counting toward the degree per se. Even when there was no such acknowledgment, however, the whole arrangement put those students who were funded in exchange for teaching-related duties into a relationship with the faculty in general, and faculty supervisors in particular, that posed a considerable threat to any possible *Lernfreiheit*. After all, when the faculty from whom you are seeking your education are also in charge of your means of funding that education, they can exercise more control—and more direct control—over the trajectory it follows than faculty without that fiscal power.

Nor is it hard to see how in the overall system constraints on any emerging *Lernfreiheit* also would have served to enhance the prospects for an American version of *Lehrfreiheit* for the field of English. As we have already seen, adding graduate students to the department's subordinate workforce (along with instructors, part-time faculty, and so on) helped generate the credit-hour surplus that enabled graduate faculty to teach fewer courses, or at least to invest less time in the courses they did teach by providing TA support—with the result, in either case, of freeing up more time for faculty research. At the same time, by concentrating this subordinate staff more or less exclusively at the lower division, and most notably in the labor-intensive composition classes, the graduate faculty could relieve itself from obligatory duty there— could, in essence, operate a kind of credit-hour factory without actually having to work in it.

Moreover, as we have also seen, the status of these graduate students *as* students in this system pretty much guaranteed that the faculty would have opportunities to teach at least some of the courses the university still required them to teach in a context that matched the German ideal: a context wherein one's research and one's professing (Graff's verb seeming to be particularly apt here) were of a piece. That is, for the purposes of teaching graduate students, the professor could afford to be the specialist whose duty began and ended with himself. And thanks to the various mechanisms for controlling graduate enrollments, a tenured graduate professor in this system could enjoy as a kind of corporate bonus access to such teaching with more long-term security than any German professor was likely to have had. For while the latter may have operated with a good deal of autonomy, his status vis-à-vis both the state and the students depended on the continuing viability of his research program. With regard to the latter in particular he had limited control: he could indeed teach what and as he chose, but there was no guarantee that anyone would enroll. By contrast, the U.S. graduate professor may have needed a strong research program to secure a good position, but once he or she held such a post, rank and seniority allowed him or her to wield considerable power— not least curricular power—regardless of whether the research continued. Thus, when it came to offering courses that might interest graduate students . . . well, as my review of enrollment-control mechanisms makes clear, whether a course was new or old, original or derivative, mainstream or marginal, there were plenty of ways to guarantee that the seats would be filled.

## The Magisterial Curriculum

The cumulative result of this peculiarly American version of graduate curricular balance—the management trainee program for College English Teaching, Inc., as it were—is what I have come to think of as the Magisterial curriculum. This was not, of course, a curriculum in any official sense, formulated, approved, and promulgated by the Modern Language Association or some other body in an effort to regulate Ph.D. production. Nor, as I have indicated, is it represented extensively in the professional literature; with teaching never really having gained sanction as an object of disciplinary inquiry, there was little incentive for faculty—least of all graduate faculty—to publish on curricular or pedagogical matters in any detail. Still, there clearly was all these years an evolving curricular industry standard, and its general lineaments are traceable. Its purpose was to complete the formalized educational portion of the process of professorial replication and corporate perpetuation: to sort and rank all the recruits who had been granted graduate status, and then to initiate some subset of that group—the chosen—into the fold, to make them into "one of us." As my review of the demographics made clear, by this point in the process a great deal of sorting and ranking would already have been done. That is, in many of the ways that really mattered—sex, race, class, national origin, educational background, and so on—the doctoral students would already have *been* "one of us." Nevertheless, the economics of the system more or less demanded a student surplus (as a source of more tuition income, more potential TA labor, etc.); it was always possible, even within such a relatively homogeneous group, to sort and rank even more finely (as the attrition rates attest); and in any case, both the curricular regimen and its constituent rites of passage performed important symbolic functions for the candidates, the professoriate, and the sponsoring institutions.

At the center of this curriculum were the graduate professors, figured once again along the lines of that idealization Sosnoski called—and hence my choice of a curricular title—the *Magister.* As suggested earlier, the *Magister* is by definition not an individual person, but rather a composite production of the field's mythology: "the sum of the ways [English] academics portray themselves officially," in Sosnoski's phrasing, a "personification of the institution's ideally orthodox [English] professor" (73–74).

In the context of the Magisterial curriculum, however, that same mythology can be said to have conferred on the graduate faculty, individually and collectively, what amounted to *Magisterial* power. Thus, Stuart P. Sherman, writing to protest the disciplinary influence of George Lyman Kittredge, characterizes him in terms that were probably effective as critique precisely because they cut so close to the prevailing, albeit more favorably disposed, view held by Kittredge's supporters. To his most advanced graduate students, Sherman writes, Kittredge was a "benignant Jove, a being of equal or greater fascination [than the Jupiter Tonans Kittredge presented to undergraduates,] but with its terrors laid by, alert, omniscient as it seemed, a hawk-eyed critic still, but of princely amenity, tireless helpfulness, and the cordialest interest in one's personal destiny" (151).

More to the point, whether the graduate faculty were cast as Olympians, gurus, or simply petty tyrants, they were by definition—and by virtue of a kind of Pauline theology—as near to the presence of the Real Thing as graduate students would ever get. The students' corresponding duty was therefore quite clear: "Imitatio *Magister,*" as Sosnoski says, "is the academic imperative given to every apprentice or examinee" (81), but with the obvious proviso that, since direct access to the *Magister* himself was impossible, students needed to make the most of their chances with the graduate faculty as members of his (mystical) body.

This imitative imperative operated in two key dimensions which, in curricular practice, functioned as two discrete stages. The first, consisting primarily of coursework leading to a set of barrier examinations, required that students come to know what the Magisterial "we" knew: in practical terms, to read what "we" had read and—by dint of certain initiatory disciplinings—to perform with that material in prescribed ways. This stage was the functional equivalent of basic training, a sort of academic boot camp: an intense (and undoubtedly often intensely humbling) program designed to weed out those whom Perry calls the "misfits" (250) and to reinforce in those who survived a proper regard for the Magisterial regime. It is not hard to follow the curricular logic here. From the corporate perspective, no mere "I"—not even a Kittredge or a Cleanth Brooks—could actually measure up to the *Magister*'s exemplary composite "we"; an entering graduate student, therefore, was a humble creature indeed. As Perry explains, the "often pitiable" situation of graduate students at Harvard (an institution that would have attracted the country's most competitive applicants) extended well beyond their finances:

> Sometimes it appeared that [a student's] college training had been grossly deficient, though his marks had been high enough. He was supposed, for instance, to be able to use French and German as tools in his graduate work, but no one had really examined him in those subjects, and often he could not use them at all. The pace set in his linguistic courses was a stiff one, and soon he felt a stitch in his side. Then he jumped to the conclusion that his real obstacle in this race was "philology," and he began to worry and then to curse and then to seek out some professor who would listen to his troubles. (250–51)

Nor was that the end or even the worst of such students' deficiencies; Perry claims that he

> could not understand why the men who were proposing to devote their lives to the teaching of literature brought with them

to Harvard such ignorance of European books and of the general history of thought. We have long ceased to expect any
familiarity with Greek, save from a very few, and it was sel-
dom that the graduates knew more Latin than their half-for-
gotten Cicero and Virgil. . . . But the great majority of them
knew nothing, at first hand, of such European figures as
Petrarch, Erasmus, Rabelais, Diderot. They did not even know
their Goethe and Voltaire, their Franklin and Jefferson. If they
had ever sat up half the night reading Rousseau and Wordsworth
for the sheer pleasure of it, they would have had some counterweight for Irving Babbitt's diatribes against the dangerous
Romanticism of these authors; but they came to his brilliant
lectures without any preparatory personal experience with the
authors whom he attacked. (252–53)

Howard Mumford Jones (1930) held much the same views. I
quoted him earlier concerning the age of graduate students, and
he has a good deal to say in the same essay about their general
state of (un)readiness:

[The entering student] has probably "majored" in English, he
has perhaps written some essays for the college magazine or
the newspaper, or perhaps a play for the college theater. He is
fond of reading, and is typically familiar with the more talked-
about contemporary writers. He has been a member of some
five or six classes in literature (besides the elementary course)
which constituted his "major" in that field. If he is the product
of a small college, these courses have been perhaps a little vague
and generalized; if he is the product of a larger school, his work
may have been more disciplined, though not necessarily so.
Under any circumstances he himself soon recognizes that his
preparation is a little sketchy; and, remembering what we know
of undergraduate values, we shall not be surprised if he tells us
that as an undergraduate he perhaps found it easy to "pass."
He is only a few years out of his adolescence, and his emotions
and his ideas are still a little vague. (469–70)

Moreover, Jones contends that this profile is accurate not only
for his own University of North Carolina but also—however re-
grettably—for English graduate programs in the United States as
a whole. Nevertheless, he counseled, if the situation was "not
very creditable to the country, the university, the graduate school,
or the state of our culture," it was "practically the condition

which student and professor have to face." Nor did he have any doubts about the corrective regimen required:

> [M]y own experience . . . is that most of the first year of graduate study, and often large portions of the succeeding years, have to be devoted to teaching the student what he is supposed to have learned as an undergraduate (that is, the salient facts of literary history); and to inducting him into the bibliography and methods of literary study as well as to disciplining and stiffening his mental processes. To attempt much beyond this is usually disastrous; our student does not yet have enough factual information to judge general theory or to form those broad views and syntheses which our critics would like to have him secure; he has not read enough, is not sufficiently experienced to make his essays in independent criticism or scholarship of value. (470–71)

As these comments suggest, the Magisterial curriculum placed a premium on a certain range of courses—those understood as most likely to instill what Jones elsewhere labels the "instrumental disciplines": developing a proper "time-sense," acquiring bibliographical methodology, and absorbing "a minimum requirement of philological discipline" (79). And, indeed, for every program and every era, there were courses that must have seemed, and that would have been presented as, indispensable: Anglo-Saxon grammar, Old Norse, Old English literature, Middle English literature, ballads and metrical romances, modern English grammar and/or linguistics, history and structure of the English language, variously conceived research method and bibliography courses, and so on. In truth, however, as the obviously fluctuating status of many such courses helps to demonstrate, the Magisterial curriculum was primarily personnel-centered. *What* was taught, especially in terms of subject area, mattered far less than *who* taught it; and the wise recruits, or at least the proper ones, were those who gave themselves over to this fact. As Perry explained to students who thought otherwise, the object was to submit to as many manifestations of the *Magister* as possible:

> I was not identified with any of the philological courses, and the graduate students who had what they thought was a literary turn of mind sought me out for advice. They had no idea

that I had ever gone through a rigid philological discipline myself, and I think that G. L. K. [Kittredge] would have been amused to hear me defend the emphasis which the Department and Division were laying upon that side of the necessary training of a teacher. To the sentimentalists who believed, in Stuart Sherman's phrase, that attention to linguistics was "killing the poet in them," I pointed out that if a poet could be killed by a year or two of hard work on the early stages of Germanic or Romance languages, the quicker he died the better. To the modernists who wished to confine their work to the eighteenth and nineteenth centuries I replied that the main thing was to learn to paddle one's own scholarly canoe, and that if some of the most skilful canoe-men at Harvard chose to exercise and teach their craft upon the rough upper reaches of the river instead of upon the broader and smoother currents lower down, it was the duty and privilege of a pupil to learn from the master on those waters where the master loved to teach. After the pupil had once learned what the linguistic specialists had to impart, he would be free to paddle his own canoe on any waters he preferred! (251)

This stage of the curriculum culminated, as it still universally appears to do, in a set of examinations. They were offered under a variety of names—qualifying, preliminary, comprehensive—and assumed a variety of forms, as well. They might, for example, have been exclusively oral, exclusively written, or (most often) some combination of the two; might have been given over several hours, or carried on for two or more days; might have been administered by a particular committee, or been open to all interested faculty; they might have given the candidates some choice over the "areas" to be examined, but might not; and so on.[3] Under whatever name or in whatever form, however, such examinations served the same basic curricular purpose, constituting the penultimate Magisterial obstacle course—a ritual gauntlet all would-be Ph.D.'s needed to run successfully—and also assumed thereby the role of emblem for the entire process, out of which they served as the only gateway. Indeed, although Perry's advice about learning to "paddle" in the masters' various favorite scholarly waters never explicitly mentions such examinations, it surely exemplifies their emblematic power in just this sense: "You had best learn to paddle on the masters' home waters now," he is in effect saying, "because you will find yourselves paddling those waters—without guidance and under masterly scrutiny—soon enough again."

By all accounts, the combined pressures of coursework and examinations did their culling work quite well, although no program appears to have kept careful track of the precise numbers involved. Obviously, some students would have dropped out before ever taking the examinations, and their ranks would have been supplemented by those who actually took the examinations and failed. Allen's 1965 survey, for example, offers some indication of the numbers involved: sixty-three graduate programs (of eighty-eight surveyed) reported failing and dropping some 212 students, or an average of 3.4 students per program in a year when those programs would grant something approaching 600 Ph.D.'s (181). Whatever the specific numbers involved, they were significant enough to provoke attacks from critics such as Sherman and, later, Wellek and Warren (see, for example, 285), but they also elicited defenses from supporters such as Perry and Jones. Indeed, from Perry's perspective the students who were eliminated had likely been done a kindness, and neither he nor Jones counted their loss as much of a problem. Jones is writing here about the students who drop out—those who found graduate work "dry and uninteresting" and the professors "mere pedants"—but his rendering of the situation no doubt extended to those who were removed by the examinations:

> Certainly the graduate school loses; but I confess that I do not view the loss with serious alarm, and I cannot agree with the late Stuart Sherman that we necessarily lose the better men, for it is my observation that those who are frightened away by the stricter mental discipline, and insistence upon accuracy which we demand of graduate students, do not in most cases achieve great things outside the graduate world. Temperamentally averse to discipline, they drift into journalism or advertising or popular fiction. (1930, 471)

Those who *did* successfully negotiate coursework and examinations, however, moved on to the second stage of the curriculum in which, in the form of the thesis or dissertation, they faced the final Magisterial challenge: learning to write what and as the Magisterial "we" wrote.[4] These students would, of course, have done a substantial amount of writing during their prethesis years, most of it in aid of acquiring the instrumental disciplines Jones describes. In other words, they would have engaged in variously configured chronological, bibliographical, and philological exercises, or, along related lines, written examinations designed to demonstrate their grasp of the material in a given course. Judging by the practices Allen's survey leads him to protest, we can surmise that in more extreme circumstances students might have found themselves "gather[ing] material for the director's next paper or book," doing "an annotated bibliography," or listing "all the variants between two manuscripts" even in coursework as advanced as a seminar (111). They may also have tried, and in some programs even been encouraged to try, those "essays in independent criticism or scholarship" Jones mentions; some such efforts presumably led him to write so disparagingly of their prospects for success. Clearly, however, the bulk of such work would have been deemed preliminary, a series of disciplinary submissions to be undertaken, per Perry's exhortation, as a "duty" and a "privilege." Perhaps the most eloquent comment on the status of these and other forms of prethesis writing is their invisibility in contemporary commentaries. Even catalogues of students' deficiencies otherwise as fulsome as those offered by Perry and Jones did not need to belabor the Magisterially obvious: those who do not know enough cannot write anything of interest or "value."

But to pass the examinations was to have demonstrated that one *did* know enough and was therefore qualified to attempt genuinely disciplinary writing. The operative word here, though, is *attempt:* although this second stage of the curriculum was no boot camp, there were no guarantees that every student would complete it. Actually, what candidates really needed to get through this stage in the process, though no one was likely to have put it in quite these terms, was a sponsor: a graduate faculty member who would publicly testify that the candidate's writing and, by extension, the candidate were worthy products of a given program. Thus, while this second stage of the curriculum had basically the same structure as the first—an extended period of professorially monitored work culminating in the public performance of the dissertation defense—the latter component seems to have acquired from very early on a more strictly ceremonial status than that held by the comprehensive examinations as the culmination of coursework. This is not to say that the dissertation defense lost its significance entirely. It clearly continued to serve, as it does even now, as an important Magisterial emblem, the ultimate rite of passage, the enactment—at least in imagination—of a tableau wherein the would-be "doctor" faces any and all challengers regarding a thesis he has affixed to some figurative door of the cathedral of learning.

Even as changes in the nature of university-based knowledge making (such as increasingly narrow specializations and higher rates of doctoral production) were raising serious questions about the possible substantiality of such occasions, however, the politics of department-based doctoral programs rendered them all but pro forma for more local reasons. Before candidates could schedule a defense, they needed approval for the essentially completed project from their supervisor and/or dissertation committee. On the occasion of a defense, therefore, any serious effort by other members of the faculty to deny the candidate's qualifications was tantamount to denying the qualifications of that candidate's supervisor and committee. For that matter, it was to raise serious doubts about the judgment of the department itself (which had, of course, already granted its approval of the principals on a number of other occasions). In short, while some candidate at some time may have failed to earn the Ph.D. on the basis of his or her performance at a defense, I have been unable to find any account of it; and all the evidence suggests that any such failure would have been very much the exception.

As a practical matter, then, all the pressure in this stage of the curriculum fell on the process of writing a document to the satisfaction of a supervising faculty member. The first step—or first two steps, perhaps—was therefore to identify a supervisor and a general topic area, not necessarily in that order and probably quite often in something like a dialectical fashion. In this as in other matters, local customs appear to have varied considerably, but it seems to have been fairly standard practice for professors to exercise default supervisory control in their general areas of expertise, so that to choose a topic area was also to identify a supervisor. Thus students would have found themselves negotiating between a cluster of their own preferred topic areas on the one hand, and the prospects for a good working relationship with the corresponding supervisors on the other. Other arrangements, though, were also likely to have been in force at one institution or another: at one extreme, students choosing their own supervisors and negotiating topics within that relationship, and at the other, having topic and/or supervisor simply assigned by the department (Allen 66–67).

Whatever pattern the arrangements followed, they involved a good deal more than a handshake agreement. A dissertation, in Jones's mixed-metaphor rendering of the standard spiel, had to "either explore territory insufficiently known or not known at all, or . . . set known facts in a fresh and important light." Before students were allowed to proceed, therefore, they needed to certify that what they were proposing would in fact constitute such a contribution—a procedure that in its purest form would have gone something like this:

> Before beginning work the student is required to traverse the whole related field of scholarship and to be certain that his particular subject has not been treated before; and if, during his preparatory work, a thesis appear from some institution, however remote, covering the same topic, he is expected to abandon his labors and make a fresh start. Moreover, before beginning to write, the student is expected by some to have absolutely exhausted the bibliographical aids, and to have read every article, however remote, which in any way bears upon his topic; and the overlooking of such articles is held to indicate a lamentable weakness in the student. (Jones 1931, 200)

As this sketch hints, the end of this topical certification process was not always precisely demarcated; even when the student had been given local authorization, the specter of that competing thesis at another institution never entirely faded. Barring any such disqualifications, however, this preliminary research would gradually segue into actual writing. The overall process was almost certain to be a lengthy one, measured in years and frequently complicated—perhaps even more than today—by the demands of teaching, finances, and family. According to Bowen and Rudenstine, for example, the median time to degree for the Ph.D.

in all fields between 1920 and 1940 was roughly between seven and eight years (115), and English seems always to have found itself toward the upper end of this range. Hence, even if students spent three to four years on coursework and exams, they would have worked on the dissertation for a minimum of three years; in fact, Allen's cohort of mid-1960s Ph.D.'s reported taking an average of three years to complete theirs (69).

Under ideal circumstances—when writer, supervisor, and committee were all in synch—those years could proceed smoothly, as witness Sherman's sketch of the benignant "Kittredge of the disciples," quoted previously. However, such pure harmony was surely more the exception than the rule. Jones writes, for example, that the rigors of the process could be such that

> it is no wonder that in the last year or two of graduate work, students become nervously exhausted, in many cases break down in health, and in most instances feel the effect of the tremendous strain which has been put upon them, for months after the degree is secured. (1931, 201)

Thirty years later, a subset of Allen's respondents—the 17 percent (315) who reported having failed to progress from their initial proposal to a completed dissertation (but eventually *did* earn the degree)—provide a concrete basis for what might otherwise be dismissed as the merely apocryphal graduate school horror stories concerning what could and did go wrong in student-supervisor or student-committee relations: "'My professor urged me to write on H. G. Wells, but I couldn't care less.'" "'The professor who encouraged the topic retired; his successor discouraged it after I had worked on it for three years.'" "'My director approved, but the committee regarded my dissertation as too narrow'" (67–68). And both Jones and Allen are describing candidates who *completed* the dissertation and were awarded the degree. Had someone thought to ask, those who did not complete it would surely have had their own tales to tell.

In the end, of course, dissertations did get written, were approved by supervisor and committee, were escorted through the ritual of the defense, and—in one form or another—were published.[5] And during this era they appear to have been pretty much what one would expect from a situation that put each of the system's most stringently selected students in the position not only of having to "either explore territory insufficiently known or not known at all" or "set known facts in a fresh and important light," but of having to do so to the satisfaction of one of the system's most stringently selected professors. In short, homogeneity was the order of the day. How could it not have been? The candidates who made it this far were, after all, those who had demonstrated a temperamental affinity, or at least a tolerance, for "stricter mental discipline" and an "insistence upon accuracy," and who had done so not least by writing precisely what was expected of them. Perhaps more to the point, they were people who had already invested at least three and likely more years in this process, survived the field's most demanding examinations, and now needed the sponsorship of one of its sanctioned masters and, even beyond that, a topic that would not be trumped by someone working elsewhere. Promises like Perry's about being free to paddle one's canoe on any waters one chose notwithstanding, how much risk—in subject matter, in method, or in form— could such people afford to take?

By all accounts, the answer was "not much." One of Jones's aims in "Graduate English Study: Its Rationale" was to upbraid commentators such as Stewart Sherman and Norman Foerster and Henry S. Canby for exaggerating the degree of conformity the system demanded, for their tendency to "unduly decry the bad and fail to appraise the good" (466). After all, writes Jones, a training regimen that could claim results such as John Livingston Lowes's *The Road to Xanadu*, Kittredge's work on Chaucer and Shakespeare, or the University of Chicago's then new edition of Chaucer or dictionary of American English, could hardly be considered a failure (466–67).

In fact, however, Jones's assessment of the situation differs very little from the versions offered by these critics, or indeed from those of such later would-be reformers as Wellek and Warren (1949) or Cameron Allen (1968). Thus, in a long footnote intended to refute charges that the system produced dissertations that were "mechanical and narrow," Jones offers his own analysis of the theses completed at Harvard (1873–1926) and Chicago

(1894–1927). Concerned in particular to challenge perceptions that philology was the all but exclusive mode available for doctoral research—a prime source of the "mechanical" label—Jones is clearly pleased to be able to demonstrate that only 30 of the 298 dissertations at these two leading institutions fall under that heading. In the process, however, he also demonstrates why the charge of narrowness would be a good deal harder to refute: he manages to sort the other 268 titles using only four additional headings, two of which—"'external' literary history" (131) and studies that "combine literary history and literary criticism (the life-and-works type is not infrequent)" (80)—account for 211 titles (467–88). By the time Jones comes to offer his own recommendations concerning the dissertation (Section VII), he finds it necessary to concede that at least in some institutions (and in fact he names no exceptions) "we must agree with Mr. Foerster as to our over-emphasis upon mechanical technique, and with Mr. Canby as to the triviality of the results" (200).

Despite these complaints lodged against it—or, indeed, as they go some way toward demonstrating—this second stage of the curriculum was clearly a logical and successful extension of the first and a fitting capstone for the entire corporate process of replication. Thus, to the extent that students wrote meticulously researched monographs on tightly defined and often rather obscure topics, they were indicating how well they had learned the lessons they had been taught: they were displaying their command of the instrumental disciplines; demonstrating, through their fealty to their respective masters, their allegiance to the *Magister*; and, finally, confirming their selfless commitment to the corporate disciplinary goal of exploring unknown territory, however remote their own tract of it might seem.

Moreover, from a management perspective this extended postexamination but predegree interval provided not only an additional source for the teaching labor needed to keep the operation running prosperously, but also—by virtue of the students' total dependence on a dissertation supervisor as sponsor—one last opportunity to secure the brotherhood's future profile, a final mechanism for quality control. Thus, while various wags over the years have commented that a foreign visitor to a U.S. English department might be forgiven for thinking that ABD (All But

Dissertation) was a formal degree designation, the corporate function of those it designated was no joke. Postexamination doctoral students—both those who would eventually complete the degree and those who would not—may not have comprised as inexpensive a teaching corps as Teaching Assistants, but they were usually no less vulnerable and in any case were still a bargain compared with regular faculty. Under titles such as "lecturer" or "instructor," they constituted a substantial portion of what Oscar Campbell in 1939 called an "academic proletariat" (181).

And the disproportionate percentage of this "underclass" who were women (Connors 76–79) testifies to the effectiveness, if not the detailed workings, of this final sorting mechanism. For whatever reasons and by whatever combination of means, this required pairing of candidate and sponsor clearly helped maintain at least one dimension of corporate homogeneity: it helped keep the Ph.D. fraternity a fraternity, as it were. Presumably this same mechanism could, when necessary, have been directed to serve the same ends in other dimensions as well.

## CHAPTER THREE

# Expansion, Contraction, and the (Surp)Rise of Heterogeneity (1950–1990)

O ver the course of its first seventy-five years, English doctoral education in the United States took its place at the top of a rather tidy corporate operation. All the key elements were in place: departments as a mechanism for converting teaching work into research time; official sanction for the Ph.D. as the ultimate certification for college teaching; undergraduate programs as a source of both employment and potential recruits; and, last but not least, a management training program—the Magisterial curriculum—as a means of corporate perpetuation. The war years (1940–1945) were difficult, with the number of Ph.D.'s granted falling to pre-1920 levels. But recovery was quick and impressive—so quick, in fact, that by 1950 the number of degrees granted had already risen to the previously unreached two hundred mark. Moreover, this immediate postwar growth spurt was only a token of things to come. The next twenty-five years constitute what I have dubbed the Great Expansion, a period during which doctoral education in English, like doctoral education in nearly all academic fields, grew on an unprecedented scale. As things turned out, this expansion proved unsustainable, and more than one generation of un- and underemployed Ph.D. holders paid dearly for its excesses. Nevertheless, this era is still often thought of as the golden age of College English Teaching, Inc., and it marked the beginning of well over half of all extant doctoral programs—including the first Ph.D. program at SUNY–Albany, which would, in its ill-fated way, provide so much of the foundation for "Writing, Teaching, and Criticism."

# The Great Expansion

The first few decades after World War II were a time of extraordinary change in U.S. higher education overall, driven in particular by the expansion of undergraduate programs. Early on, much of the impetus for that expansion came from the GI Bill, which in its initial form (the 1944 Servicemen's Readjustment Act) helped boost postwar enrollments in higher education by more than 50 percent over 1939–40 levels. In subsequent legislative incarnations, this program helped cushion what would otherwise have been an even more serious decline in enrollments through the 1950s (a decline that reflected, more than anything, the nation's low Depression-era birthrate).[1] Ultimately, however, this long-term expansion in enrollments was sustained and subsequently pushed to its highest levels by the arrival of the baby boom generation. There were any number of complementary and complicating factors involved: the expanding postwar economy; an overall increase in the percentage of the population enrolling in postsecondary education; increased federal support for higher education through programs in addition to the GI Bill (especially the National Defense Education Act [NDEA]); the civil rights movement; the Vietnam War-related draft and its deferment provisions; and so on. Still, the sheer demographics of the bulge are unmistakable: after small but gradual increases in the late 1950s, undergraduate enrollments between 1960 and 1970 jumped from something on the order of 3.5 million to almost 8 million students.

This pattern of growth in undergraduate education was paralleled by, and in large part responsible for initiating, a similar boom in doctoral education. Certainly this was the case for English; the increase in Ph.D.'s awarded over this period was simply meteoric. The 237 degrees awarded in 1950 had more than doubled by 1963, to about 500; by 1972 they had more than doubled again, falling just short of 1,400. To no small extent, this rapid expansion was itself a function of the increase in numbers of undergraduates with an interest in English. The recruiting system, described in Chapter 1, seems to have worked on a percentage system more than on a simply quantitative quota basis, so that the increase was in part a matter of what Bowen and Rudenstine call a "scale effect" (47): if 500 English majors, say, produced 50 potential graduate students, then 5,000 would produce 500.

There was also a connection between employment prospects and this pattern of expansion. Bowen and Rudenstine are careful to argue that the connection between the academic job market and Ph.D. production is not a simple or direct one, and, as we shall see throughout this chapter and the next, this has proven true for English. Nevertheless, demonstrable existing needs presumably had some impact on the increase in Ph.D. production during this boom era. That is, given the status of the degree as "the sine qua non" for teaching at all universities and more and more colleges (Allen 15), this increase in degrees granted represented an effort, at least in part, to keep up with the rapid growth of undergraduate enrollments. The tone of Allen's description reflects some of the urgency that tended to characterize discussions of the situation:

> The shortage of fully trained teachers of English has unfortunately been increasing in an order that is not consonant with the increase in undergraduate enrollment. In 1953–54 only 29 percent of all new teachers of English had a doctorate; ten years later, this surprising percentage had fallen to little more than 12 percent. . . . The decline in trained personnel revealed by these percentages for English is true of all other disciplines but not to the same degree. While the number of beginning English teachers with Ph.D.'s was being halved, the average for all fields was falling from 31 percent to 25 percent. It seems almost a natural law that the more trained English teachers are required, the fewer are available. Can this shortage be solved or should we regard it as chronic? (17–18)[2]

Moreover, as his closing comments suggest, these existing shortages were not the only concern. The drive to increase the number of available English Ph.D.'s was also fueled by an acute anxiety about, along with some obvious corporate ambitions regarding, the future. Among other things, Allen points out that while there were six million undergraduates enrolled in 1965, "government experts at forecasting enrollments, who have been regular underestimators by about 10 percent, predict that there will be 7 million undergraduates in 1969 and 9 million in 1975" (16)— the implication being, of course, that English was at present desperately ill-equipped to deal with its projected share.

The institutional alterations undertaken to meet these current and projected demands for Ph.D.-holding college professors dramatically changed the profile of English doctoral education, transforming the "close corporation" described in Chapter 1— an enterprise that was not, after all, much more than a cottage industry—into something more like an industry proper.[3] Not surprisingly, a significant portion of this shift played out on the same campuses that had always produced the bulk of the degrees. Thus, in 1958 the institutions with graduate programs ranked in what Bowen and Rudenstine call Tier I—a fairly stable group that included the likes of Columbia, Harvard, Yale, Chicago, Stanford, and so on—produced 235 (of 333) doctorates; by 1972 that number had risen to 700 (of 1,370) (1992, 387). The number of programs represented in these figures shifted a bit over these fourteen years, from 25 in 1958 to 29 in 1972, but the rate of growth is still remarkable: It means that on average each Tier I program went from granting 9 to 10 doctorates per year to granting something on the order of 24.[4]

As the total number of degrees for these years makes clear, however, the Tier I programs by no means accounted for all of the increase. In 1958 the 235 degrees awarded by the 25 Tier I programs represented about 70 percent of the total 333, meaning that the 35 programs in Tiers II through IV (there were 60 English doctoral programs altogether) granted 98 degrees, or about 30 percent (387). By 1972, however, while the 700 degrees granted by the Tier I programs obviously constituted a major increase in their output, those 700 degrees were only 51 percent of the 1,370 awarded overall—they represented, that is, a substantially smaller *proportion* of the national total. By that year, in other words, the programs ranked in Tiers II through IV, the number of which had grown to 95, nearly matched the Tier I programs in total output, at 670, thereby accounting for 49 percent of the United States' English Ph.D.'s (386–87).

Moreover, a good many of those 95 programs were what Bowen and Rudenstine classify as "new": those "that awarded at least one doctorate . . . in some [even-numbered] year after 1958, but no degrees in 1958" (391).[5] Perhaps the single most striking measure of what was happening with English doctoral education during these years is this increase in the total number of programs offering the Ph.D.: from 60 in 1958 to 124 in 1972 (386). And these new programs, nearly all of them ranked in Tiers II through IV, definitely made an impact. Bowen and Rudenstine indicate that in 1960 28 of a total 386 degrees were awarded by new programs, or about 7 percent. By 1972 that raw number was up to 387, and the new programs' share of the total degrees awarded had quadrupled, to 28 percent (388).

From what I have been calling a corporate perspective, these were clearly heady times, and in fact Cameron Allen's *The Ph.D. in English and American Literature* can be seen as a peculiarly appropriate memorial to them, albeit in two somewhat conflicting senses. On the one hand, the book commemorates the commissioning of the study that produced it and thus marks a special moment in the discipline's corporate history: the moment at which English doctoral education can be said to have officially entered the educational big time—or, to put it a bit more pointedly, to have officially tried to (re)claim corporate control and/or responsibility over an enterprise that had gotten out of hand. Allen explains the undertaking's genesis, and I quote him at some length because the persona he offers of the aging, self-deprecating Renaissance scholar pulled reluctantly into a world of surveys, statistics, and foundation grants effectively mirrors the corporate self-image of College English Teaching, Inc. during this period of professional transition:

> At the 1965 meeting of the Modern Language Association in Chicago, the Secretary, Professor John Fisher, abetted by the first Vice President, Professor Nathan Edelman, urged me to undertake the study of the Ph.D. in English and American Literature under the aegis of the Advisory Committee. "Morally" weakened by fifteen years of service on the Editorial Committee and physically disturbed by the approach of my sixty-third year, I agreed to abandon my normal habits of life and become (for a season) a statistical debauchee. At the moment of decision, I assumed there would be small risk to life and limb (brain damage already had been sustained) because it was then supposed that the Modern Language Association would bear the

costs; hence, the labor would be fantastically modest. However, these expectations were dashed when the Danforth Foundation generously offered to support a report on a larger scale.
For this support, I, the Advisory Committee, the officers of the
Modern Language Association, and, perhaps, the profession
are very grateful. (vii)

On the other hand, sadly, the book's publication also marks
the completion of that study and the discipline's official endorsement of it, and in doing so commemorates a moment of colossal,
if understandable, corporate misjudgment. Allen's report is terrific in a number of ways: it is arguably the sanest, best-grounded,
and most comprehensive analysis of the subject ever published.
Among other things, it draws on the responses of some 1,880
recent Ph.D. recipients, 1,170 graduate professors, and 88 chairs
or directors of graduate departments; it also features thoughtful
and usefully provocative recommendations concerning everything
from language requirements and teacher training to coursework
and dissertations—all dedicated, as he humbly puts it, "To all
the graduate students who have endured me and who will wish I
had seen the point sooner" (v).

However, as Allen's account of the "shortage of fully trained
teachers of English" quoted earlier makes clear, everything in the
report—especially its recommendations—was based on the assumption that there were far too few Ph.D.'s in English and,
moreover, that despite the dramatic increases made in the rate of
production since World War II, the system for producing new
ones was *still* too slow to close a gap that seemed like it might go
on growing indefinitely. The field's primary imperative, therefore, was to streamline the process of doctoral education, shear
it "of its unrealistic accretions" and convert it "into a serviceable
and uniformly administered procedure sensibly adjusted in all its
requirements to the public obligations of the profession in this
century" (31).

Unfortunately, that basic assumption—and therefore that
primary imperative—turned out to be badly flawed, a serious
corporate misreading of the situation. Even as the book was being published in 1968, most members of the three largest graduating classes of English Ph.D.'s ever (1972, 1973, 1974) were
already in the pipeline. And those new degree holders, almost

4,000 strong—to be joined before the decade ended by some 6,000 others—would find themselves facing not the boom in academic employment that Allen's report might have led them to expect, but something much more like a bust: a situation that featured not growth and opportunity, but rather what we would now call downsizing and underemployment. Obviously, Allen and the MLA Advisory Committee do not deserve all the blame for the fate of those generations of scholars. The forces he and the committee misjudged so badly were underway even as the study was being commissioned and would likely have done considerable damage no matter what the report had recommended. Nevertheless, their failure to recognize conditions for what they were surely made the damage worse. In the process—and perhaps even more tragic in the long run—that failure led them to squander an opportunity that had been almost a century in the making. *The Ph.D. in English and American Literature,* which might have been the blueprint for the first serious, discipline-wide curricular reform of doctoral education in the field's history, became instead another victim of—was, in effect, discredited by—the sequence of events here called the Great Contraction.

## The Great Contraction

The beginning of the end of the Great Expansion for doctoral education in English can be traced to changes in the enrollment patterns of those same 1960s undergraduates who had represented for Allen such a promising, if challenging future. To be fair, his reading of the situation was partly right: the number of B.A.'s awarded in the United States did continue to grow until 1974 or so, and even then did not tail off very sharply. Subsequently, although very gradually, the number even moved beyond that early peak again, a process that began in the early 1980s. English as an undergraduate major, however, did not share in this continued growth. On the contrary: interest in English peaked in the middle of the 1960s; after a rather gentle decline through the end of that decade, its share of majors fell off sharply through the 1970s, from a 1967–68 high of almost 7.6 students/ hundred graduated to a 1983–84 low of 3.4.[6] This decline—a kind of academic recession, if you will—eventually constricted the enterprise of English doctoral education in two ways.

First, it was one factor in a parallel decline in the candidate pool for English doctoral study. Other factors were involved in this decline, and relationships among them are complex. So, for example, the end of 2-S draft deferments for graduate study, effective as of 1968, not only moved students from graduate school rolls into the armed services, but also seriously eroded the plausibility of long-term study for men eligible for the draft. There was clearly less incentive to begin the long haul toward an English Ph.D. when the process could be interrupted at any time by a letter from Uncle Sam.[7] In addition, the winding down of some of the educational support systems of the boom years—the National Defense Education Act, for instance, expired in 1973—no doubt helped sustain the downward momentum as well. The net effect of these and presumably other factors can be measured in terms of what is sometimes called Ph.D. proclivity, the tendency among all B.A.-earners of a given year to complete a doctorate. For English this proclivity peaked in 1962 for men (just over 6 percent) and in 1964 for women (at just under 2 percent), and then, thanks almost exclusively to a decline among the former, dropped rather severely well into the 1970s, leveling off below 2 percent overall. Thus, while it may be hard to establish clear causal relationships among such factors, it seems safe to say that a lot of students began to get the message that English might not have much to offer by way of a future, and they began to get it fairly early on.

The second effect of this undergraduate shift away from English shows up, at least initially, at the other end of the doctoral enterprise— placement—and it followed a fairly straightforward marketplace logic. This decline in the number of English majors constituted a loss in what was for College English Teaching, Inc. both its repeat undergraduate customer base and its strongest institutional argument for claiming long-term (i.e., tenure- track) personnel resources. In short, departments with significantly fewer majors to teach needed fewer professors to teach them.

Here again the downward spiral set in motion by the decline of English as an undergraduate major was supplemented by other factors. In this instance, a key and not unrelated influence was the trend among colleges and universities toward relegating more and more "service course" teaching—especially composition, but also lower-division literature courses—to (less expensive) non-tenure-track professionals and TAs. Indeed, according to Bettina Huber's retrospective analysis of the MLA's periodic surveys of Ph.D. placements (1994), there has been only one occasion since the first survey in 1976–77 when more than 50 percent of those Ph.D.'s with known employment status reported finding tenure-track positions (51.1 percent in 1991–92), and yet the percentage of those who have reported finding employment in postsecondary institutions has averaged 83 percent (48). In other words, in each of the surveyed years over 30 percent of the Ph.D.'s who managed to find post-secondary employment accepted non-tenure-track and/or part-time teaching positions—in most of which, it seems safe to assume, they would mainly be teaching lower-division courses to nonmajors.[8] These years also witnessed the leveling off in the founding, and therefore staffing, of new postsecondary institutions and also of the trend to convert institutions such as normal schools into colleges and universities. Therefore job creation on a more wholesale scale diminished quite seriously as well. Together, these changes combined with the Great Expansion's peak years of Ph.D. hyperproduction to create the nightmarish job market crunch of the late 1970s and early 1980s.

For a time, both these effects were likely cushioned, or at least disguised, by the continuing overall growth at the undergraduate level—a phenomenon that no doubt helps to account for Allen's and the Modern Language Association's misreading of the situation. The still-rising number of students entering higher education maintained the pressure on English's service-course workload, at least for a while; not all of that pressure would have been absorbed by the move to alternative labor arrangements—or, again, at least not right away. (Indeed, anecdotal evidence suggests that it was not unheard of during these times for institutions— particularly universities—to hire fairly large groups of new Ph.D.'s to do mainly service-course teaching, and subsequently to deny most of those junior faculty members either contract renewals or continuing appointment.) Likewise, the fact that the total number of students being awarded B.A.'s was still rising helped for a time to mask the decline in the *percentage* opting to pursue doctoral study in English; a smaller portion of a larger number of students, in other words, helped keep doctoral enrollment numbers up. Eventually, though, the process of contraction set in: immediately following those peak years of 1972–1974, the annual total of Ph.D.'s granted began to drop off nearly as precipitously as it had risen, falling throughout the next decade: to 1,214 in 1975–76, 952 in 1979–80, 733 in 1983–84, on down to a low of 668 in 1986–87.

## The (Surp)Rise of Heterogeneity

It is crucial to recognize, however, that the Great Contraction did not simply constitute a reversal of the Great Expansion, a move back toward a kind of pre-1950 version of Ph.D. business-as-usual. In terms of sheer scale, of course, it was clearly a setback for the United States' postwar experiment of opening up access to higher education, for it eventually reduced both the number of places for and the career prospects of those aspiring to advanced study in English. Within the constraints imposed by that reduction, however, other portions of the Great Expansion's legacy—at both the institutional and individual levels—can be said not only to have survived but—however surprisingly—to have thrived.

On the institutional level, this legacy took the form of a doctoral education enterprise that became, as Bowen and Rudenstine put it, "far more distributed, more variegated, and more extensive in terms of participating institutions" (62) than ever before. Taking "more extensive" first, one of the most striking features of this period of contraction was that while the number of degrees granted was *de*creasing so dramatically, the number of programs offering the doctorate actually continued to *in*crease, from 124 in 1972 to 132 in 1988 (and even higher in the 1990s) (Bowen and Rudenstine 386). Moreover, since much of the decrease in enrollments and total number of degrees conferred was absorbed by the older, larger, more established programs, the process of redistributing the share of degrees granted that had begun during the Great Expansion easily sustained its momentum. By the time the contraction bottomed out in 1988, those programs Bowen and Rudenstine place in Tier I (still at 29) produced 300 of the total 717 degrees, or 400 fewer than in 1972. Obviously, the programs in the other three tiers also produced fewer total degrees—417 in 1988 compared to 670 in 1972—but their *share* of the total output had continued to increase, rising from the 1972 level of 49 percent to about 58 percent in 1988. Moreover, a good portion of this increase in share went to the new (i.e., post-1958) programs: their 1972 share of the total output—28 percent—had risen to 41 percent by 1988 (388).

These two kinds of change—rapid proliferation and the ongoing redistribution of degrees granted—account for much of the increase in programmatic variegation, as well. In any field, of course, there are differences among the doctoral programs mounted at different institutions, and there had always been such differences in English. The Magisterial curricular arrangements were often, as I noted earlier, personnel-driven, so that depending on staffing one program might favor Renaissance English studies, another early American, and so on. Even so, before 1950, when the number of programs was still relatively small, there seems to have been a fairly strong sense of what I call a curricular industry standard, especially among the 15 to 20 programs dominating the field; Ph.D.'s from Harvard or Yale or Columbia might not have been identical, but they were understood to be more or less equivalent. Programs mounted by other institutions were generally measured against this standard: they were seen, that is, as attempts to mount programs in the image of a Yale or a Columbia, but in the unfortunate absence of the same resources. Schemes for ranking programs, such as the Bowen and Rudenstine Quality Tiers I have been citing, obviously both reflect and perpetuate this view of the system. Based on such measures as program size, perceived quality of faculty, quantity and quality of support available for students, size of library, and so on, these rankings imply that an acknowledged industry-standard program really does exist; that those ranked in Tier I offer it; and that those ranked in lower tiers could, with the right level of investment, come to offer it as well.

While this notion of an industry standard may operate to some extent even now, however, the programmatic reality has gradually become something much more like an academic version of niche marketing. This shift began with the Great Expansion, during which the ambitious university presidents, and deans, and department chairs at the seventy or so institutions creating new programs sought to distinguish their English Ph.D.'s (and for a time, their D.A.'s) from those offered by their competitors. As I have already suggested, the Allen report was published at least partly to combat precisely this problem: in other words, to promote and (re)establish a "uniform" degree program, thereby protecting the credibility of the Ph.D., with this latter concern explaining why the book's subtitle calls it a report not only to "the profession" but also to "the public."[9]

But it was the Great Contraction that played the larger role in promoting this new range of variegation. The numbers we have already reviewed indicate that the group Allen calls "the great departments" (24) lost a considerable portion of their degree-granting dominance during this period. In 1972, for example, the average Tier I program was cranking out 24.1 Ph.D.'s a year, Tier II 8.9, Tier III 9.1, and Tier IV 4.1. By 1988 those outputs had drawn into a much tighter cluster: Tier I 10.3, Tier II 5.6, Tier III 4.0, and Tier IV 3.3. Thus programs in all tiers were much closer to being "average" (5.4) in terms of degrees granted per year (Bowen and Rudenstine 386–88).

And these emerging constraints on size ran directly counter to the field's long-standing propensity to multiply the specializations sanctioned for doctoral study—a propensity which, no doubt also spurred by market pressures, seemed to accelerate during this same period. The result was a very real squeeze. Even if departments at the wealthiest or most ambitious institutions had been able to expand their faculties and libraries to keep pace with all the field's various specializations (most usefully defined, in this context, in terms of the positions listed in MLA's *Job Information List*)—and that is unlikely enough—they could hardly have afforded to do so when their programs were working their way *down* toward graduating some ten Ph.D.'s a year. Either those students would have had to take endless years of coursework, or else many of the graduate faculty would have found themselves idle most of the time.

What happened instead is that while all doctoral programs still sought to claim, for purposes of accreditation, some version of a basic or comprehensive English doctoral curriculum, they in fact increasingly came to foreground a more limited number of emphases that played to their faculty strengths, their student-recruitment base, and their ambitions in or share of the job market. Within this new arrangement, there no doubt was still a place for something imagined to be a "traditional" comprehensive preparation, and to the extent that this perception influences recruiting and/or placement, older and better established programs maintained some advantage. More and more, however, specific programs claimed, were ceded, or otherwise acquired more specific, and in some instances mutually exclusive, specializations.

The most visible example of this trend has been the emergence of rhetoric and composition as a specialization. Before 1972 no English department we can find offered a doctorate with a primary emphasis in this area, nor would any department have been likely to advertise a position in it. By the end of the 1980s, however, approximately two dozen programs in rhetoric and composition served a job market featuring plenty of positions calling for just this specialization. Similar if less dramatic developments have occurred under all sorts of other rubrics. That is, in addition to featuring various (sub)specializations under British literature or (that now well-established upstart) American literature, programs have claimed emphases in creative or technical writing, variously configured work in feminist studies, literary and critical theory, cultural studies, and so on.

On the level of the individual student, meanwhile, the legacy of the Great Expansion took the parallel and surely related form of bringing into English a substantially altered demographic mix of students. Thus, while the actual number of people earning— and presumably enrolling to earn—Ph.D.'s in English steadily decreased from 1974 until 1988, their *diversity* as measured along any number of dimensions increased, in some cases quite dramatically. The most striking of these shifts, and one that represents a marked departure from the post-World War II effects of the GI Bill, was in the balance between the sexes. As noted earlier, for most of the field's history the overall percentage of English doctoral recipients who were women is unlikely to have topped 20 percent; certainly for the immediate post-World War

II era, it seems to have stayed well below that margin. Beginning in 1964, however, that percentage rose steadily and without any interval of decline before leveling off in the late 1980s in the 50 percent to 60 percent range, where it has since remained.[10]

I have already described two of the key factors in this shifting balance: the diminishing impact of the GI Bill and the end of 2-S draft deferments. For all of its history, the GI Bill had obviously aided far more men than women into higher education and on into graduate school. Indeed, it was so effective that, especially during its first twenty years, women interested in graduate study were actively displaced both by the sheer numbers of male applicants and by the priority given to veterans (Solomon 189–90).[11] By the mid-1960s, however, the program's direct demographic impact had lessened considerably. This development, combined with the increasing number of available doctoral programs—created to some extent in response to GI Bill-promoted enrollments in the first place—made more spaces available for women. Moreover, the 1968 cancellation of 2-S deferments accelerated this profile change. As explained earlier, insofar as that cancellation affected Ph.D. demographics, it did so by removing far more men from the rolls than women. Bowen and Rudenstine note, for instance, that between 1966 and 1968 the Ph.D. proclivity of the B.A. cohorts in English for men fell from 5.2 percent to 3.1 percent, and by 1970 to about 2 percent—largely, it appears, in reaction to draft issues. Over the same span, the proclivity for women remained between 1 percent and 1.2 percent (51–52).

While this change in the balance between the sexes may have been the most dramatic alteration in the demographic profile of English Ph.D.'s, however, others were significant as well. For example, I noted earlier that the percentage of doctorates earned by non-U.S. citizens more than tripled between 1972 and 1988, from 4 percent to 13 percent. Additionally, while the number of degrees earned by U.S.-resident minority students over the same span did not increase on anything like the same scale (in 1988, for instance, the data indicate that only forty-four such people were awarded Ph.D.'s in all, just one more than in 1982), these small but steady enrollments mark a real departure from the field's first one hundred years. And in a period of such serious overall decline, even holding constant produced a slight increase in share, edging up from about 5 percent to 7 percent.

Finally, this changing student body also included an increasingly varied mix of socioeconomic and educational backgrounds: there was, in other words, movement across what passes in the United States for class boundaries, as well. Hard data on the magnitude of this kind of change, especially hard data specific to English, are not easy to come by. Still, the general trend seems quite clear, and certainly the anecdotal information is strongly suggestive. Thus we know with considerable certainty that overall the GI Bill produced this effect. A substantial number of the veterans who took advantage of it would not have attended college otherwise—estimates range as high as 20 percent—and at least some of those people no doubt made their way into English doctoral study.

In addition, a sizable proportion of the students enrolling in and graduating from the proliferating Tier III and IV programs came from less prestigious undergraduate institutions and less privileged socioeconomic backgrounds than did the average Ph.D. earner of the pre-1950 era. They would have earned their B.A.'s at public colleges or regional universities, as opposed to Oberlin or Princeton or Chicago, and they would have done so not least because, whatever their academic abilities, neither family tradition nor family finances would have directed them otherwise. For that matter, some portion of these undergraduates—assisted, possibly, by campaigns designed expressly to diversify Tier I and II student bodies in various ways—surely had some effect on the Ph.D. cohorts of those upper tier programs, gaining at least a slightly greater share of the available places, and bringing with them both a different brand of training and a different orientation toward their place in the academy.

# The Crisis of Identity in English Studies and the Demise of the Magisterial Curriculum

T he net effect of the postwar developments was to produce what I am inclined to call—without, I think, unwarranted melodrama—a crisis of identity in English as both a discipline and a profession, a crisis with serious implications for doctoral education. Let me summarize the process we have been tracing. Beginning in 1946, graduate students of steadily greater diversity in terms of sex, class, national origin, educational background, and race enrolled in and graduated from doctoral programs in English that, for reasons having to do with both their rapid proliferation and limitations in size and resources, had themselves become increasingly variegated. Thanks in no small part to variously formulated and implemented affirmative action policies—and despite the post-1975 softness in the job market—these new Ph.D. holders gradually established themselves in the academy and the profession. The process was not of course as smooth or as easy as this rendering might imply; these new members of the profession often faced substantial difficulties, even active opposition. Nevertheless, steadily, inexorably, they made their way in: they found tenure-track positions; secured continuing appointment; and wrote, taught, and served their ways into and up through the ranks of College English Teaching, Inc.[1]

## What *Is* English?

The cumulative effect of this process, one obviously still at work, was to create an English of a diversity in these several demographic and disciplinary senses unprecedented in the field's institutional history, and to do so, moreover, during an era when the resources available for negotiating such differences proved to be more than usually constrained. In *Professing Literature,* Gerald Graff argues convincingly that the field's traditional means of handling its differences—all of them framed, for his purposes, in doctrinal as opposed to demographic terms—has been a form of institutional compartmentalization based primarily on the principle of "field-coverage" (6–10), a practice made possible for most of this century, and most dramatically during the Great Expansion, by the relatively consistent growth of higher education in general and English departments in particular. To put it crudely, new specialties have mostly been absorbed by addition, building a new wing, as it were: "Yes, fine, we'll hire one or two of those [American literature scholars, New Critics, creative writers, etc.]."

Beginning in the mid-1970s and continuing through the present, however, such expansion became a more and more unaffordable luxury for most institutions. In terms of full-time tenure-track faculty, English departments for the most part have either remained relatively stable, so that new lines have been issued mainly to replace retirees, or else have begun to shrink somewhat, so that lines freed by retirement have either left departments altogether or—in a widely decried but rarely remedied practice—been parceled out in non-tenure-track and/or part-time hires (or even, ironically, in assistantships designed to help produce more Ph.D.'s).

Adhering to the field-coverage principle during this era, then (and the success of the doctoral program variegation described previously suggests that many undergraduate-oriented departments tried to do just that), forced some very hard choices and rendered peaceful coexistence by compartmentalization increasingly untenable.[2] The scenarios can be multiplied endlessly: when a department's Miltonist/eighteenth-century person/Emersonian/ director of first-year composition retired, should it hire another Miltonist, etc., or a deconstructionist, a fiction writer, a scholar in African American literature, someone expert in computers and writing, a postcolonialist, etcetera, etcetera? Both this decision-making process and the subsequent search came to be further complicated by demographic (not to mention ethical and legal) considerations: man or woman? Ivy League, land grant university, or smaller niche program? U.S. citizen or not? White, Hispanic, African American, Asian American, Native American? Or, to invoke what has become yet another class marker in this context, what was to be done with a candidate whose first degree not only was not from a Princeton or an Oberlin, nor even a Cal-State Northridge, but from a Mohawk Valley Community College? In short, departments found themselves having to decide again and again what it meant to "cover the field" when, on the one hand, that field—conceived in terms of both the constituent areas of expertise *and* the bodies of those who populated it—had diversified beyond anyone's experience, and, on the other hand, the resources available for carrying out any such coverage either remained the same or became scarcer.

Hence my use of the term *crisis*. English has never been a particularly stable or coherent disciplinary enterprise, an assertion amply documented by such studies as Graff's, or Arthur Applebee's *Tradition and Reform in the Teaching of English*; and it might well be said to have had long-standing problems with this dimension of its identity. It also might be argued that the discipline has faced challenges to its demographic identity before: when the first women, or the first public school undergraduates, or the first Catholics or Jews, or the first children of Italian or Polish or Hungarian immigrants, say, found places in doctoral programs, were awarded degrees, secured positions as professors, came up for tenure.

I would contend, however, that the situation it faced during this Great Contraction—and indeed still faces—was unique in its severity, different not merely in degree but kind. The enterprise had never faced either disciplinary or demographic challenges on this scale. It had never had to deal so extensively with both at the same time, nor in ways that were so often intertwined (i.e., so that an individual's disciplinary credentials might be explicitly connected with personal characteristics). And it had never been forced to meet such a set of challenges when the available resources were so grossly inadequate to the task at hand.

One of the more visible manifestations of this crisis, subtle but quite insistent, was the gradual emergence of English Studies as the disciplinary designation of choice. As oblique or inadequate as "English" alone must often have seemed over the previous century, it had nevertheless managed to hold off all challengers, doing duty as the cover term for an impressive variety of activities—a successful corporate trademark if ever there was one. Through the 1980s, however, the sheer range of constituent modes and methods, and even more the increasingly ferocious demands by the devotees of each that the integrity of their particular favorite be properly acknowledged, seems to have prompted the tacking on of "studies," at first with the small s, but gradually capitalized. It was as if, with departments no longer able to expand to encompass the field's diversities, its name had to be stretched to do the job instead.

But of course the crisis qua crisis was made visible in much more standard ways, as well; as the concern of commissions, professional meetings, publications, and so on. The list of these is long and diverse and includes what amounts to a decade's worth of study by the MLA (the Commission on the Future of the Profession, followed by the Commission on Writing and Literature). Probably the most notable of these responses to the situation, however—and certainly as close as there was to a disciplinewide summit during this era—was the 1987 Wye (Maryland) English Coalition Conference. This three-week meeting sponsored by the field's eight major professional organizations brought together sixty representatives from three "levels" (elementary, secondary, college/university) in an effort to get a handle on just what enterprise those assembled imagined themselves to be engaged in.[3] The results most germane to postsecondary education appeared in two books (published jointly by MLA and NCTE): the official report, *The English Coalition Conference: Democracy through Language* (edited by Richard Lloyd-Jones and Andrea Lunsford, 1989); and Peter Elbow's more revealingly titled *What Is English?* (1990). Elbow's opening paragraph is an accurate, albeit bravely upbeat, assessment of his own and the field's situation (and please note the appearance, despite his title, of a lowercase "studies"):

> "What is English?" The title is not intended as a question I can answer with my book, not a slow lob that I can try to hit for a home run. The title *is* my answer, my summing up, my picture of the profession. This book is trying to paint a picture of a

profession that cannot define what it is. I don't mean this as scandal, and I don't take our not knowing as the most important news from the English Coalition Conference (if it was news). Yes, it might be more comfortable and convenient if we knew just what English studies is, but this very absence of comfort and convenience in the profession is probably a good thing. English is percolating at various levels, and I don't think anyone can know where it's going to end up. On good days I even say, "It's about time we finally don't know what we are." (v)

# Reinfiltration and the Demise of the Magisterial Curriculum

Inevitably, this crisis of identity cycled its way back around to affect the doctoral programs. As we have seen, these programs had played no small role in fomenting the crisis in the first place, slowly (re)populating the profession with their increasingly variegated graduates. But it was one thing to alter the disciplinary and demographic mix of entry-level Ph.D.'s, and quite another for that new mix to affect in its turn the practices of doctoral education. After all, of the more than 3,500 English departments in U.S. higher education at which a new Ph.D. might be hired, there were still only 140 or so in the business of awarding doctorates—and for the most part, they were not hiring during these years as frequently as they once had.

As always, the vast majority of the field's professionals would go their entire careers without having any direct hand in training their eventual successors. True, these new members of the profession could exercise substantial indirect influence: they could exert pressure from below, as it were, through such means as publication; participation in professional organizations; the kinds of training they provided for their own undergraduates; and, perhaps most pointedly, the sorts of credentials they pressed for when their own departments had openings to fill. Opportunities for direct influence, however—teaching in and having voting rights as a member of a doctorate-granting department, let alone acquiring the seniority and/or political wherewithal to exercise such rights with any real impact—these would come to relatively few and considerably more slowly.

Still, such opportunities did arise, and the mechanisms that made them possible were basically the same as those operating elsewhere: affirmative action policies, which altered the (replicatory) hiring practices of even the most demographically conservative English departments, and the continued use of the field-coverage principle as a guide to hiring, which provided spaces for at least some of the emerging new specialities. Here again, I do not want to suggest that creating or realizing such opportunities was simple or painless. Given in particular the idiosyncracies of the academic tenure system, this upper echelon of College English Teaching, Inc.'s corporate hierarchy was probably at least as conservative as any other in U.S. culture, all the more so in its handling of those who, like a gradually increasing number of these postwar Ph.D.'s, found themselves having to operate therein with few ready disciplinary and/or demographic role models and mentors.

It is also worth noting, however—a measure of compensation, perhaps—that partly because this was an era of straitened resources, and partly because the proliferation of specializations eroded the primacy of seniority as a credential for graduate teaching, the opportunities that *were* thus created shifted the balance of power in doctoral programs more rapidly than would likely have been the case in any earlier era. To return to my earlier scenario: if the retiring senior Miltonist in a department of thirty-five was replaced by an assistant professor in rhetoric and composition, the department's voting balance would be altered a good deal more than if, following the pattern of flusher times, resources had allowed the appointment of both the rhetoric and composition specialist *and* the replacement Miltonist. Moreover, whether a department was in a position to expand or not, faculty hired mainly for their credentials in new specializations were quite likely to leapfrog over more senior colleagues into the rotation of graduate courses, examinations, and dissertation work—a reordering made all the more likely when, as in this example, it was reinforced by the realities of the job market.

As the 1980s drew to a close, this reinfiltration had progressed far enough that a majority of English doctoral programs were ready to acknowledge that the long reign of what I have been calling the Magisterial curriculum had come to an end: mounting a doctoral curriculum designed to make some B.A.-holding "them" into a Ph.D.-holding "one of us" was no longer even a plausible fiction in either disciplinary or demographic terms. To a considerable degree, of course, Elbow's comment on the profession's inability to define what it is fits here, too: such an acknowledgement was not exactly news. As my discussion of programmatic variegation made clear, between its additive propensities ("A new specialization? Well, we'll just add another grad course.") and its tendency to be personnel-based, the Magisterial curriculum's disciplinary coherence, never all that stable to begin with, had been showing ever more visible signs of strain since at least the Cameron Allen era. Now, by most accounts, it had crumbled altogether. This disciplinary collapse was made as official as such things can be in April 1987, when "invited representatives from eighty [of the nation's 139] Ph.D.-granting departments"[4] assembled in Wayzata, Minnesota, for the Conference on Graduate Study and the Future of Doctoral Study in English, the official proceedings of which were published as *The Future of Doctoral Studies in English* (1989). The purpose of the gathering was

> to consider what it is that can now be said to constitute our discipline: the connections among the subjects we teach and the foci of our scholarly efforts; the nature of the profession for which we train and into which we socialize our graduate students, a profession that they, in turn, will define through their own theoretical interests, institutional assumptions, and pedagogical practices. (Lunsford, Moglen, and Slevin v)

The result of these considerations, this assembly's collective answer to the question at issue—What is it that can now be said to constitute our discipline such that it can inform our efforts in doctoral education?—was unequivocally *that they did not know*. "[N]o unanimity on any significant issue emerged during the conference," report the editors of the proceedings, with the near, albeit negative, exception of a "dominant view" that neither "historical coverage" nor "canonical unity" could "guide our conceptualization of curricula. As a consequence," they conclude, "there was little certainty about what our graduate students should know both as developing scholars and as apprentice teachers" (vi).

In short, if these representatives agreed on anything at all, it was on their disagreement and uncertainty. The editors of the proceedings characterize the situation as follows, and their interesting (even hilarious) mixing of metaphors in the first paragraph seems particularly apt:

> What did become clear [at the conference] is that our subject has been destabilized and that our methodologies are being radically questioned. Foreground and background have disappeared. Towering figures who once marked the focal points of an inherited tradition have been swallowed up by the crowds that surround them, barely noticed before. The coronation parade has been lost in the shifting but disciplined realignments of marching bands at half-time ceremonies. Feminists, Marxists, new historians, colonial-discourse analysts, and many other schools or orientations in current literary theory call the tune.
>
> The text is no longer bound and self-contained, a discrete object of painstaking and definitive analysis. It is transformed, rather, by the discourse in which it is situated—cultural, historical, deconstructive, psychoanalytic, phenomenological—its meanings determined by the context that defines its reading and writing. Neither we nor our students can claim expertise on major authors, literary periods, genres, or traditions when all these categories are the sites of heated contestations. To many [conference participants] it seemed that we could only familiarize ourselves with the variety of theoretical approaches, making these theoretical constructs themselves the center of our disciplinary education. (vi)

In short, whoever the disciplinary "we" may have become (and surely the rhetorical problems presented by that pronoun, both in this passage and throughout the volume, are symptomatic in their own way[5]) they no longer agreed among themselves to any significant degree on what or how to read or write or teach, let alone on what might constitute a suitable doctoral curriculum. And their disagreements were very much on display in the kinds of coursework, examinations, and dissertations their programs featured. One major schism, of course, is reflected in the title of Bettina Huber's Appendix to the proceedings, "A Report on the 1986 Survey of English Doctoral Programs in Writing and Literature": the field had reached the point at which it was necessary to make a formal distinction between degree programs in rhetoric and writing (N = 42) and those in literature (N = 103).

Even these two presumably stable entities were shaky at best. According to Huber's survey of required courses, the courses which ought to be the mainstays of a discipline's identity, the most common requirement on the literature side was in bibliography and research methods, mandated in 75 percent of the programs reporting. Beyond that, however, there is nothing even close to unanimity: 53 percent required courses in literary criticism; 45 percent in critical theory; 39 percent in historical scholarship; 38 percent in linguistics; 32 percent in rhetoric, writing, or composition; and 22 percent in textual criticism. The variation on the rhetoric side is less extreme, but there is no unanimity either. The most commonly required courses (however ironically) were in British and American literature, at 86 percent; followed by theory of composition at 81 percent; and rhetoric at 79 percent. After that, the spread begins for real: 57 percent of the programs required linguistics, 55 percent bibliography and research methods, 48 percent history of the English language (which had almost disappeared as a requirement on the literature side, where it had once been a fixture), and 14 percent social science or experimental research methods.[6]

As might be expected, the level of disagreement was even greater in other parts of the curricula. Thus the list of courses offered as electives by the responding programs included not only all those listed as sometime requirements (with all the variability possible under those rather broad headings) but also courses in such areas as creative writing, technical writing, film, and folklore. Moreover, this fuller range of course offerings was reflected in the breadth of options available for examinations and dissertations, thereby affirming even more pointedly than the range of possible coursework just how serious was the profession's lack of agreement concerning what constituted advanced disciplinary work. Hence, while 99 percent of the 126 programs reporting allowed examinations and theses in what the survey characterizes as British and American literature and 86 percent sanctioned work in critical theory, only 58 percent did so in rhetoric, writing, or composition; 25 percent in creative writing; 18 percent in linguistics; 14 percent in what Huber calls "specialty literature" (including such things as Canadian literature, and children's literature); and 10 percent in technical writing.

To make Magisterial matters worse—the coup de grâce, as it were—English also could no longer claim the sort of "we" that had for so long provided its more durable demographic foundation. There appears to have been little explicit attention paid to such matters at Wayzata. With the exception of Helene Moglen's pointed analysis of the domestication of poststructuralist modes of criticism (Moglen 86–90) and the occasional acknowledgment of the importance of feminism (although not always of women), there is little mention of bodies, faculty or doctoral student, in the proceedings. Even James F. Slevin's otherwise excellent (and much needed) response essay, which is devoted exclusively and quite passionately to (re)placing doctoral students as participants in the professional conversation, never actually addresses the question of who, in this demographic sense, those students *are,* or where they come from.

Whatever the reasons for this omission, however—and I recognize that it was then, as it is now, a complex and often fraught topic—there can be no question about the significance of demographics in the demise of the Magisterial model. As we saw in earlier chapters, for the better part of one hundred years the students who had arrived to enroll in, and to an even greater extent the Ph.D.'s who graduated from, the Magisterial curriculum had constituted an "us" in ways that had little overt connection with disciplined modes of inquiry as such: that is, they were predominantly white male U.S. citizens from relatively comfortable socioeconomic backgrounds holding B.A.'s earned at one of a very select group of institutions.

Even for some years after the demographic profile of enrollees had begun to change, the curriculum appears to have demonstrated a considerable ability to absorb the differences thus embodied—to render them invisible, as it were. At least until the degree had been earned, and often until tenure had been granted, the *Magister* could demand—and expect to get—a conformity in disciplinary and professional behavior that belied heterogeneities of other kinds. The primary means by which the earliest challengers to this long-standing demographic norm survived was necessarily a form of what might be called in other contexts "passing": in this case, writing and (at least for public purposes) reading, teaching, and speaking, even dressing and behaving, in keeping with a Magisterial image probably best embodied in popular iconography—and with allowances for an English professor's somewhat lower standard of living—by John Houseman's craggy Professor Kingsfield from the film *The Paper Chase*. Thus a woman or an African American or a child of working-class parents or, to put it in composite form, the daughter of working-class African American parents, could, should she have made her way to graduate school in English, aspire to this image. But it would *be* this image against which she would be measured, and for the most part her differences would be constructed as lack, as defects to be overlooked or handicaps to be overcome.

Ultimately, however, following the pattern I have been sketching throughout this chapter, even the Magisterial reach turned out to have its limits. Ph.D.'s, once awarded, could not be taken back. Gradually, thanks to the processes of tenure and promotion—along with substantial measures of both courage and mutual forebearance, and in a perpetually complex relationship with disciplinary practice—the profession not only came to include women and nonwhites and non-U.S. citizens and the non-middle-class-or-higher and non-Ivy League- or Research I-educated people in variously substantial numbers, but it did so in ways that more and more acknowledged *who they were:* it admitted them less in spite of and more because of those differences (albeit often controversially and never entirely). The reinfiltration process promoted as tight a spiraling effect in this regard as in others. Thus the usually hard-won success of works such as Judith Fetterley's *The Resisting Reader,* Geneva Smitherman's *Talkin and Testifyin,* or Henry Louis Gates's *Black Literature and Literary Theory,* coupled with the presence of these and other Magisterially iconoclastic scholars in doctorate-granting departments, made possible a coalition with incoming doctoral students that closed the circle begun so modestly—and surely with little sense of the ultimate consequences—by the GI Bill, and thereby launched a new era in the history of English (Studies?) as a discipline and a profession.

## Looking to the Future: Dissolution, Corporate Compromise, Fusion

In the end, probably the most appropriate way of characterizing the Wayzata conference—at least given my corporate theme—is to cast it as a meeting of that majority subset of College English Teaching, Inc.'s board of directors who, having finally engineered the ousting of the long-time (Magisterial) CEO for alleged incompetence and amid rumors of senility, gathered to figure out what the hell to do next. It was a daunting task, for despite the apparent confidence suggested by the titles of both conference and subsequent proceedings, it seems clear that these representatives were aware of just how difficult it would be to predict *The Future of Doctoral Studies in English,* and that something more like Elbow's offering—*What Is the Future of Doctoral Studies in English?*, say—would almost certainly have been a more accurate description of both the deliberations and their results.

Indeed, compared with their counterparts at the Conferences on the Ph.D. in English and American Literature held twenty years earlier in conjunction with Cameron Allen's efforts,[7] this was a much chastened corporate group. The comforting topical assurance of "English and American literature," of course, is gone; and while the symptomatically revealing *studies* gets finessed—deployed, despite rather obvious clumsiness, elsewhere (Conference on Graduate *Study* and the Future of Doctoral *Study* in English, *The Future of Doctoral Studies in English*)—it nevertheless manages to pop up in the very first line of the Introduction to the proceedings: "For the past ten years, the executive director and Executive Council of the Modern Language Association have encouraged and facilitated an extensive process of self-examination within the profession of English *studies*" (Lunsford, Moglen, and Slevin v, emphasis added).

Moreover, this was a group that had learned some hard economic lessons from hard economic times; the decade of self-examination appears to have brought about a greater sense of the vulnerability of both the entire enterprise and many of its members.[8] Whereas Allen's rhetoric of urgency was harnessed in aid of corporate ambition—dreams of efficiency and expansion—here it is reserved for corporate compassion and responsibility.

"[O]ur current debates about literature and composition," write
the editors,

> have a special urgency. In the last two decades, our depart-
> ments have come increasingly to rely on faculty members who
> are poorly paid, ill-treated, marginal, and temporary; more than
> one-fourth the English faculties in four-year colleges, and as
> many as half the English faculties in two-year colleges, teach
> only part-time. . . . Our desire to reconceptualize who we are
> and what we do derives in part from a more basic desire to
> challenge these institutional practices and to make possible a
> mutual respect for all areas of our instruction and scholarship.
> (vii)

Nevertheless, it is possible to discern among the varied and
for the most part candidly uncertain contributions to *The Future
of Doctoral Studies in English* three major strategic options that
this gathering expected the field, its doctoral programs, and in
particular its doctoral curriculum might pursue. The first and, at
least from an outside perspective, the most obvious of these options was dissolution. That is, College English Teaching, Inc. could
simply formalize the process long since underway and divide
English Studies into more specialized new disciplines: literary studies and rhetoric/composition as the obvious initial pair, and after
that whatever others faculty could muster the savvy or institutional leverage to establish (e.g., American literature/studies, cultural studies, creative writing, etc.). Such a move would have the
curricular advantage of replacing the implausibly varied pattern
of course offerings outlined in Huber's survey with a set of two
or more post-Magisterial unities, so that degree programs—to
the relief of candidates and prospective employers, at the very
least—could then move back in the direction of reasonably defensible industry standards. Such a move would do much to rees-
tablish the graduate faculty's Magisterial authority, albeit on a
smaller scale. Assuming that these new units did reasonably well
establishing themselves in college and university economies, they
could—long term—help create new positions at both the graduate and undergraduate levels. In short, if English could no longer
sustain even the illusion of a single disciplinary "we" into which
to initiate students, wouldn't it make sense to split the field into

the two (or three or four) units that *could* each constitute a workable "we," and let doctoral students—and subsequently employers—choose from among them?

Despite its obvious plausibility, however, this option receives little visible consideration in *The Future of Doctoral Studies in English*. We can be fairly certain that it was present at the conference. For one thing, such a breakup was clearly part of the motivation for the gathering in the first place, and it lurks just beneath the surface of many of the published papers. For another, we know that at least one speaker, Maxine Hairston, openly advocated the "secession" of rhetoric and composition from English, a course of action she had previously recommended as chair of the Conference on College Composition and Communication (1984). (The Wayzata version of her position is not included in the proceedings, but Gary Waller—letting the cat out of the bag?—refers to it [112].) And frankly it is impossible to imagine that the topic did not erupt, fierce and impatient, at small group discussions and in corridors and over coffee ("Let them take their Freshman Comp and go!" or "I'm sick of carrying these snooty bastards! Let's make the break!").

Still, there is little sign of such deliberations in the official record, and it is easy enough to guess why. I have traced at some length the advantages this Magisterial corporate model traditionally had provided for graduate professors. For those assembled at this conference, a corporate breakup—especially after ten of the most economically traumatic years in the profession's history—would simply have posed too much risk in pursuit of too nebulous rewards. Even those whose professional credentials were mainly in the writing field and who therefore presumably stood to gain the most from such a split (and who were ably represented among the editors by Slevin and, even more especially, by Lunsford) are characterized as concurring with the following view: writing people need to be understood as "those in a marginalized area of the profession—'comp,'" understandably desiring "to locate their projects within the larger, legitimating structure of more privileged groups" (Lunsford, Moglen, and Slevin vii). So, while there was undoubtedly a strong desire to take the occasion of the Magister's demise to *redistribute* the system's rewards—

with the threat of secession and thus dissolution as a constant if mostly silent feature of the negotiations—very few among the graduate faculty assembled were (as yet) seriously inclined to risk killing the College English Teaching, Inc. goose that lay what were still reasonably valuable golden eggs.

For much the same conservative reasons, the most palatable corporate option, the one most in evidence in the proceedings and, I would assume, at the conference, involved holding the conflicted enterprise together, however loosely, and then—for curricular purposes—finding some way to present *and* preserve all of its competing interests: a strategy that might be called corporate compromise. The proceedings offer a number of proposals along these lines, the most common model being to offer some synthesizing term as a way "of posing and organizing our questions about writing and reading" (these two concepts, however problematic themselves, operating here as the irreducible common core of English studies) "so that they take account of many different cultural contexts, including—ultimately—our own," and thus become the basis for a greater disciplinary self-knowledge (Lunsford, Moglen, and Slevin viii). Not surprisingly, *rhetoric* is the favorite among these synthesizing terms, with Jonathan Culler apparently making a particular splash during the conference with his presentation of it (Lunsford, Moglen, and Slevin vii). But variously defined notions of theory ("literary, critical, cultural, textual" [viii]) are not far behind. There is also frequent mention of the related strategy proposed by Gerald Graff in *Professing Literature* and since encapsulated in the catchphrase "teaching the conflicts": that "the disagreements [among the field's subdisciplines] could themselves constitute the substance of reading and writing in English studies" (x).

Any of these versions of corporate compromise offered College English Teaching, Inc., and particularly its graduate professors, three substantial advantages. First, such a strategy would sustain at least the illusion of disciplinary unity for institutional purposes. For much of its history, English had tended to be the largest department in the humanities, and frequently one of the largest—and in that sense most influential—in U.S. colleges and universities overall. By following this compromise strategy, then, its members would be better able to maintain that size advantage rather than, as with dissolution, having to take their chances in smaller, untried, and likely more institutionally vulnerable units.

Second, this sort of compromise would insulate graduate professors from most of the pressure and the punitive learning curve of having to change, to somehow retool professionally in response to the discipline's crisis of identity. Under this arrangement, the apparent vice of that crisis becomes, if not precisely a virtue (although even that argument could be made; see, e.g., Lunsford, Moglen, and Slevin viii), then at least a standard and defensible feature of its stock-in-trade. In other words, once there was agreement that the curriculum was going to concentrate on, say, "teaching the conflicts," it would become at least acceptable and maybe even desirable for the faculty to keep those conflicts alive: to keep doing, for the most part, what they *had* been doing.

Which leads to the third and closely related advantage of this compromise strategy: that while it would operate in the absence of the Magisterial curriculum, it would nevertheless allow the graduate professors to maintain something akin to Magisterial power in the doctoral classroom. This power would not be entirely undiminished, of course. To institute even the most rudimentary teaching-the-conflicts curriculum formally invites students to undertake an intradisciplinary scrutiny, and thereby possibly gain a disciplinary leverage, that the *Magister* would never have allowed. (To recall Bliss Perry's woodsy image, teaching the conflicts would amount to pitting the masters against one another in no-holds-barred canoe races, perhaps even trying to sink a colleague's craft—surely a most unseemly and, finally, impossible prospect.) Even so, the graduate faculty would still wield considerable control over when and where and how students might be able to *exert* any such leverage within a given program. In other words, professors might teach the conflicts, or teach some other approach to metadisciplinary analysis, and they might well require students to write *about* them. But these same professors would be under no particular obligation to allow students to exercise what they learned from such study during, let alone on, the course in which they were learning it. The invitation would be to watch and analyze the conflicts, not participate in them. To do the latter, one would need to get at least as far as the qualifying examinations, and maybe through to the degree itself. In this sense, the corporate compromise strategy is very much in the Magisterial tradition: a new subspecialization—in this case, the history and politics of English Studies—simply gets added to the list of requirements students need to fulfill. To become "one of us," students would now also need to demonstrate that they knew how nonunitary that "us" was, and why.

Considering the advantages offered by this corporate compromise option—not to mention its appeal to the self-interest of graduate professors—it may be hard to credit that the Wayzata conferees seriously contemplated a third possible strategy, but the evidence suggests that they did. Like the other two, this third approach is conceptually simple and, given the field's situation, easy enough to deduce a priori: fusion, it might be called; bringing disparate elements together under sufficient pressure and with sufficient energy to transform them into a single new entity, one quite distinct from any of the original components. Or, to put it in terms specific to English Studies: rather than ending the field's divisions by breaking it up along the lines of conflict (dissolution), or packaging those conflicts for the purposes of curricular delivery (corporate compromise), the object would be to harness the energy generated by the conflicts in order to forge some new disciplinary enterprise altogether.

It might be argued, of course, that the corporate compromise strategies represent cautiously framed versions of this approach; that they have, as an implicit ultimate goal, just this sort of transformation. That may be the case, but the move from implication to application, particularly on the curricular level, seems to me to involve three fairly dramatic commitments that those writing in favor of corporate compromise do not appear to have been ready to make. First, it requires that representatives of the field's disparate elements who are also members of some substantive entity—the department being the obvious choice—need to be sequestered in the disciplinary and professional equivalent of a locked room for what amount to do-or-die negotiations. Nobody gets to go home until some resolution has been reached. Gary Waller's account of Carnegie Mellon University's (CMU) Ph.D. program, "Polylogue: Reading, Writing and the Structure of

Doctoral Study," quite eloquently addresses both the importance of taking this step and its possible consequences. At the time, the CMU program featured two strands, one in rhetoric and one in literary and cultural theory. As chair Waller was anxious to promote what he insists is a crucial interaction between these strands but one that also represents for him an interaction crucial to the discipline as a whole. "[A]t the very least," he writes, the program must bring the students and the faculty from the two strands together "at key points in the curriculum" for colloquia or seminars. However, even this modest step turns out to present a fairly serious challenge. It seems that the faculty groups involved tended to have another agenda, "each group . . . anxious to preserve 'its' integrity and 'its' students" (118). Given such concerns, the sort of dialogue Waller has in mind—his vision of the locked-room dynamic—suggests that those groups had good reason to be anxious. The stakes in this "interaction" have the potential to become very, very high:

> The discipline has relied on all too predictable ways to categorize, valorize, regard, and empower. The promise of interaction is that we can establish new patterns for empowering, and competing, that cut across traditional boundaries . . . . That will mean that these key faculty members [those who "look to actively promote dialogue, discussion, debate in their own work as in the courses they teach"]—in my own department distributed, I am happy to say, across all ranks and within programs—must be prepared to engage, in their own work, in something less genteel than a polite pluralism or social reconciliation. The new approach must involve an acknowledged clash of paradigms, frameworks, languages, and methodologies, an understanding that some will not survive the battle and many will find themselves led into conversations they did not expect. Interaction is risk taking at its finest, and the discipline will rely heavily on those willing to take a chance. There is a very real danger of factionalism and intellectual war. (118)

The second commitment required by this fusion strategy, and the one that perhaps most visibly sets it apart from the teaching-the-conflicts approach in particular, is that doctoral students must be afforded a major role in the deliberations. They must be participants, not spectators. Such a commitment is implicit in Waller's vision, and elsewhere in his essay he insists that "[w]e are inviting our students to enter the conversation" (116). But the importance of this invitation is spelled out more fully, if still somewhat guardedly, in James Slevin's "Conceptual Frameworks and Curricular Arrangements: A Response." The immediate provocation for his essay, he explains, is the conference presenters' rather consistent figuring of the graduate student as victim. It may be that this image "focuses our problems, evokes sympathy, and so may help to bring about change; but it risks further marginalizing our graduate students, ignoring their desires and subverting their potential to collaborate with us in transforming the profession" (Slevin 31). To escape this trap, Slevin proposes that those assembled "bring our dialogue here [at Wayzata] into our graduate programs," to which end he offers ways "to open up some curricular space within which our graduate students can learn about and participate in this critique of the profession" (31). *Participate* is very much the key word:

> Reconceiving the graduate program . . . ought not to be the work of the faculty only. I am concerned with how we can effectively involve graduate students in the consideration of the graduate curriculum itself and, through this involvement, in the shaping of their professional goals and the scrutiny of ours. A new kind of integration for our graduate programs could emerge from this involvement. What I hope for, at least, is a drawing together: of graduate faculty members and students in a shared exploration of issues; and of courses in the graduate program, where coherence, for the time being at least, might derive from a shared *process* of inquiry. (36–37, his emphasis)

Ultimately, however, the third commitment is the most dramatic and clarifies just how radically this fusion strategy breaks with the Magisterial tradition. It goes like this: the graduate faculty must be willing to renegotiate their disciplinary and professional status vis-à-vis the doctoral students in their programs. Here again, elements of this commitment can be seen embedded in the other two: Waller's warning that "some will not survive the battle" and Slevin's image of a "new kind of integration" both hint at how much the professoriate will be required to put on the table—to flat-out risk—if this transformation is to proceed. However, Helene Moglen's "Crossing the Boundaries: Interdisciplinary Education at the Graduate Level," offers the proceedings' fullest articulation of what is involved. Taking as her point of departure the work of feminist critics and theorists, Moglen's ambition—like Waller's—is to activate in English Studies a process that disrupts old relationships and forges new ones,

> the reconceptualization of power relations in order to acknowledge that resistance and conflict—as well as contradiction—are always inscribed in discursive practice and that we are all situated in many different places in those intersecting and often conflicting discourses. Understanding *how* we are situated, we can begin the process of re-situation: of resistance and change. (Moglen 88)

Moglen also makes it clear that this process—*all* of it—needs to constitute a defining curricular practice, and that the clearly post-Magisterial "we" she has in mind includes both faculty and students. In other words, this is not a matter of teaching students how "we" are all situated with regard to one another and then having an examination to make sure they remember. Rather, she intends this enterprise of *re*-situation to be taken quite literally. Once the process is set in motion, she expects that "the changed focus of the graduate program, and of the larger intellectual effort that it represents, might well help to redefine the relationship of faculty members to graduate students and graduate students to one another" (90). Moreover, she predicts that this redefinition will take place in and through that most jealously guarded of professional and disciplinary prerogatives, writing:

> it is the writing—produced by both students and faculty members, all participating in an exploratory and innovational project—that could allow individuals and groups that formerly viewed themselves as being in hierarchical and competitive relationships to redefine themselves genuinely as colleagues. (90)

In the post-Wayzata era, all three of these strategic options came to have their supporters. Thus, while dissolution has still not become a widely acceptable topic for discussion—so far as I know no return trip to either Wye or Wayzata for the purpose of officially dismantling English Studies is in the works—there are plenty of signs that the possibility continues to percolate (Elbow's verb). So, for example, a number of writing programs have moved out of English to form their own administrative units—including, significantly, separate departments. And while these moves have to this point involved primarily undergraduate programs, they make it distinctly more possible that more units will follow the lead of the Syracuse University writing program which, having separated from the English department some years ago, has now developed its own Ph.D. program.

Meanwhile, of course, the vast majority of doctorate-granting departments have opted to keep working through their respective versions of the corporate compromise strategy, comparing notes by means of such groups as the MLA-sponsored Association of Directors of Graduate Study in English, while at the same time trying to secure a recruitment- and placement-market niche by featuring distinctive emphases. Perhaps the single best indicator of this strategy's dominance is the growth in programs claiming some strength in rhetoric and composition. Huber's 1986 survey, you will recall, identified forty-six such programs; a spring 1994 special issue of *Rhetoric Review,* by contrast, identified over seventy. (If you can't fight 'em . . . .)

Finally, however, out on what might be called—at least from a corporate perspective—the radical fringe are those departments that have chosen to pursue some version of the third option: to put themselves in that locked room to see what comes out. The English Department at Carnegie Mellon is often mentioned in this connection, as are Illinois State University and the University of Pittsburgh. And of course that list also includes the English Department at the University at Albany, State University of New York. Its efforts are the subject of the next section.

# WRITING, DOCTORAL EDUCATION, AND THE UNIVERSITY AT ALBANY'S PH.D. PROGRAM IN "WRITING, TEACHING, AND CRITICISM"

(with BARBARA A. CHEPAITIS, DAVID COOGAN, LÂLE DAVIDSON, RON MACLEAN, CINDY L. PARRISH, JONATHAN POST, AND BETH WEATHERBY)

I t may be, as one early reader of this manuscript commented, that the plot driving the previous four chapters contains notably messianic overtones: 120 years of English doctoral education leading, by way of denouement, to the University at Albany's Ph.D. program in "Writing, Teaching, and Criticism." Obviously, I want to be very cautious in handling implications of this sort. The historical outline I offer does indeed lead to Albany—but only as one among many possible places. Other versions of much the same material could easily be made to lead elsewhere and to provide a context for describing other, very different programs. As I noted in closing Chapter 4, the doctoral programs that have chosen to pursue the fusion option represent a small minority, a relatively radical fringe. And, although the Albany program, like the others in this group, is ambitious in lots of ways, no one involved has ever (at least publicly) gone quite so far as to proclaim it the savior of English doctoral study, the One and Only Way.

At the same time, however, my collaborators and I do not want to wax falsely modest. As explained in the Introduction, Albany is a particularly apt representative for the post–World War II generation of English doctoral programs—"poster-child" was our mildly irreverent label—both brought into being by and thereafter largely uninsulated from the forces that have so dramatically altered the face of U.S. higher education in the latter half of the twentieth century. To recap some of the institutional events-cum-credentials that warrant such a claim: in the thirty-two years following its host institution's transformation from teacher's college to university center (in 1962), the Albany English Department launched its first Ph.D. program (1963), followed a few years later by a D.A. program (1971); that first Ph.D. program was deregistered after a State Education Department review (1975), with the deregistration subsequently challenged—unsuccessfully—in court (1976–1978); in the aftermath of that loss, the D.A. program prospered (1978–1992), providing the foundation for a second Ph.D. program (1992) and ultimately leading to an internal decision to suspend admissions to the D.A. Program (1994).

But Albany's suitability to represent this post–World War II generation of English doctoral programs is also grounded in the profile of its English Department faculty. In some ways, the official listing (reproduced on page 81 from the 1989–90 *Undergraduate Bulletin*, which features the group that implemented the curriculum on which the new Ph.D. would be based) has a very traditional, downright Magisterial look to it; certain features are reminiscent of an NYU or Columbia roster from 1950. All but five of the forty-three faculty listed hold Ph.D.'s, with one D.A., one Ed.D., one M.A., and two B.A.'s. Almost half of those degrees are from the nation's oldest, most prestigious, and traditionally most prolific doctoral programs, all but three in the East: five from the University of Pennsylvania, three from Brown, two each from Harvard, Yale, Cornell, Wisconsin, and Columbia, and one each from Chicago, Michigan, and Johns Hopkins.

In other ways, however, the composition of this faculty clearly reflects the effects of events traced in Chapters 3 and 4. One such effect can be seen in the number of Ph.D.'s from midwestern universities, both public and private. In addition to Chicago, Wisconsin, and Michigan—and where one might well have expected to find a Princeton or an NYU—there are Ph.D.'s from Indiana (four), Washington University (two), Iowa, Illinois, Kansas, and Northwestern—a flow of academic talent from (mid)west to east that runs counter to much pre–World War II tradition and repre-

# Department of English

**Professors**
Jeffrey Berman, Ph.D., Cornell University
Ronald A. Bosco, Ph.D., University of Maryland
Sarah Blacher Cohen, Ph.D., Northwestern University
Robert A. Donovan, Ph.D., Washington University
William A. Dumbleton, Ph.D., University of Pennsylvania
Judith Fetterley, Ph.D., Indiana University
Eugene K. Garber, Ph.D., University of Iowa
M. E. Grenander, Ph.D., University of Chicago
William Kennedy, B.A., Siena College
Walter Knotts, Ph.D., Harvard University
Daniel \. Odell, Ph.D., Cornell University
John M. Reilly, Ph.D., Washington University
Harry C. Staley, Ph.D., University of Pennsylvania
**Associate Professors**
Judith E. Barlow, Ph.D., University of Pennsylvania
Lillian Brannon, Ed.D., East Texas State University
Donald J. Byrd, Ph.D., University of Kansas
Randall Craig, Ph.D., University of Wisconsin
Diva Daims, Ph.D., Union Graduate School
**Deborah Dorfman, Ph.D., Yale University**
**Helen Regueiro Elam, Ph.D., Brown University**
**Sandra Fischer, Ph.D., University of Oregon**
**Warren Ginsberg, Ph.D., Yale University**
**Richard M. Goldman, Ph.D., Indiana University**
**Judith Johnson, B.A., Barnard College**
**Cyril H. Knoblauch, Ph.D., Brown University**
**Eugene Mirabelli, Ph.D., Harvard University**
**Rudolph L. Nelson, Ph.D., Brown University**
**Stephen North, D.A., State University of New York at Albany**
**David C. Redding, Ph.D., University of Pennsylvania**
**Barbara R. Rotundo, Ph.D., Syracuse University**
**Martha T. Rozett, Ph.D., University of Michigan**
**Joan E. Schulz, Ph.D., University of Illinois**
**Frederick E. Silva, Ph.D., Indiana University**
**Donald B. Stauffer, Ph.D., Indiana University**
**Myron W. Taylor, Ph.D., Washington University**
**Assistant Professors**
Lana Cable, Ph.D., Johns Hopkins University
Jennifer Fleischman, Ph.D., Columbia University
George S. Hastings, Ph.D., University of Pennsylvania
Edward M. Jennings, Ph.D., University of Wisconsin
Mark J. Schenker, Ph.D., Columbia University
Thomas H. Smith, M.A., Harvard University
Carolyn Yalkut, Ph.D., University of Denver
**Lecturers**
Barbara A. McCaskill, Ph.D., Emory University

Adjuncts (estimated): 10
Teaching Assistants (estimated): 24

sents to a considerable degree the aggressive policies of such programs during the Great Expansion. A similar effect has to do with
the gradual mixing in of degrees from less established and/or less
storied programs: doctorates from places such as Maryland, Syracuse, and the University of Oregon, which are of course hardly
obscure, but also Emory, Denver, Union Graduate School, East
Texas State, and Albany itself, along with the B.A.'s from Siena
and Barnard (these last two held by faculty in creative writing).

Meanwhile, in terms of demographics, this group is most
demonstrably typical of its generation on two counts not entirely
visible in this particular kind of listing: age and the proportion
between men and women. As a function of its rapid expansion
from the late 1950s into the early 1970s, the Albany English
Department as listed here was, like many of its counterparts, still
numerically dominated by white males—26 such men to 17
women, 10 to 3 among full professors.[1] Primarily as a function
of age, however, that dominance was diminishing, and quite rapidly. Between 1980 and 1989, for instance, the department had
had 11 retirements among its 43 members, all of them white
males over 60. By 1996 another 18 of the faculty listed here (all
of them also on the 1980–82 roster) would retire (16) or die (2),
all but three of them also white males. In other words, of 29
retirees (or decedents) between 1980 and 1996, 26 were white
males. The net effect (in concert of course with the demographic
changes in candidate pools, the continuing impact of affirmative
action, and a slightly amplified version of the overall downsizing
pattern in higher education in the 1990s) has been to bring the
department's 1997–98 male-female ratio into line with what might
be called the millenial profile for English Studies: 17 women, 12
men (7 to 5 among full professors).

For our purposes, though, the more significant ways in which
this department can be said to represent post–World War II doctorate-granting departments are those that reflect the changing
nature of English Studies as a discipline. Under what has been
the most common post–World War II system for disciplinary head
counting, it would be reckoned that 18 of the 43 1989–90 faculty listed here had been hired primarily in British literature and
17 in American literature. However, while such a degree of par-

ity across the British-American divide might itself be considered an interesting measure of long-term change in the discipline, in truth it makes more sense to argue that by the end of the 1980s this whole mode of classification had become entirely, demonstrably inadequate as a means of accounting for a field as variegated as English Studies had become. Its most obvious failure with this roster lies in the eight appointments that are simply left unaccounted for: three in rhetoric and composition (Brannon, Knoblauch, North), three in creative writing (Garber, Kennedy, Johnson), one in journalism (Yalkut), and one in literary theory (Elam).

But there are other important disciplinary developments that this customary mode of counting obscures. For example, one of the Americanists listed (Nelson) holds a degree in American rather than English Studies. Three others (Barlow, Fetterley, Schulz) had by this point in their careers established themselves sufficiently in feminist scholarship and women's studies—an area of specialization all but unthinkable during their own graduate training—that their primary credentials could no longer be adequately characterized, as they once might have been, under such headings as "Twain scholar" (Fetterley) or "expert on O'Neill" (Barlow). Another pair, one senior (Reilly) and one junior (McCaskill), could claim disciplinary expertise in African American literature—very much a post-Magisterial option—and in fact the latter was hired in large part on the strength of her work in that area, a first for this department. And, last but not least, especially for our concerns, this listing includes three faculty who, responding primarily to the D.A.'s emphasis through the 1980s on writing, can be said to have shifted from the literature to the writing side of the ledger. Two did so by emphasizing their own status as writers in both publication and (especially graduate) teaching to such an extent that, in discussions of departmental hiring priorities, they came to be accounted first as a poet (Byrd) and a fiction writer (Mirabelli) and only second as Americanists. The third (Jennings) had been hired as a seventeenth-century British specialist, but his extensive and pioneering work with computers and writing over the better part of two decades had resituated him quite firmly in rhetoric and composition.

The presence of so variegated a range of post-Magisterial specializations—and there are others—as part of a mix that also included all those faculty whose professional identities remained firmly grounded in period and/or figure (the medievalist, the Shakespearean, the American Colonial expert, the Poe scholar, the Victorianist, etc.) reflects very clearly the situation in English Studies as a whole, the situation on such unnerving display at Wayzata and in *The Future of Doctoral Studies in English*. In short, whether or not its efforts warrant messianic ambitions, the Albany English Department had the representative wherewithal to mount a curricular experiment on the doctoral level of considerable interest to both other institutions and the field in general.

The powerful disciplinary presence of writing at Albany—greater here even than at Wayzata, where its growing influence can be said to have brought that conference into being—makes this effort at fusion particularly worth watching. Here is an English department in which nearly a quarter (ten) of the tenure-track faculty locate their primary professional identities not in some branch of literature—not literary history or literary criticism or literary theory, although a number of them can claim expertise in such areas—but in writing: in rhetoric and composition, in creative writing, in journalism. Nor is their presence of merely numerical significance. This group had figured powerfully in the department's graduate offerings, and particularly the D.A., for more than a decade. Between 1980 and 1989, for example, they had (along with Knoblauch's predecessor, C. Lee Odell) directed the vast majority—some 70 percent—of the department's completed dissertations (fifty-two of seventy-three, according to the department's records) and were generally accorded much of the credit for the success that degree program had enjoyed. Indeed, two of these ten faculty members—(Garber and Brannon) served on the five-member committee that spearheaded the development of the new Ph.D. proposal, a level of representation on any such body almost certainly unprecedented in the history of English Studies.

Hence the visibility—indeed the primacy—of writing in the new program's title ("Writing, Teaching, and Criticism"), its crucial role in the curricular experiment that title represents, and its consequent status as the focal point of this study overall and of this section in particular. In a shift of emphasis that has nearly always distinguished writing-based English curricular models from those that are literature-based, the Albany Ph.D. curriculum situates the students' work in writing—their work as writers of all kinds—at the center of their educational experience. As will become clear in the chapters that follow, all the other activities associated with doctoral education in English (including the field's traditional locus for its disciplinary core experience, reading) are still very much present and still play an important role in the overall curriculum; this is not, to use the pejorative frequently invoked in standard writing-versus-literature discussions, "merely" a "studio" program. Nevertheless, where traditionally all such activities would have been understood as focusing on the students' reading of primary texts—what Graff has called, in a related context, "literature itself" (10)—here they are centered around, and ultimately in the service of the students' writing.

Chapter 5, then, explores the nature of this doctoral program, with a particular emphasis on the ways in which its approach to writing departs from the dominant traditions in English Studies. The next four chapters then examine in greater detail some of the uses of writing thus promoted. Chapter 6, "Writing to Get Situated: Learning to Stage a Reading," focuses on what is usually called informal writing, or—in writing-across-the-curriculum circles, writing-to-learn/learning-to-write-in-the-discipline. Chapter 7, "Charting Courses (1): Extended Work in a Preferred Mode" looks at how students go about representing the program's constituent perspectives in what they write for different courses: poetry in the History of English Studies, 1880–Present, for example, or fiction in the course on Models of History in Literary Criticism. Chapter 8, "Charting Courses (2): (Re)Combinatory Writings," considers what are essentially new forms—that is, textual forms generated in response to the peculiar mixing of discourses that is at the heart of the Albany enterprise. And Chapter 9, "Writing beyond Coursework: The Qualifying Examination and the Dissertation," examines the impact of the program's principles on those most highly formalized writings in doctoral education, qualifying examinations and dissertations.

## CHAPTER FIVE

# Albany's Ph.D. in English Studies: "Writing, Teaching, and Criticism"

The 1992 proposal that serves as the charter for Albany's Ph.D. in "Writing, Teaching, and Criticism" is quite explicit about the program's local genealogy. "The new Ph.D. proposal," it explains, "takes its direction not from the previous Ph.D. but from the current D.A. program" (5). Part of the message here is that this program would not be cast, as the department's first doctoral effort had been, in the post–World War II image of the Magisterial tradition. On the contrary: it would deliberately abandon, much as the Wayzata conferees had, both historical coverage and canonical unity as the "invariable reference points" of a doctoral curriculum in English (Lunsford, Moglen, and Slevin vi). Thus, whereas the curriculum of the department's first Ph.D. had "centered on courses in literary periods, genres, and authors," with only 10 percent of the course offerings providing for the study of "criticism, language, and issues of topical interest," less than 5 percent for "rhetoric and pedagogy," and none for work in creative writing ("Proposal" 5), the new program was to have both a different organizing principle and a different curricular profile.

## An Integrative Dynamic

In particular, then, this new effort was to "build on and extend" the integrative dynamic—"the emphasis on what might best be called intra-disciplinary study" (5)—that a generation of students had made the hallmark of the D.A. Program, and that in turn had put that degree program on the national map:

Even before the new curricular offerings were put in place in the fall of 1990, students in the Albany D.A. engaged and put into relationship issues in writing theory and practice, critical theory, and language theory, as well as the issues that rise from the study of literary history. In addition, they set these concerns in the context of their implications for teaching theory and practice. These emphases are reflected in recent doctoral examination areas and in dissertations. Because of these interests the Albany D.A. has achieved national recognition. In *Professing Literature: An Institutional History* (Chicago, 1987), Gerald Graff mentions Albany as one of fifteen departments that have developed programs he views as significant departures from the traditional doctoral format. ("Proposal" 5)

What these students had been managing to do, in other words, was to bring together in productive ways (to engage and put into relationship, in proposalese) the various but also largely insular disciplinary discourses to which they were being introduced by the faculty in courses. The Doctor of Arts had appeared in U.S. higher education as a college teaching degree, the single most ambitious effort ever undertaken in this country to correct the poor fit between the research orientation of Ph.D. training and the teaching careers many of the degree's holders actually pursued.[1] The aim of the version mounted by the English Department at Albany, very much in keeping with this originary conception, was to produce well-rounded but also coherent generalists, people prepared primarily to teach undergraduates at two- and four-year colleges.

In pursuit of well-roundedness, students would take a wide range of courses: say, in rhetoric and composition, creative writing, literary theory, Chaucer, early American literature, the British novel, and so on. There was, however, a catch of sorts. Following the pattern of professionalization in the field as a whole, each such course tended to be essentially discrete and would, if anything, encourage students in the direction of greater and more discrete specialization. In other words, it would direct them further and further into rhetoric and composition, literary theory, or early American literature but rarely outward toward any broader construction of English Studies as a larger, let alone coherent, whole.

Which is where the postcoursework requirements of the D.A. program—examinations, internship, and dissertation—would take over. From the program's inception, the qualifying examinations in particular had been designed to promote precisely this sort of broadly constructive effort. *Synthesize* was the operative term: instead of requiring students to work from traditional comprehensive lists or a menu of possible period-and-genre choices, these examinations were based primarily on each individual student's coursework and represented an occasion for making retrospective sense of—synthesizing—his or her journey through sixty-odd hours of coursework. And this process tended to carry over into the internship (nearly always in college teaching) and dissertation as well, the former providing an immediate opportunity for (re)situating this emerging synthesis in various classroom contexts, and the latter for carrying it on in a more sustained way than the temporal and generic constraints of the examinations permitted.

As the excerpted passage from the proposal indicates, these efforts had proven valuable for both the students and the program. The successful D.A. graduates were able to carry on a brand of disciplinary inquiry different from, and in some respects superior to, that of their mentors, and the profession had recognized and indeed welcomed their work. What the passage does not quite say, but what is equally true, is that the process had had a considerable influence on the participating faculty as well. These D.A. examination and dissertation committees routinely brought together professors from across the various sectors of English Studies represented in the department, matching one from creative writing, say, with a second from rhetoric and composition, and a third from literary theory or early American literature or the Renaissance—any number of combinations was possible (standard committees had three faculty members).

Once they were thus assembled, the exigencies of the situation accomplished what neither the department as a whole nor the larger profession had been able to manage nearly so well: they engaged these disparate faculty in sustained intradisciplinary inquiry that was not only motivated by a shared concern for education (as opposed to self-interest, academic turf, and so on), but even went so far as to include the person whose education was at issue—the doctoral student—in a substantive way. Far more than in the comprehensives of the Magisterial tradition, the candidate played a crucial role here: the candidate was the one who had moved across the intradisciplinary boundaries under discussion; who had, by virtue of completing the required coursework, both necessitated the committee's meetings and set their agenda; and who would subsequently be expected to enact through his or her teaching and writing any synthesis the group's work might help produce.

In short, these committees gave participating faculty considerable experience—for the most part very positive —with what it might be like to pursue the fusion option in the context of a doctoral program. True, the operative scale was small and the duration relatively short; four people can establish a working relationship of this kind, especially in aid of a specific task, more easily than the forty or more involved in a Ph.D. curriculum. And the stakes, while obviously important, were still limited; the disciplinary positions held by all members of these committees may have been open to investigation, but the results of the inquiry, and hence any *sustained* challenge to those positions, could be sent out into the world in the person of the candidate, and (therefore) need not return directly to the department itself.

Nevertheless, a decade of success with the dynamic generated in these minifusion sessions proved both intriguing and promising enough that the department determined to place it at the center of—indeed, to make it the engine for—its second attempt at a Ph.D. program. Thus, the new program would feature this intradisciplinary emphasis not only in its handling of examinations and dissertation—both of which would take their lead from the D.A. in ways we will detail further in Chapter 9—but also throughout the entire curriculum, thereby "promoting *within* courses the fruitful dialogue that had until 1990 tended to take place primarily *between* courses" ("Proposal" 5, original emphasis).

This decision is realized most visibly in the way the curriculum is structured. Courses are organized into "seven interrelated branches of study" ("Proposal" 10)—Writing in History, Writing Theory and Practice, Rhetoric and Composition, Critical

Theory and Practice, Teaching Theory and Practice, Language
and Language Theory, and Literary History—but with the emphasis very much on *interrelated*. (So, for example, while students are required to undertake coursework in a minimum of
four branches, they are also strongly advised—and generally inclined—to include more.) And in this sense the paradigmatic
member of the group—the branch that sets the tone and establishes the programmatic context for the others—is the one listed
first, Writing in History:

> The courses in this category are designed to effect the synthe-
> sizing intentions of the curriculum. Each course is conceived to
> include the interests of the program's various constituents—
> rhetoricians, creative writers, literary scholars and theorists; to
> bring into relation in a single conversation the issues addressed
> by the remaining six branches; and to inform the work that
> goes on elsewhere in the curriculum. Designed around the un-
> derstanding that all writing of whatever kind—creative, criti-
> cal, theoretical, instructional—takes place within an historical
> and social sphere which it both shapes and is shaped by, and
> that the teaching of writing and interpretation as an academic
> profession occurs within an institutional context which has it-
> self an historical and social dimension, these courses invite all
> students to view themselves within a complex set of historical
> conditions. (10)

It is crucial to the program's operation, however, that the
"synthesizing intentions" set in motion by this branch—and particularly by its core course (one of only two required courses in
the program), The History of English Studies, 1880 to the
Present—carry on through all the courses in all the other branches:
this branch should, as proposed, "inform the work that goes on
elsewhere in the curriculum."[2] Thus, while the other six branches
correspond in fairly recognizable ways to both historically established concerns of English Studies and constituencies within the
Albany faculty,[3] they do not signal the kind of tracking—the development of increasingly exclusive specializations—that the
Ph.D. has traditionally required and that moves students further
and further away from intradisciplinary inquiry. On the contrary,
these branches need to be understood as marking points of entry,
places from which to *enter* that inquiry-in-progress. To this end,

each branch features a core introductory course that explores not only "the basic theory, pragmatics, and problematics of that aspect of English studies" but also—and insistently—"its relationship to the overall curriculum" ("Proposal" 10). Furthermore, while subsequent courses in each branch necessarily move toward some degree of specialization, they nevertheless remain in touch with the enterprise as a whole: *all* courses, explains the proposal, "are intended to invoke the central elements of the program—writing, teaching, and criticism. That is, they are intended to be pedagogically and critically self-reflective and to place the act of writing at the center of inquiry" (10).

Ultimately, this relentlessly integrative structure functions as a version of what we described in Chapter 4 as the locked room necessary for any fusion experiment: it represents, that is, not a system for parceling out a body of knowledge by way of replicating a certain kind of expert (the Magisterial model), but rather a coordinated series of occasions for negotiating claims about who knows what, how, why, and to what ends. It might still be said that the purpose of the curriculum is to make participants "one of us," but only with the powerful qualification that the "us" in question is both more local and more contingent than in the Magisterial tradition. On the one hand, then, in the absence of any widely accepted disciplinary coherence—the legacy of Wayzata, if you will—the Albany curriculum is grounded much more, and much more consciously, in an "us" that refers to those-who-are-gathered-here-now:

> [I]n many respects the most innovative feature of the degree, which distinguishes it most sharply from the traditional Ph.D., is the way its curriculum gains coherence not primarily from period courses but from the integrated interests of those who teach and take the classes. Every course, whatever its focus, explores its subject from the perspectives which creative writers, students of rhetoric and composition, and literary critics bring to bear on it. This interplay of responses will inevitably challenge the belief that literature is discrete and neatly classifiable into periods or that any one approach to it is unproblematically more valuable than another. Ultimately, it will make traditional distinctions between composition, creative writing, and literary criticism difficult to maintain. ("Proposal" 2)

On the other hand, but for much the same reasons, any coherence thus generated is understood to be temporary, open to further, and in principle endless, negotiation. Or, as the proposal puts it,

> programmatic coherence is dynamic. Each part of the program interacts with and interrogates the others. Such interaction has the twofold effect of keeping the program open to changing relations between subjects and making the program continually aware of its own assumptions and practices. The areas of writing, pedagogy, and literary criticism are thus interwoven by a sustained critique of the nature of understanding and of the history by which such understanding comes to be. The aim of these interrogations is not, obviously, to provide a determinate and stable context for each area of investigation but to unveil the ways in which competing and interlocking interests and ideologies affect our understanding of a field of study and the questions we raise about it. Such a critique provides within the program a space for constant re-evaluation and revision, even as it makes possible a dynamic relation of subjects and questions. (3)

## Classroom Effects

You can see how this curricular model departs not only from the Magisterial tradition but also from the corporate compromise proposals so prominent at Wayzata. One such difference lies in the very way it configures English Studies: in other words, in the (sub)divisions of the field it assembles for its declared mission of intradisciplinary inquiry. Clearly, putting "rhetoricians" on an absolutely equal footing with "literary critics" in an English Ph.D. program constitutes a fairly radical move, a serious break with tradition. As any number of sources can be called on to demonstrate, the former have almost universally been treated as at best poor cousins, sometimes tolerated but rarely (if indeed ever) embraced as full disciplinary partners. And it is even more radical to expand this core group to include "creative writers," and to grant them equal status as well. So far as we can tell, this is a triumvirate which, *as* a triumvirate, is entirely without precedent in the annals of English doctoral education. Certainly none of the essays in *The Future of Doctoral Studies in English*—even the most far-ranging—so much as hints that it might be a possibility.[4]

However, a second crucial difference between Albany's fusion experiment and both the Magisterial tradition and corporate compromise strategies has to do not with *who* interacts, but *how*. It is not hard to see how such a program would have been anathema to the kind of mastery that anchored the Magisterial curriculum; whatever disagreements there may have been behind the scenes, the facade of curricular solidarity was not negotiable. And the situation is not entirely dissimilar in terms of corporate compromise. As explained in Chapter 4, the basic aim of the dominant post-Wayzata approach is mutually profitable coexistence: holding the conflicted enterprise together, however loosely, and then—for curricular purposes—finding some way to present, but at the same time preserve, all its competing interests. Hence the conservative attractions of such notions as "teaching the conflicts." Under such a curricular model, "real" disciplinary activities—both the various investigations and "the conflicts" that arise from and among them—are understood to take place elsewhere, in arenas accessible only to the properly licensed. Thus when in a given class faculty describe or analyze or even dramatize the tensions among the discipline's divisions ("teach" the aforementioned conflicts), they are exercising and even enhancing their disciplinary authority, not opening it up to challenges: they are (re)enforcing both a particular version of the field and their claims to a position in it. Students, meanwhile, are situated outside the knowledge-making enterprise by definition—so far outside, in fact, that they scarcely qualify as spectators, let alone participants, since they do not so much witness the conflicts as learn about them second- or thirdhand.

By contrast, the aim of a fusion strategy like Albany's is not preservation but transformation, the production of new versions of English Studies that will make sense—gain coherence—not by reference to activities underway elsewhere, nor to any other externally imposed norm (e.g., "period courses"), but as a function of "the integrated interests of those who teach and take the classes." Hence the pedagogical imperative: "*Every* course, whatever its focus, explores its subject from the perspectives which creative writers, students of rhetoric and composition, and literary critics bring to bear on it" ("Proposal" 2; emphasis added). It would not be enough to represent these perspectives in separate tracks and then establish distribution requirements that would also allow faculty to "teach the conflicts" among them. That would simply postpone, as the D.A. had, any sanctioned intradisciplinary inquiry until after coursework and thereby force any earlier efforts outside the curriculum proper, back to the hallways, coffee shops, and TA offices where students have always gathered to make what sense they can of departmental offerings. Worse, it would effectively remove (excuse) the faculty from any extensive participation in such inquiry, with the result that the exploration of interrelatedness, and any consequent refiguring of the discipline, would have to be done in the absence (and even in spite) of the teachers who were ostensibly sponsoring it. In short, in this program all courses have to be an occasion, and every classroom a location, for its fusion enterprise. Strictly speaking, there is never any "elsewhere" to defer to: real disciplinary activities—again, both the field's highly various investigations and "the conflicts" that arise from and among them—are not so much taught in these classes as embodied, enacted, engaged.

It follows, too, that such an imperative requires a substantial shift in the classroom roles of, and relationship between, professors and doctoral students. In the Magisterial tradition, as we have seen, faculty members derived their curricular authority (their mastery, to recall Bliss Perry's term) from work in one or another disciplinary discourse, and they would be assigned to teach graduate courses on that basis. The student counterpart to this specialty-based mastery, in turn, was a specialty-based apprenticeship. Thus, while presumably no one has ever really imagined that doctoral students enter English graduate courses with no disciplinary perspectives of their own (although the Jones and Perry characterizations quoted in Chapter 2 come awfully close to making such a claim), they have nevertheless traditionally been expected to conform to the discursive trajectory of each course in which they enroll—a conformity most visible and, given the means by which students are evaluated in such courses, most important in what they (are assigned to) write.

So, for example, in the fairly standard period-based curriculum of Albany's first Ph.D. program, three students whose own eventual credentials might be grounded in such divergent specializations as stylistic variations in the writing of computer scientists, the contemporary reception of *Uncle Tom's Cabin,* and the fiction of Dorothy Sayers, could all quite easily have found themselves in a Chaucer seminar working up an extended paper on *The Legend of Good Women,* or in a course on the Transcendentalists preparing a presentation and subsequent essay on *The Dial.* To recall Perry again, it was the pupil's "duty" and "privilege" to "learn from the master on those waters where the master loved to teach" (251).

This basic arrangement inevitably holds true for the corporate compromise strategy, as well. One of its principal advantages for graduate professors, as we saw at the end of the last chapter, was the extent to which it allowed the faculty to preserve their classroom authority. Thus, while a teach-the-conflicts faculty would certainly abandon the Magisterial pretence of a united front—so that a latter-day Bliss Perry, say, would be a good deal less sympathetic concerning the Harvard Ph.D. program's obsession with philology, and might even mix it up in classroom debate with Kittredge for the students' benefit—its members would just as definitely *not* surrender the authority of their individual specializations. Students would therefore find themselves in much the same situation as in the Magisterial curriculum, with the specialized mastery that licensed the faculty for graduate teaching in the first place determining both what courses were offered and each student's discursive *raison d'être*—including, of course, the professionalizing "what we write" that students have enrolled to gain mastery over.

In the current Albany curriculum, however, this traditional configuration of authority necessarily changes, and with it these discursive *raisons.* We don't want to exaggerate the magnitude of this shift. Each course is still likely to feature what might be called a sponsoring perspective, if only as a function of the interests and training of the faculty member assigned to teach it. Moreover, it is important for students to engage that perspective and its corresponding disciplinary/professional discourse in at least some of the same ways they always have: reading texts that represent it, responding to that reading, and so on. Building on "the integrated interests of those who teach and take the classes" clearly requires as much. Besides, for all its transformative ambitions, the institutional aim of Albany's doctoral program remains professionalization, to which end the shutting out of the licensed professionals—instituting a monopoly of student perspective(s), as it were, in place of one imposed by teachers—would be more than a little perverse.

Nevertheless, as a primary challenge, each class also faces the task of fulfilling on a daily basis the program's promise to "explore[s] its subject from the perspectives which creative writers, students of rhetoric and composition, and literary critics bring to bear on it"—of making sure that the sponsoring discourse is only one of several represented. In part, this is a matter of conception and design: course titles and bulletin copy that frame subjects amenable to approach from these multiple perspectives (e.g., Writing and Revision, Theories and Practice of Creativity, Theories of Language); reading lists that feature texts from across this range of perspectives; classroom practices designed to promote dialogues—indeed, polylogues—instead of monologues, and so on.

More than anything else, however, this exploration requires a fundamental change in the relationship among teacher, students, and subject matter. Thus, instead of being *the* master of *the* perspective the course exists to explicate, the teacher must learn not merely to include but to negotiate, and negotiate with these other perspectives and their distinctive ways of approaching—indeed of constituting—each course's subject matter. Correspondingly, when the teacher is not simply the "master," the students obviously cannot afford to be simply apprentices, either. If these other perspectives are in fact to be represented, it will be up to the students—"those who . . . *take* the classes"—to do the work. Instead of conforming to some dominant perspective in every individual class, then, each student must adopt, even if only provisionally, a disciplinary perspective and a professional identity— rhetorician, literary historian, fiction writer, etc.—with the concomitant right and substantial responsibility to "bring [that perspective] to bear" on the subject of the course.

# Be Sure to Get It in Writing

It is crucial that this change of relationship extend to the *writing* in these courses. Indeed, it might be more accurate to say that such a change can *only* happen in writing, or at least that it has to happen there most, first, above all. After all, English Studies, like most disciplines in the U.S. academy, is writing-based: from the dissertation to the article to the book, its knowledge-making processes—and much of its credentialing—are grounded in (published) writing. As we have argued from the beginning, this holds true for its doctoral education as well: even in the Magisterial tradition, with its heavy curricular emphasis on coverage (i.e., reading), the coin of the realm—from the précis to the annotated bibliography to the seminar paper to the qualifying examinations to the dissertation—has always been the written text.

It would be a fairly empty gesture, therefore, if the courses in the Albany curriculum invited participants to work from—and move toward integrating—their perspectives as creative writers, students of rhetoric and composition, and literary scholars and critics when they read and think and talk . . . but not when they write. Given the relationship between writing and evaluation in the credit-based economy of graduate school, students especially would be rightly skeptical of invitations to represent alternative perspectives if that representation did not extend to the writing they were invited or required to do. For the program to have any chance at success, this "interplay of responses" ("Proposal" 2) to the subjects of all courses absolutely must take place in and through writing.

Obviously, Albany is not the first English department in which these perspectives and their attendant forms of writing have ever crossed paths in the context of doctoral education. Quite the opposite: in one combination or another, albeit usually behind the facade of Magisterial solidarity, they have been competing with one another—and with other perspectives—for disciplinary and curricular space since very early in the field's history. Mind you, in a pattern that itself is symptomatic of the tensions involved, renderings of that history are rarely constructed as though such competition has had much to do with disciplinary writing practices in general, let alone with writing practices in doctoral programs. The story of English Studies tends to be framed in terms of concepts that are broader and more abstract: methods, which is how I would characterize Graff's approach, for instance; bureaucratic "self-reproduction" (Connors 63); the means and ends of "literary education" (Myers 13); or, as in our first four chapters here, demographics.

Nevertheless, institutional logic alone tells us what there is also considerable evidence for, which is that sooner or later, especially at the university level, many of this discipline-cum-profession's key interactions had to play out over something someone had written or wanted to write: over what a journal or a review or a press would or would not publish; what an English department or a university would or would not accept as textual evidence that someone was employable, tenurable, or promotable; or, our direct concern here, what a would-be Ph.D. could or could not write in a course, present on an examination or—that most critical of sanctions—submit for a dissertation. And since we also know that for various periods in the field's institutional history each of the perspectives featured in the Albany program has been the outsider—the challenger, the interloper—we can be certain that the modes of writing sanctioned by each perspective have also had to do a good deal of jostling to make their way into doctoral education, and indeed have had to do so more than once. Time after time, in program after program, one or another doctoral candidate—with or without faculty sponsorship—has had to challenge the local and/or disciplinary status quo with something that he or she wrote . . . or at least tried to write.

Thus, as Graff explains so patiently in *Professing Literature*, both the literary historical and the literary critical perspectives, which in the post–World War II era have acquired the patina of permanent fixtures—*the* modes of *the* Establishment—emerged separately, each an upstart in its own right: the historical in tension with the philological beginning in the 1890s; and the critical in a struggle with both the philological and the historical, beginning at about the same time and carrying on (especially with regard to the latter) well into the 1950s (Graff 193). And although the professional literature is not exactly awash in accounts of how this competition played out in the country's early Ph.D. programs, Stuart Sherman's "Professor Kittredge and the Teaching of English" offers what is at least highly visible testimony that at one institution—Kittredge's Harvard—trying to write against the grain was no simple matter.

So, for example, Sherman reports that in courses—and this is *not*, despite its apparent tone, heartfelt praise—"[f]ired by that unrelenting [philological] ardour" Kittredge inspired,

> one fixed one's attention with as intense a concern upon a disputed comma in the [sic] Canterbury tale as one could have felt for the most momentous crisis in the affairs of a nation. One could sit for week after week copying down under [Kittredge's] dynamic dictation an endless ballad bibliography that one never used, nor ever hoped to use, and yet maintain through it all the spellbound gravity of one hearkening to a seraphic discussion of fate and foreknowledge absolute. (Sherman 151).

Sherman claims to have asked one of Kittredge's favorite pupils, "What did you learn in those graduate seminars that was permanently useful to you?":

> "To verify my references," was the reply, "and to transcribe quoted passages with punctilious accuracy." That was, of course, a jest. What the speaker meant was that he had carried away the technique and the ideal of scientific research. That, as we take it, is what Professor Kittredge has principally desired to impart to graduate students. (153)

What was worse, this philologically-based perspective dominated the entire program, from coursework through dissertation. Alternative conceptions of English as a discipline, alternative modes of inquiry, and, it seems safe to assume, alternative modes of writing were simply, albeit quietly, not allowed:

> When, in conformity with the printed invitation, the candidate for the higher degree unfolded to the Department his plans and desires for work in modern literature, a majestic figure [Kittredge] waved him to a more removed ground [Kittredge's own preferred territory, the Middle Ages]. There was nothing

on paper to indicate objection to his enterprise, but after a few weeks he began to perceive that the modern period was not, so to speak, in good odour with those in authority. There was the system which incorporated the leading ideas of the Chairman of the Division of Modern Languages, and which prepared one for research in the Middle Ages. The core of the course was prescribed and the rind very strongly intimated—Germanic Philology, Romance Philology, Historical Grammar, Old Norse, Anglo-Saxon Grammar, Beowulf, Cynewulf, Old Irish perhaps, Ballads and Metrical Romances, Chaucer, Shakespeare, another course in the Drama also desirable. It was notorious that in the grand ordeal of the far-dreaded final examination serious inquisition into your scholarship would, in nine cases out of ten, end with the Fourteenth Century. (Sherman 154)

In short, while the historical and the critical would ultimately achieve not merely respectability but dominance in doctoral education, they did so only after a conflict that not only claimed a good many outright casualties—e.g., all those would-be poets Perry was so willing to see killed off—but that also exacted a substantial price from many who survived. As Sherman says quite bitterly elsewhere, many of the doctoral candidates "who have been constrained to submit . . . have been rather subjugated than pacified" (Sherman 152).

Meanwhile, rhetoric and composition's first attempts to win doctoral status for its methods and modes of writing came at about the same time, albeit with far less success. While this area of study is most widely perceived as having emerged on the doctoral scene in the late 1970s and early 1980s (so that by the mid-1980s, as we saw in Chapter 4, it had established enough of a presence to leverage the Wayzata conference) it had made other, and much earlier, appearances. In 1901, for example, the MLA's pedagogical section, under the leadership of the section's president, Fred Newton Scott, issued a report on "The Graduate Study of Rhetoric," evidence that even at the turn of the century there was "a group well aware of what serious graduate work [in this field] could be" (Brereton 187).

In fact, as Robert J. Connors explains in "Rhetoric in the Modern University: The Creation of an Underclass," Scott's entire career might be understood as an ongoing effort to renegotiate the place of rhetoric vis-à-vis English, particularly at the doctoral level. From the earning of his own 1889 Ph.D. at Michigan's Department of English and Rhetoric, to his establishing of a "separate and equal" Rhetoric department at the same institution, to that department's eventual remerger with "the powerful and secure English Language and Literature" in 1929 (Connors 65), he carried on the kind of campaign that a Howard Mumford Jones or a Stuart Sherman, say, or later an Allen Tate or John Crowe Ransom would conduct on behalf of the historical and the critical. In one sense, as Connors indicates, that campaign was ultimately unsuccessful: "written rhetoric—increasingly called composition . . . was afterward to be found, and despised, in departments of English" (65). In another sense, though—taking the long view, if you will—the campaign was by no means a total loss: Scott's own work as a scholar and a teacher, coupled with the work of his many graduate students (149 M.A.'s and 23 Ph.D.'s), made it possible for the rhetorical perspective to influence disciplinary and doctoral writing practices until at least the 1930s.

Finally, there is the troubled history of the perspective identified in the Albany program as creative writing. Like the others, it has been a feature of the doctoral mix for a long time. For example, in the oft-cited series in *The Dial* that became *English in American Universities* (edited by William Morton Payne), Charles Mills Gayley of the University of California offers in 1894 what might be called the liberal version of the Magisterial position on creative writing's status (in contrast with the conservative position, which would not accept "creative" or "imaginative" work toward the earning of the Ph.D. under any circumstances whatever):

> To graduate courses of information and of research might legitimately be added courses having a third purpose: the encouragement of literary creation. We have as yet none such in the University of California, unless one denominated Special Study, under which we announce ourselves ready to assist and advise competent graduates in approved plans of work, may be construed as sufficient for the emergency. Academic scholarship does not look with favor upon the attempt to stimulate or foster creative production. But, if charily advised, sagaciously circumscribed, and conducted under the personal supervision

of a competent critic, constructive literary effort may surely find a place in the curriculum of an exceptional graduate,—never, of course, unattended by other study with informative or disciplinary purpose in view. There is, nowadays, no reason why genius should be untutored or its early productions unkempt. (Gayley 58)

Variations on this position turn up again and again over the course of the century. Its most famous manifestation, of course, was at Iowa, where in 1930 Norman Foerster took advantage of the newly formed School of Letters to create a Ph.D. program that would "permit the substitution of a poem, play, or other work of art for the more usual type of dissertation" (*Daily Iowan*, qtd. in Wilbers 44). But the possibilities were clearly on other, and other high-profile, minds over the years as well. For example, in "The Study of Literature in the Graduate School" (Chapter 20 of the 1949 edition of *Theory of Literature*), Rene Wellek and Austin Warren point the way toward Ph.D. reform by identifying, among other things, some "hopeful signs" in "the world of professional magazines." Not only have the

"learned journals," including the *PMLA* . . . increasingly admitted articles (theory, literary criticism, studies of contemporary writers like Joyce, Proust, and T. S. Eliot) which, before, would either have been rejected or never received. . . . But our magazines of "literary scholarship" include also, and centrally, the critical or critical and creative quarterlies—the late *Criterion* and *Southern Review*, the current *Scrutiny, Sewanee Review, Kenyon Review, Partisan Review*, and *Accent*. (289)

Moreover, they seem ready to extend this broader range of discipline-sanctioned writing to "the doctoral thesis," which, they contend, "should be conceived of as flexibly as we conceive of professional literary distinction" (294).

And if Wellek and Warren were not absolutely clear about just how capacious their notion of "professional literary distinction" might be (although elsewhere in the chapter they specifically consider "poet" as one of the "types of mind and method" that it might be good to include in a staffing policy [291]), Don Cameron Allen, writing some twenty years later in aid of the same kind of reform, leaves no doubt whatever:

If good sense suggests that the thesis should be greatly short-ened and made more to the point, does not good sense also suggest that something other than the traditional dissertation is sufficient evidence of a candidate's literary ability? Many theses are now of a so-called critical nature and would have been turned down coldly before 1935. May we not go further and, granting that the student follows the usual doctoral pro-gram, accept an original work of literary merit? We cannot say we are unable to judge this merit. If we do, we should give up our profession. (115–16)

Of course, as his proviso about "granting that the student follows the usual doctoral program" suggests, the liberal posi-tion offered by Gayley was clearly still intact in the late 1960s. The ambivalence it reflects does not noticeably diminish over the next two decades, either, and is very much on display at Wayzata. Thus, according to Huber's 1986 survey (1989), while more than two-thirds (67.5 percent) of the 126 programs responding re-ported offering courses in creative writing (Tabulation i, 139), only one-quarter (24.6 percent) allowed examinations and dis-sertations in this area (Tabulation j, 141), a rather striking dis-parity even for a field with considerable experience at this particular form of institutional hypocrisy.

In short, creative writing has had the roughest doctoral-level row to hoe of any of Albany's constituent perspectives. Never-theless, given its longevity, its resilience, and its impressive list of supporters—far more illustrious in terms of Magisterial star power than that for rhetoric and composition[5]—it too has undeniably been a player in terms of who has gotten to write what in doc-toral education in English.

Ultimately, however, these long-standing competitive relation-ships can hardly be said to constitute any significant *interplay* among perspectives, particularly at the curricular level, and even more particularly in terms of their attendant forms of writing. In the Magisterial tradition—and under the field-coverage model—disciplinary perspectives might be added in or booted out of the curriculum, but not mingled, cross-pollinated, integrated. A case might perhaps be made that the historical and the critical, after years of overt feuding, came closest to reaching something like a workable "understanding": that, as Graff puts it in explaining the prevailing attitude of the 1940s and 1950s, "[c]riticism and history, it was agreed, were complementary, and no sound literary education could forgo either" (Graff 183). But as Graff himself responds, at the faculty level this understanding was based almost entirely on the *absence* of interplay—so that, in keeping with the theme that dominates *Professing Literature,*

> a set of conditions that might have created an atmosphere of edifying disputatiousness became assimilated in the polite congeniality wherein old antiquarians and new critics, insofar as they continued to think of themselves as opposing types, tactfully *left each other alone.* (194; emphasis added)

It seems most unlikely that any more productive engagement would have taken place in their respective, Magisterially insular, doctoral classrooms.

And of course neither rhetoric and composition nor creative writing has gotten even that near to a rapprochement with other disciplinary perspectives. As the statistics on courses, examinations, and dissertations cited over the past two chapters help make clear, no majority of Ph.D.-granting faculty in this country has yet stood ready to expand on even so rudimentary an "understanding" as the sort Graff describes: to say, in other words, that not only literary criticism and literary history, but also creative writing and rhetoric and composition are complementary, so that no sound doctoral education in English could forgo any of the four, let alone that such an education ought to be grounded in the mutual exploration, and even the integration, of their respective modes of writing.[6]

All of which is what makes the design of the Albany program such a marked departure from previous disciplinary practice, the most radical experiment to date in pursuit of the fusion option. "Writing, Teaching, and Criticism" takes precisely such an understanding as its point of departure, then challenges students and faculty to see where that acknowledged complementarity might lead, what sort of new disciplinary enterprise their collective efforts might forge. Chapter 4 featured the quotation from Gary Waller's agonistic vision of what intradisciplinary inquiry might be like, with its "acknowledged clash of paradigms, frameworks, languages, and methodologies, an understanding that some will not survive the battle" (118). Albany's version of such interaction is to Waller's what integration might be to civil war: an attempt to achieve disciplinary coexistence without the presumption of antagonism, of violence, and one that depends heavily on the next generation—in this case, the students more than the faculty—to work their way toward the new order. And writing is the key, figured not as a weapon on the academic battlefield but as the primary medium for both negotiations and new possibilities. It is to some of those uses for writing—what some students in the Albany program have actually done—that we will now turn.

## CHAPTER SIX

# Writing to Get Situated: Learning to Stage a Reading

One of the most significant early developments in the Albany program—predictable in retrospect, perhaps, but not much anticipated, and certainly not evident in any of the formal planning documents—has been the emerging importance of the writings designated in this chapter's title by their function: writings in which students work at *situating* themselves within the program and among its constituent discourses. In some sense, of course, all the writing students do in a doctoral program serves this purpose. But we are referring here to kinds of or occasions for writing—informal, if that's the right term, or pre- or extra- or protodisciplinary—specifically designated to serve this purpose, and operating for the most part outside of the program's graded evaluation system: journals, logs, response papers, letters, and so on.

Writing along these lines is obviously not peculiar to or original with this curriculum. Advocates of undergraduate writing-across-the-curriculum (WAC) programs, for example, have long supported such practices, most recently under the dual heading of writing-to-learn and learning-to-write-in-the-disciplines. As this rubric suggests, there are two closely related impulses at work in such initiatives. The idea behind the first—writing-to-learn—is that it is possible to harness writing's power as a technological aid to or extension of consciousness as one means (among several, usually) of gaining control over some activity or set of operations. Strictly speaking, such uses of writing need not be understood as leading to other related and/or more disciplined uses of writing per se. So, for instance, persons studying subjects as diverse as calculus, painting, and computer programming might all benefit from keeping some sort of regular learning log as one means of developing fluency in these activities—activities that obviously do not in and of themselves involve much writing in natural languages. At its best writing can serve as an adjunct discipline that, in return for time invested in the peculiar mode of consciousness we usually call composing, provides a specialized (and, because it is written, cumulative and reviewable) kind of feedback in aid of whatever the primary discipline might be.

As a practical matter, however, WAC programs have devoted much of their efforts to working in disciplines that *do* feature a good deal of writing as a central activity. Hence the second impulse, learning-to-write-in-the-discipline, stands as something of a special case of writing-to-learn: writing serves less as a separable adjunct discipline than as both the means by and the medium through which students work to gain control over the textual conventions of a given discipline. This arrangement is obviously not without its institutional complications. As David Russell's *Writing in the Academic Disciplines, 1870–1990* illustrates all too convincingly, postsecondary institutions in this culture have too long a history of using writing more or less exclusively as a means of summary evaluation to be readily, reliably, or consistently comfortable with uses that are more formative.

Nevertheless, at least in principle the pedagogical aims of learning-to-write-in-the-discipline are essentially the same as in any writing-to-learn situation. The teacher, working in concert with the students, tries to establish a discursive space within which entering writers, however new to a discipline, can work toward (and, along the way, comment on, speculate about, argue with, etc.) a given disciplinary perspective from wherever they need to begin. For selected writings in a given course, the teacher agrees not to hold students to some full set of disciplinary conventions (or whatever quasi-disciplinary conventions operate in formal classroom assignments) but instead invites them to operate somewhere between that full standard and whatever their particular backgrounds allow, with the ultimate purpose of helping them move toward whatever would constitute full disciplinary fluency.

It is not hard to see how this general line of WAC reasoning can be extended to graduate education in English (or in any number of fields). Graduate students are as likely as undergraduates to benefit from using writing to get situated in either of these senses: (1) as an adjunct discipline in aid of coming to terms with some other activity that is part of their training (such as teaching), or (2) as a medium in and through which they can move—with an instructor's guidance—toward the production of full-fledged disciplinary writing.[1]

In the context of a doctoral program, such writing turns out to have a third possible function as well, and one that gives it an even stronger claim to a regular presence in graduate rather than undergraduate curricula. English Studies has a long-standing tradition of writing that operates across and outside the conventions of formal academic discourse. In correspondence especially, licensed inquirers of many persuasions have long carried on negotiations that were, in a strictly disciplinary sense, behind the scenes. Further, both the volume and the importance of this kind of academic exchange appear to have increased as the Magisterial era has wound down: in traditional letter writing still, but also increasingly by e-mail and on listserves and at Web sites, the ever more variegated corps of English Studies professionals write their way into a professional "conversation" that is governed neither by the *MLA Style Manual* nor any editorial board. Such writing may never be published, or even become fully public, but it nevertheless plays an important part in the life of the discipline.[2] Its general use in English doctoral education might be defended, therefore, simply by invoking the logic of professionalization: this is a kind of writing even the fragmented post-Wayzata "we" does, so it ought to be part of the curricular mix.

Such a justification becomes even stronger in the context of a fusion-based graduate program. Although some portion of this behind-the-scenes writing in English Studies is exchanged across the field's many and various divides—playing its part in fractious intradisciplinary negotiations—the far more common tendency is centrifugal: participants gravitate toward those whose disciplinary preferences are most like their own, forming more and more specialized and increasingly insular pockets of interaction. As we have seen, however, a curriculum like Albany's is designed to create a more centripetal dynamic, one that puts pressure on faculty and students alike to enter and sustain precisely such negotiations. This pressure creates a considerable need in this context for something like a programmatic lingua franca: a "hybrid language," as *The American Heritage Dictionary* puts it, "used as a medium of communication between people of different tongues," with the "tongues" in this case being grounded in the program's disciplinary constituents.

To date students at Albany have found this sort of writing useful for getting situated in a number of relationships—a means of working out their positions vis-à-vis their own students (in the classroom, the writing center, discussion groups, etc.), vis-à-vis their faculty mentors (in classes and elsewhere), and vis-à-vis one another (most notably on a very active listserve). Perhaps the most consistent and visible student use for such writing to date, however, and our (illustrative) concern here, is how they have used such writing to situate themselves vis-à-vis the texts they are assigned to read in the courses they take.

## Learning to Stage a Reading

If anything in the long history of English doctoral education can be characterized as a curricular constant—can be identified, that is, as *the* central disciplining activity—it would have to be the business of teaching graduate students to situate themselves properly with respect to whatever are imagined to be, in a given time and place, the discipline's key texts. Descriptions of this process have most often been framed, as indeed they still appear to be, in terms of such essentially invisible activities as "reading" or "knowing." In fact, however, what the graduate faculty of any era—from philologists to New Critics, from process-not-product compositionists to postmodernist materialist feminists—have perforce always looked for is competence in writing what are imagined to be the public (re)presentations[3] of (disciplined) private acts: the textual ability, as it were, to stage a reading.[4]

This priority has certainly held true for the Albany program. As we indicated in the last chapter, all courses feature assigned texts that, coupled with the teacher's sanctioned disciplinary expertise, constitute a proprietary discourse. In negotiating a relationship with that discourse, the students must demonstrate that they have come to terms with those texts: they must stage readings that satisfy not only the professor but also their own emerging sense of disciplinary and professional identity. And one of the key means by which such negotiations have been carried on—not universally, but frequently, and with what we believe are noteworthy results—is in what are generally called response papers. The usual procedure calls for students to write in reaction to the week's assigned readings (but they might also include, as a term proceeds, comment on the cumulative body of readings, class exchanges, earlier writings, etc.). Length requirements are not strict; the rule of thumb calls for about an hour of thoughtful writing, resulting in texts about three to five pages long. These writings then become a feature of the class discussion based on those readings; they are read aloud to the whole class or small groups, selectively duplicated on a rotating basis, and so on. They are then subsequently read again, and responded to in writing, by the teacher and/or other students.

To some extent, the rationale for such writings is short-term, classroom-based, and logistical; they function as a form of writing-to-learn. Doctoral students in English at Albany, and we presume elsewhere, routinely face 500–1,000 pages of required and optional (or, more aptly, less urgently required) reading each week, everything from Faulkner novels to their own students' papers to *Das Kapital*. Their ability to recall any particular portion of that reading, and recall it well enough to participate in a discussion of it, obviously increases if they engage that portion in some kind of writing. Indeed, given the extraordinary reading and writing demands of doctoral student life, composing even a straightforward summary can be useful as record and/or reminder. To a far greater extent, however, the value of these writings accrues over the longer term. As part of the larger cycle of discussion, composing, and response, they provide a series of curricular occasions for students to take a crack at staging disciplinary readings—or, since such writings are treated as formative rather than summative, to run rehearsals by way of preparing to do so.

## The Personal/Expressive Register and Louise Phelps's *Composition as a Human Science*

The range of variation available for this kind of writing is obviously considerable, but we have selected excerpts from five response papers that should help illustrate the possibilities. To provide some additional contrastive leverage, the first three are all taken from responses to the same text in the same course: Louise Wetherbee Phelps's *Composition as a Human Science,* assigned in English 521, Composition Theory, the core course under the program's Rhetoric and Composition rubric.[5] For the author of our first excerpt, Laura Lane, this course constitutes her first extended exposure to the professional literature of rhetoric and composition. Quite reasonably, then—especially given the widely acknowledged difficulty of the Phelps book[6]—she situates her narrator at a considerable remove from any sort of full-fledged disciplinary reading performance:

> It's difficult for me to enter into any sort of debate that this book stages. The debate(s) are so abstracted. Anyway, I could see some similarities between Phelps' "personal need for theory" and the desire for a rhetoric of composition illustrated by Victor Vitanza. His article "Critical Sub/Version" is a foray into postmodern culture, rhetoric and composition theory—just as her *Composition as a Human Science* is. She says that she attempts "to discover what problematics of postmodern culture lie behind . . . composition."
>
> One of the things that she wrote in Chap. 9 seems "postmodern": "theories make us aware of the relativity and finitude of concepts." I'm not sure, exactly, why that's postmodern (to me). I guess "relativity" and "finitude" remind me of Derrida's sign system in which meanings are relative.
>
> One thing that struck me about this book is how she brings in so *many* thinkers and ideas. I mean, the "Name Index" is a separate piece because she brings in so many names. Does this mean, then, that she doesn't have a "Phelpsian" idea? . . .
>
> Anyway, another spot at which I noticed a "debate" that I am familiar with is when she is trying "to accommodate all the strands of" Composition's scholarship. I thought she was doing pretty much the opposite of what [Stephen North's *The Making of Knowledge in Composition*] does. *MKC* pulls apart the strands, and problematizes the concept of composition having a 'central' "practical mission."
>
> Isn't it weird how inquiry into Composition always takes up the question: "is writing central to: learning? democracy? the State's indoctrination? all subjects learned in school? self-reflection?" I mean, the list for why writing is so important gets carried away. (1–3; Lane's emphasis)

What this text presents—what Laura constructs—is a performance in which the narrator-as-reader is situated on the threshold of disciplinarity in at least two senses: she is making only preliminary, rather tentative movements toward a disciplined reading in the area of rhetoric and composition, and she is doing so without claiming, at least in an overt way, any particular disciplinary identification of her own. This is partly a matter of rhetorical positioning. Laura operates here in what we would call a personal/expressive register,[7] an extremely popular choice for these response papers. It is characterized most notably in this instance by the insistent first-person singular narrator, who introduces this performance by declaring that while she has been able to read Phelps's book, she cannot yet identify, let alone enter, any debate(s) it might be "stag(ing)"; she then reinforces this claim by offering frequent updates on her uncertainty (e.g., "I guess," "I think," "I'm not sure," etc.). It also includes the concomitant construction of an audience of sufficient intimacy, mutual trust, and shared context that she, he, or they require nothing whatever in the way of direct address, either in these excerpted portions or elsewhere.[8]

But the narrator's threshold location is borne out, too, by the nature of the (reading) performance itself. To be sure, the piece features a number of identifiably academic strategies. For example, the whole idea that Phelps is staging and/or engaged in a larger debate is a basic academic-cum-disciplinary presupposition. And it is followed up throughout the response by efforts to get a handle on that debate—on what might be at stake—by making connections between this book and other texts, other writers, other more recognizable debates. Thus the opening paragraph juxtaposes Phelps's ambition "to discover what problematics of postmodern culture lie behind . . . composition" to Vitanza's "Critical Sub/Version" in the context of postmodernity; the fourth paragraph compares Phelps's aim " 'to accommodate all the strands of' Composition's scholarship" with North's less accommodating approach in *The Making of Knowledge in Composition*; and the last couple of pages in the response (not quoted here) compare Phelps's intellectual range (as exemplified in part by the book's extensive Name Index) to the similarly eclectic Ann Berthoff (3–4). Ultimately, however, none of these individual strategies gets carried very far, nor do they accumulate to produce any particularly sustained reading of Phelps. Rather, they serve as a series of related queries, organized more or less associatively, and offered as possible points of departure for anticipated discussion, response, and further inquiry: "writing," as James Britton and his colleagues put it in one of the better audience taxonomies ever developed, "as part of an ongoing interaction; and in expectation of response rather than formal evaluation" (overleaf).

One measure of progress in this program, however, lies in learning to stage readings that move the writer beyond such threshold positions—learning to offer performances, that is, in which the writer carries on more sustained, recognizably disciplinary re-presentations, and does so from a more fully articulated disciplinary position of her own. Our second excerpt, from Deb Kelsh's response to the Phelps book, helps suggest what such development might entail:

> I was reading Phelps while I was trying to write my "talking paper" [a text to serve as the basis for an oral examination in the course]—but I found I couldn't do both at once. Phelps is getting at (I think) exactly what I'm trying to say in my talking paper, but she's coming at the issue from a different place. What's she trying to get at? She's trying to say that the composition teacher—who is neither fish nor fowl, practice nor theory, but rather mediator—is the center of Composition as a Human Science, which itself is neither fish nor fowl, but rather a yin-yang sort of entity wherein practice and theory engage in the mutually limiting dance of discourse. That is, Composition is a (s)p(l)ace where different views can meet and talk. I, too, am trying to explain Composition as a mediative space.
>
> Really, though, I don't think Louise would agree that we're doing the same thing. A couple of things she says make me think this—
>
> 1. "Carol Gilligan clarified the gender sources for this theme [tension and response] and linked it to development. . . ." (xii)
>
> She doesn't mention Gilligan (or feminist theory—except for a backward glance at "negative critique" [p. 9] which I'll get back to) anywhere else, though. She doesn't develop what could be the revelatory gender sources for this theme.
>
> I think that's what I'm trying to do, though.

2. "A natural pedagogy provides the values, but not the intellectual framework and critical understanding necessary to work with these realities from day to day" (120).

The natural pedagogy is pretty much—as she describes it in chapter 5—the same thing as mothering and women's connected and constructed thinking. Louise isn't interested in providing the values—but I am. Why? Because I disagree with Louise that values don't inform intellectual framework. I see Gilligan's whole argument as saying that values DO inform ways of thinking, and Belenky et al. explore how.

And really, I think Louise arrives at this point, too: "Phronesis together with the universality of reflection as a human potential creates for composition a structure that is not primarily hierarchical, but parallel and interactive" (237). If she ain't talking about values, and if that don't sound just like Gilligan's ladder and web metaphors, then I'm a spent penny.

So, I am trying to:
1. develop the gender (possibly revelatory) sources for the theme of tension and response as a basis for Composition and Ethictheory; and
2. argue that women's values—which inform their thinking—inform Composition.
Maybe they're both the same thing. (1–2)

We can begin by noting the obvious: that for this sort of writing in this program, making progress does not necessarily require abandoning the personal/expressive register.[9] Indeed, Deb's response might be said to deploy it even more fully than Laura's, in that the first-person narrator is an even more insistent presence—is given far more time on stage. Laura's narrator introduced herself as the uncertain but deferential auditor, a disciplinary outsider/novice trying to piece together some version of a larger debate or debates; most of the textual space, therefore, is given over to juxtaposing possible participants therein. Deb's narrator, by contrast, comes on as the interrupted writer, a disciplinary fellow inquirer who, student status notwithstanding, is at work on a text (her "'talking paper'") that will serve as an entry in the school-sponsored extension of the debate to which *Composition as a Human Science* is a contribution. As a result, both the narrator's reading of Phelps *and* her writing-in-progress are fair game for re-presentation.

This rhetorical shift in situation carries over into Deb's construction of an audience, as well. Thus the absence of direct address, coupled here with a style that is more overtly meditative than Laura's (i.e., more contraction-, dash-, and parentheses-laden, more prone to metacommentary ["What's she trying to get at?"], occasionally arch-colloquial ["spent penny"]), again invokes an audience of considerable mutual trust, a reader or readers willing to follow a fairly convoluted set of textual twists and turns. In this instance, the implied shared context invokes an even greater level of intimacy: narrator and audience alike are cast as disciplinary insiders, persons for whom the "Phelps" of the first paragraph can become the more familiar "Louise" thereafter and for whom the book under discussion accordingly can be rendered as far less monumental, roughly comparable for rhetorical purposes to the narrator's off-stage talking paper—a sort of utterance-in-progress, something Louise is "trying to get at."

As in Laura's response, however, the narrator's claim to disciplinary location is borne out by the actual performance. Accordingly, and despite its grounding in a personal/expressive register, this response moves much further than did Laura's into the academic milieu: it deploys more extensive citation of and quotation from the target text (including a careful accounting of page numbers) and, along with these, concise summaries of some of the book's major themes; it demonstrates a greater fluency with relatively specialized terms (e.g., "mutually limiting dance of discourse," "revelatory gender sources," "connected and constructed thinking"); it brings to bear other sources (in this case from outside the course readings), and in ways that move well beyond simple juxtaposition—Gilligan and Belenky et al. in the excerpt, but later also Sara Ruddick ("Maternal Thinking"), Annette Kolodny (on "pluralism"), Nina Baym ("Melodramas of Beset Manhood"), Judith Fetterley (*Resisting Reader*), and Peter Elbow (on the "believing game"); and it offers, albeit in a rough form, an explicit argumentative textual framework (i.e., the repeated 1 and 2, which mark Deb's paper-in-progress as a response to Phelps).

Taken together, these strategies also provide Deb's narrator with a workable disciplinary identification: a place to be coming from, as it were—feminist theory—so as to engage with Phelps' book, which is figured as coming out of composition. Just as important, the terms of this engagement cast Deb's narrator in a much more active role than Laura's, and one that seems particularly well suited to both the theoretical position being articulated *and* the Albany program's stated goal of placing the student-as-writer at its center. Thus the interrupted writer-reader-narrator does not claim to be doing what we might expect—is not saying, for instance, "I couldn't read Phelps and write my talking paper at the same time, so I decided to completely set aside that paper and give myself over to a readerly analysis of Phelps's book." Rather, as we suggested earlier, the two texts are handled as if they were contemporaneously under way—so much so, in fact, that at one point Phelps's book is treated almost as if it were a commentary on Deb's text-in-progress and not the other way around: "Really, though, I don't think Louise would agree that we're doing the same thing. A couple of things she says make me think this—."

In the end, of course, this response paper makes no pretensions to being full-fledged public disciplinary writing. Even taken on its own terms, it is clearly offered as preparatory to—a gloss of sorts on—a text-in-progress, Deb's talking paper, which is represented as operating in the formal disciplined prose of rhetoric and composition. Nevertheless, taking Laura's threshold position as a sort of starting point, Deb's response paper exemplifies one sort of programmatic trajectory, one angle from which to enter the Albany program's discursive matrix. Our third respondent to the Phelps book, Wilma Kahn, suggests another. The first three sections of her six-section response (which totals six typed, double-spaced pages) deal with Phelps's prose style, the instructor's comments on Wilma's previous response paper, and Phelps's feminist tendencies, respectively. The fourth, and our concern here, occupies two pages and focuses on Chapters 5 and 6 of the Phelps book, "Literacy and the Limits of the Natural Attitude" and "The Dance of Discourse":

> Do you remember my Neel paper <her response to Jasper Neel's *Plato, Derrida, and Writing*>? All my remarks on meaning? Well, naturally, I was interested when Phelps started to discuss gestalts and meaning. However, her emphasis (through p. 106)

has been on interpreting language and not on symbols and subtext—my interest. However, I can see that what she is talking about can be made to stretch to cover my particular interest. When she talks about intended meaning, I think she is talking about intended overt meaning. I am more interested in intended covert meaning. However, whether readers are interpreting overt meaning or covert meaning, they must make gestalts.

It is possible that a writer may not consciously intend a covert meaning, i.e., his or her unconscious mind may be providing a constellation of details which add up to a covert meaning he or she is unaware of. Nevertheless, a reader may gestalt the unintended covert meaning as an interpretation of the writing. I have posited elsewhere that a fiction writer trained in exegesis most likely will read his own work in progress and gestalt *as a reader* meaning he created unconsciously. Thus, his reader and writer selves can decide to excise the covert meaning, enhance it, or leave it alone. [Maybe I should have written my final paper on this topic, because it fascinates me so, but "meaning" seems like such a huge, unwieldy topic, difficult to limit.] (3; Kahn's emphasis, parentheses, and brackets )

Even in this short excerpt, you can see that Wilma's response shares a number of rhetorical tendencies with her classmates'. Certainly its use of the personal/expressive register is similar. The response as a whole begins (in a passage not excerpted here) with its own version of a process-based stage setting: "Showing great restraint, I waited until I hit page 160 before writing any cogitations on Phelps. Here goes—" (1). Moreover, while there is actually direct address in this instance (and from evidence elsewhere in the text, it is quite clear that the "you" of "Do you remember" refers to the instructor), it is equally clear that this "you" is configured along much the same lines as the audiences in Laura's and Deb's responses. In fact, insofar as Wilma's entire response offers only one direct quotation from the Phelps book, it can be said to posit an even more intimately shared context for narrator and audience than Deb's. By including only the most minimal gestures of textual reference (the mention of a few key terms here, a page number there), the narrator invokes a reader who is as fresh from, or at least as immediately familiar with, *Composition as a Human Science* as she is. Finally, and along much the same lines, while Wilma's style does not rely on the same devices as Deb's to generate its meditative effects (e.g., the entire six-page document features only a single contracted verb form and three dashes), it nevertheless offers its own equivalents—most notably, perhaps, a half dozen of the bracketed asides we see at the end of this excerpt.

Strategically, however, the reading that Wilma stages is grounded in a disciplinary identification quite different from either Laura's or Deb's. Neither the deferential novice nor the disciplinary co-inquirer, Wilma's narrator is instead the fiction writer with an ongoing interest in what might be called an applied hermeneutics. Thus, while this narrator, like Deb's, engages Phelps at a point where their lines of inquiry intersect—in this passage, the role of "gestalts" in the construction of meaning—it is an engagement primarily in aid of advancing that narrator's work in doing and understanding fiction writing, particularly her own fiction writing, not engaging any debates in composition as such. Hence, in the second paragraph of the preceding excerpt the narrator relocates Phelps's discussion of the "dance of discourse"—a discussion that emphasizes mainly the interaction *between* a writer and a reader—into the context of her own argument ("posited elsewhere"), so that the emphasis shifts to how that dance plays out *within* the individual fiction writer. And this extrapolation is taken even further, and rendered in more applied terms, in a proposal that occupies most of the next paragraph:

> [How about this: self-case study, sort of like Freud did on himself: I, a writer and a reader, analyze my *own* revision, pointing out my intentional covert meaning, and picking out unintentional covert meaning. Do I keep the unintentional? Do I throw it out? Do I enhance it? Choices and more choices. Reader self and writer self work together to do the job. And sometimes the reader will pitch in and do some of the writing and sometimes the writer will do some of the reading. Amazing! This is the closest I've ever come to describing what I *do* when I write fiction.][10] (4; Kahn's emphasis and brackets)

Wilma stages a reading in which her narrator claims to be traveling, and with considerable momentum, along a programmatic trajectory whose coordinates have been determined by discourses not identified with composition theory, a trajectory that also, therefore, frames and limits the terms of her engagement with *Composition as a Human Science*. Thus, while for Deb's narrator this encounter with the Phelps book is characterized as the beginning of a sustainable, long-term engagement, and one that will see that narrator move much further into the discourse of composition studies, for Wilma's narrator, the convergence is briefer, a crossing of paths that, though it can be said to inform and even energize her movement through the program as a fiction writer, does not seem likely to alter that movement's trajectory dramatically.

## Rehearsing a Disciplinary Stance

Taken together these responses would appear to represent the three logical possibilities for readings staged in this personal/expressive register: the as-yet-uncommitted spectator, as in Laura's; the committed participant converging, as in Deb's; and the committed participant diverging, as in Wilma's. However, as popular as readings staged in this register have proven to be, and as much flexibility as it affords, we are compelled by both curricular logic and classroom experience to illustrate two further alternatives. The first might be seen as an extension of Deb's converging-participant stance, in that the writer, bypassing the personal/expressive altogether, tries to move directly into the course's sponsoring discourse. Our example comes from one of Jeff Van Schaick's weekly responses (called "reader's reports") in a course on British women novelists offered under the program's Seminar: Texts/ Authors and Their Critics rubric.[11] This excerpt, from early in the term, is in response to Barbara Pym's *Excellent Women*, and takes as its point of departure a quotation chosen from a list the professor distributed at the first class by way of suggesting the issues the course might address:

> "For readily discernible historical reasons women have characteristically concerned themselves with matters more or less peripheral to male concerns or at least slightly skewed from them. The differences between traditional female preoccupations and roles and male ones make a difference in female writing." (Patricia Meyer Spacks, *The Female Imagination*)

This passage would seem to have a great deal of relevance if one is discussing Barbara Pym's *Excellent Women*. The female characters in the novel indeed appear to be, for the most part, separated from their male counterparts in terms of both occupation and role. Further, there is even a degree of stratification within the female gender itself as to role and status. Mildred, Dora Caldicote, Winifred, and several others are lumped together under the title "excellent women," and this title has certain consequences. Such women are apparently destined to remain unmarried, with lower level public service or charity jobs, spending a great deal of their time performing the various functions which keep their local parish functioning. They are a female support system once removed from the housewife: Mildred is perfectly capable of providing comfort to Julian Mallory, editing assistance to Everard Bone, and personal advice (as well as tea) to Rocky Napier. This is not necessarily a favorable or attractive role which Pym has created for these "excellent women:" despite Bone's appellation near the close, "Excellent women whom one respects and esteems," one must question the status Mildred and the others inhabit. (1)

Clearly, this is a very different sort of performance from the first three we reviewed. To begin with, the textually represented occasion for it is not the reading of the assigned text (Pym's novel) but rather the passage from Spacks—a shift which, at least in Jeff's handling of it here, significantly alters the rhetorical dynamic. What was for Laura, Deb, and Wilma an occasion to (re)present their individual efforts to engage *with* Phelps's *Composition as a Human Science* for a relatively intimate audience becomes for Jeff an occasion to participate in a discussion *about* Pym's *Excellent Women* that is essentially *with* the passage from Spacks, and for an audience consequently construed in considerably more public, formal terms. No insistent first-person narrator here, nor any locational commentary about debates unengaged, writings interrupted, or pages read before responding. Instead, Jeff offers his version of the dispassionate third person that has served English so faithfully as an analogue to the objectivist narrator of the sciences: one for whom, or perhaps within which, individual and/or private acts of reading are subsumed by an objectivist rhetoric of unmediated observation. Thus the only trace of anything that might be called rhetorical agency— overt nominal or pronominal reference to reader(s), writer, or audience—comes in the venerable "one" who "is discussing" in the first line (by Jeff) and "must question" in the last (and who might well be edited out in subsequent drafts). And while the response clearly acknowledges the fictive status of Mildred, Dora, and the others as "characters in the novel," they are nevertheless rendered throughout in language that is not only empirical, but that indeed goes so far as to posit their existence in that peculiar perpetual present that is a hallmark of this critical tradition: "Such women *are* apparently destined to remain unmarried, with lower level public service or charity jobs, spending a great deal of their time performing the various functions which keep their local parish functioning"; or "Mildred *is* perfectly capable of providing comfort to Julian Mallory"; and so on.

This is not to say that Jeff's response therefore constitutes a full-fledged disciplinary performance. As with Laura's, Deb's, and Wilma's, this would not be true even on generic grounds: by definition, the reader's report is a school genre, a rehearsal, an occasion for learning-to-write-in-the-discipline. Moreover, we chose this particular text—by no means Jeff's most polished or fluent—in part because it helps illustrate the difficulties such rehearsals allow students to work through. In this case, while it is easy enough to see how the Spacks excerpt might have prompted the line of argument Jeff follows, the response's handling of it—in particular, the nature of its "relevance" to the novel—is clearly problematic. In ways that the full context of *The Female Imagination* would make it easier to see, Spacks is most directly concerned in this passage with the historical situation of female writers.[12] Broadly speaking, then, it would probably be best suited as a prompt for commentary along biographical lines, suggesting in this particular instance, say, that Pym's lived experience of "traditional female preoccupations and roles" made "a difference" manifested in *Excellent Women* as an example of "female writing."

As it happened, though, when Jeff wrote this report—prior, significantly, to even the class meeting on *Excellent Women*—it was only the second or third week of the term; he had only the Spacks excerpt to work from; and he would have had, in any case, only limited biographical information on Pym. It is not really surprising, therefore, that he should apply the excerpt as he does, constructing a reading that shifts the emphasis to the ways in which the novel's *characters* bear out the claim Spacks makes in her first sentence. In other words, just as "'[real, historical] women have characteristically concerned themselves with matters more or less peripheral to male concerns or at least slightly skewed from them,'" so, Jeff's narrator argues, "[t]he female characters in the novel indeed appear to be . . . separated from their male counterparts in terms of both occupation and role." What gets a bit lost in the shuffle is the second sentence of the Spacks passage, and particularly its concern with the production of something called "female writing." It might be argued, perhaps, that Jeff's response can be seen as a compressed and narrowly mimetic extension of Spacks's reasoning, to the effect that *historical* differences between traditional female preoccupations and roles and male ones are manifested in "female writing" as directly corresponding *fictive* differences. It seems more plausible, though, to understand this response, just like Laura's or Deb's, as a reading with a future: as one that might itself be revised, or else as one in a series of approximations through which Jeff will move closer to a publishable disciplinary fluency. In this sense, even if he has not handled the Spacks excerpt in quite the way he might in some later context, he has nevertheless used it to generate an interesting reading of *Excellent Women*, and one that could easily provide the basis for subsequent consideration of the concept of "female writing."

Our final example of a staged reading is to Jeff's roughly what Wilma's was to Deb's. Like Jeff, John Latta works directly in a mode sanctioned by one of the program's constituent discourses. Unlike Jeff, however—and in this he is like Wilma—John is not working in the course's sponsoring discourse, but rather in one that represents his preferred disciplinary identification. The course is The History of Rhetoric, and John responds to each of the semester's readings—Aristotle, Plato, Cicero, Augustine, Coleridge, Langer, Foucault, and so on—with a poem. Here is "Reading the *Biographia Literaria*," quoted in full and including the sort of closing comment John provides for all his entries:

"So immethodical a miscellany" is how Coleridge tagged it.
And so we plunder its districts, its lanes, or we random
its historical particulars, aloof as orphans,

mapping out the cruel logic of our dissection in order
to justify another life gone haywire, all evasive
in its passions, foregone in its appetites, unstomached

by first love, first failure. Poor Coleridge.
He characterized himself as "indolence capable of energy,"
he named himself Nehemiah Higginbottom.

In the splendid roar of youth he heard voices
talking pure sprung epithets, doubling and singing together
"to tame the swell & glitter" into voluble

fractals, inaustere and movable visions, perpetual un-
foldings. Later, opium-doubt, careering lassitude and an odd
    fear
of plagiarism made him insist on the perspicuous, fear

"half-meanings" and admit "the sense of impossibility
quenches all will." He turned to philosophy
and, unsprung, without a permanent home,

what he remembered was "the most astonishing image"—
that of a whole black rookery that flew up out of a giant's
    beard,
flushed by the tiny voice of one Tom Hickathrift.

A kid's book naturally. Ineffable itch of memory.
So Coleridge contemplated contemplation, the act
of which made contemplation itself rise up into existence

like that dark whirring dispersion of blackbirds,
a nascent vision unfolding and unfolding but curiously empty—
contemplation needing form and music,

needing, say, frogs, those *brekekekex-ko-ax-ko-ax*-ing things
Aristophanes made rise up so Bacchus—in a snit
about the counterfeit nature of poetry—could retrieve

the "old and genuine poesy" of frog-
voice and, imperfect mimic, have at the real thing himself.
Poor Coleridge. Poor Coleridge. He decided

he could only become himself by the act of constructing
himself objectively to himself. Blessed be the knotty,
the unmusical, the abstract. He took,

to this end, to practicing such constructions in public.
He constructed himself as a swimmer, a breaststroker,
and practiced with wide scooping arm-

motions and long glides propelling himself sensationally
down a long London street only to be cornered
by two burly bobbies who suspected him of being a pickpocket,

a thief. No. He was *thieved*. At the end poetry becomes *other,*
criminal, something we must *prepare* ourselves for—
a different terrain, different furnishings, not for the parlor,

not for the social circles of common fan-talk and tea-sip,
there where the eruption of metaphor ices the polite
conversation and produces "a sort of damp

and interruption for some minutes after." No. Poor
Coleridge, if "the burthen of the proof lies with the oppugner,"
I shoulder it and admit: *I hate it that you quit.*

I hate it as if you were that manchineel fruit, that tree,
that metaphor forbidden as "suiting equally well
with too many subjects." That manchineel

fruit grows on a tree so poisonous
men have been known to perish by standing in its shade.
And Coleridge, we all stand in that shade.

A curious piece. I can't seem to bounce off poets without getting personal. My sense that Coleridge "failed the brotherhood"
[?] pervades this piece. That he gave up something like "trust-
ing the music," stopped writing poems, gave up his utopian
dreams, radical politics, etc. I play more off the little factoids
of the *Biographia* than the philosophy. The story of Coleridge
practicing the breaststroke in a London street comes from a
recent review in *The New Yorker* of a book called *Haunts of
the Black Masseur: The Swimmer as Hero,* by Charles
Sprawson.

Of the five responses we have considered, this one comes closest
to achieving that standard we keep invoking, the full-fledged dis-

ciplinary performance. This is absolutely *not* to say, of course, that it is the "best" response of the five. Given the occasions for and purposes of these writings, such a distinction is neither possible nor meaningful. But we have already invoked a continuum of programmatic development calibrated in terms of the extent to which reading performances constitute sustained (re)presentations offered from articulated disciplinary positions—and in those terms, we would place John's response furthest along that continuum. Like Jeff's—and with the exception of the endnote—this response is a public performance, driven in particular by the narrative "we" of the first stanza. That is, while the poem does feature a first-person singular narrator in its last three stanzas, its primary suasory tactic is to construct an audience of *Biographia* readers willing to go along with (we almost want to say "be implicated in") what amounts to a lament. This audience is not immediate and local (does not consist, say, of the course instructor or the other members of the class as such) but larger and more generalized: in essence, an audience consisting of members of a transgenerational "we" who, taking their cue from "poor Coleridge" himself, began puzzling over the man even during his lifetime, and for whom the *Biographia* has therefore tended to function, as it does here, mainly as an occasion to wonder—however guiltily—about the life, and in particular about its failures, its having "gone haywire." And while nothing in the text of the poem absolutely restricts the membership of this "we" to those who would identify themselves as poets, certainly the form constitutes an appeal in that direction, as does the line of argument. Whoever "we" might be, we are at home with these three-line, free verse stanzas; we are ready to nod at the reference to Aristophanes, smile at the play on the Beatitudes; and are able to accept a plot in which Coleridge's decision to abandon poetry dumps him unceremoniously onto the streets of London to make this pathetic, suspicious spectacle of himself.

By the time the response switches to the first-person singular in the seventeenth stanza, the narrative "I" who appears is firmly established as a member of this larger group: he emerges to speak not as Albany graduate student or History of Rhetoric class member, but as poet. This narrator exercises his authority in two different spheres. In the realm of poetry, he goes further than the narrators of Deb's or Wilma's or Jeff's responses and situates himself not as an equal with the author of the text under study— as a co-inquirer, say, with the Coleridge of the *Biographia*—but as in some sense superior to him: one qualified, as a member of this larger "we," to be disappointed and angry with the author, "to hate it that you quit," and indeed even to associate the Coleridgean legacy with the poisonous manchineel. (Imagine the other responses framed in similar terms: "Poor Phelps," say, "I hate it that you failed feminism.") Given the context of the course, however, this stance also has repercussions in the realm of rhetoric, implying as it does that any significance Coleridge's philosophical speculations might have for the history of rhetoric are qualified by their origins in the failure, not to say the perversion, of his poetic abilities. Put it this way: if Coleridge's legacy for poets is associated with the manchineel, but if he is nevertheless of value to rhetoricians, what are we to make of the relationship between rhetoric and poetic, the toxicity of their divergence?

We will close this section with one last recital of what has become our standard disclaimer. Despite its relative fluency and completeness, John's response is still clearly—by definition and otherwise—an occasional piece, brought into being by and for an ongoing classroom-based conversation, and in that sense best understood, like the others, as in-progress: disposable or recyclable rather than completed, permanent, monumental. Indeed, John's endnote frames his response as very much a performance in just this sense, with its own "I"—this time constructed rather more pointedly as John Latta, graduate student/poet—stepping back to comment, almost with surprise, on this "curious piece." Thus, while of this set of five responses it might stand the best chance as a text of escaping the classroom orbit to appear, say, in the poetry pages of *College English* or, better yet (if it had a poetry section), *Rhetoric Review*, it is more likely to wind up as a traceable influence in some larger, later work, or, more likely yet, simply to become one in an endless series of textual engagements wherein the exact significance of any single entry is beyond our capacity to measure. This is the status, after all, of most of the writing most of us do most of the time. Even framed in terms of this last scenario, however, you can see how, given the aims of the Albany program, the kind of performance John stages—

negotiating across intradisciplinary lines—holds considerable promise for writers and readers assembled to explore the interrelationships among the field's various branches.

## CHAPTER SEVEN

# Charting Courses (1): Extended Work in a Preferred Mode

I f the writing-to-get-situated we described in the last chapter was a somewhat surprising feature of this new doctoral curriculum, the writings gathered under this heading—extended work in a preferred mode—were surely its most anticipated development. As we have seen, in the Magisterial tradition the writing that doctoral students undertook in their courses was very much a function of the specialty-based apprenticeship. Each course followed a particular discursive trajectory, and student writings were expected to conform to it: to run not only parallel to but essentially coterminous with it, matching up not only formally but topically and methodologically, too.[1] That is, student writings were not only expected to take the form favored by the professor-as-master, or at least to be an exercise leading thereto, but they were also expected to be on topics—"about" something in a fairly narrow sense—understood as fitting within course parameters. These writings were also supposed to (re)present one or another similarly sanctioned method of inquiry, not only in terms of deploying various evidentiary systems, but also in a more overtly behavioral sense, wherein textual conventions are assumed to regulate (or at least to signify the regulation of) the students' investigative activities.[2] Indeed, the ideal outcome in such courses, though not often framed in quite this way, would be for the apprentice to produce a text that could plausibly have been written by the master.

As we have also seen, however, the Albany program is based on a different faculty-student relationship, so that the writing the students do in their courses needs to be conceived of in a different way. The curricular logic we traced in Chapter 5 is simple but compelling. If each course is to "explore[s] its subject from the perspectives which creative writers, students of rhetoric and composition, and literary critics bring to bear on it," and if writing is to continue to be the discipline's primary medium of exchange, it is inevitable—and necessary—that students should carry out at least some of these explorations on topics, in forms, and according to methods sanctioned by those constituent perspectives. For the purposes of this curriculum, then, students' discursive trajectories are best understood not as (pre)determined by instructors, but as negotiated in context: students chart their own courses, seeking to pilot the chosen vehicle of some preferred mode through that portion of the (force)field of English Studies represented by a given class and its general subject area. As we shall see, these arrangements do not absolutely preclude the kind of formal, topical, and methodological convergence between student and professor that was *de rigueur* in the Magisterial tradition. It does, however, substantially alter the status of such convergence, making it only one possibility among many. To the extent that such convergence becomes anything *other* than an occasional curricular happenstance—begins, that is, to exert a Magisterial dominance—the Albany curriculum would have to be judged a failure on its own terms.

## Writing (and) the History of English Studies, 1880 to the Present

By design the effects of this altered curricular dynamic are most concentrated, and therefore most visible, in the core courses of the program's seven branches, and most especially in the core course of the program's paradigmatic branch—the core course of core courses—The History of English Studies, 1880 to the Present. All the courses in this branch (i.e., Writing in History), you will recall, are "designed to effect the synthesizing intentions of the curriculum" ("Proposal" 10), but none more forcefully than The History of English Studies. The subject matter is interesting in its own right; it may be that every English doctoral program should feature a course which, as the program proposal describes this one, foregrounds institutionality and provides an occasion for inquiring how the history of academic institutions has shaped the theories and practices of contemporary writers, rhetoricians, and literary scholars, and how current institutional configurations determine, constrain, and facilitate the acts of writing, teaching, and criticism. (10)

What makes the course especially important in the Albany program, however, is the way this "occasion for inquiring" is enacted. As *the* required course in *the* paradigmatic branch, it is consistently guaranteed as broad a mix of doctoral students as the program can generate, and therefore it is also the best first place to examine the kinds of writing this mix makes possible: to see what happens when these students explore a subject from their perspectives as creative writers, students of rhetoric and composition, literary critics, and so on, and do so in forms, on topics, and following methods sanctioned by those perspectives. The catalogue copy for the course reads as follows:

> The course explores the history of English as a subject of study in universities and colleges, its relation to other disciplines, its evolution in the 20th century, and its place in the current relationship between the humanities and sciences. Particular attention is given to the connections between graduate school education and public school policies and practices, to the history of writing instruction within the discipline, and to the role played by social and political issues in the evolution of the discipline. (*English Graduate Study* 11)

The exact curricular details vary from section to section, but the reading list is typically built around such books as Gerald Graff's *Professing Literature,* James Berlin's *Rhetoric and Reality,* and D. G. Myers's *The Elephants Teach: Creative Writing since 1880,* and then supplemented both by historical documents (e.g., of the kind assembled in Gerald Graff and Michael Warner's *The Origins of Literary Studies in America: A Documentary Anthology* and John Brereton's *The Origins of Composition Studies in the American College, 1875–1925: A Documentary History*) and any number of commentaries: Kermit Vanderbilt's *American Literature and the Academy,* say, or David Shumway's *Creating Ameri-*

*can Civilization*; Susan Miller's *Textual Carnivals: The Politics of Composition* or Robin Varnum's *Fencing with Words: A History of Writing Instruction at Amherst College during the Era of Theodore Baird, 1938–1966*; Jed Rasula's *The American Poetry Wax Museum* or R. M. Berry's "Theory, Creative Writing, and the Impertinence of History"; and so on.

Likewise, while specific course requirements also vary from year to year, students are typically asked to engage in broadly conceived historically based work in two forms: to take on one project of more or less "standard" academic history, an essay in the manner of Graff, Berlin, or Myers, and a second in a form of their own choosing, with the further proviso that one of these projects must also form the basis for a class presentation. To some extent, we can suggest the range these projects have covered by means of various lists. In terms of the topical, for instance, we can say that students have focused on such subjects as literary societies at a specific New England college in the eighteenth and nineteenth centuries; the canonical status of female modernists; various aspects of the rise of New Criticism; the shape of English instruction in postsecondary educational institutions devoted primarily to Native American or Hispanic students; the function of the MLA during World War II; the status of women in English as a profession; the impact of computers on the teaching of writing; the development of writing centers; gay, lesbian, and queer studies in English; the role of Asian Americans in the profession; Marxism and Marxists in English departments; and so forth. We can offer a similarly suggestive list of the forms such work has taken: we can say that in addition to the essays students have carried on this historical work in short stories, text-only and text-and-image collages, poems, taped audio performances (in the manner of a radio broadcast), plays and scripted skits, StorySpace constructions and Web sites, first-person narratives, puzzles, videos and multimedia productions, and so on.

To do either the curricular dynamic or the students' work in this course anything like real justice, however, we need to complement these lists with a more detailed examination of how topic, form, and method have come together in specific projects. To this end, we offer here three examples, one identified with each of the perspectives—literary scholars, rhetoricians, and contemporary writers—referred to so often in the program's literature. The first of these, identified with literary scholarship, is Christiane Farnan's "A History of Recovery: 19th Century American Women Writers," and we begin with it because it represents the kind of undertaking we assume most of our readers would expect from such a course. Her essay opens with this emblematic description:

> In a small, local, liberal arts college library, the works of Nathaniel Hawthorne sit on a black metal shelf that is placed in the almost exact middle of a dusty and dim basement room. Many of Hawthorne's books are limp with age and use, their soft blue and green bindings unraveling and trailing knotty thread. Others are of a mellow middle age; the covers are worn enough to be comfortable in the hand or lap, but the pages have not yellowed. The new editions of Hawthorne, the young books, those between two and ten years old, have firm covers and pages the milk-white of baby teeth. The titles of these books, stamped or printed onto the bindings, are crisp and clear. *The Scarlet Letter* especially runs the gamut of the ages, as eight copies of the novel are lined up one after the other upon the shelf, each the product of a different publishing house, each bearing the marks of youth, middle or old age—a visual representation of the publishing history of Hawthorne since the 1930's. Below the shelf that bears Hawthorne's primary works—all in all a collection of twenty-two books, counting the multiple copies—run two more shelves of books filled with critical essays and chapters based upon Hawthorne's work, and biographies reciting the facts of his life.
>
> Across the aisle from Hawthorne, about twelve feet to the left and two shelves down, is a book originally published four years after *The Scarlet Letter* in 1854. Reprinted in 1988 through the efforts of the American Women Writers Series, the fire-engine red binding and wallpaper-pattern cover make the book easy to spot. It is *The Lamplighter,* the novel by Maria Susanna Cummins which sold 100,000 copies between 1854 and 1855 and prompted Hawthorne's now famous phrase concerning the "damned mob of scribbling women" who controlled the literary market during the nineteenth century and erased any of Hawthorne's hopes for financial success.
>
> The book stands alone. No other works by Cummins surround *The Lamplighter* . . . and no critical works or biographies are anywhere to be seen. Since Cummins' novel was reprinted, almost ten years have passed. (1–2)

The essay's aim is to account for the general—and obviously gendered—situation for which this imbalance between Hawthorne's and Cummins's holdings is the type: to take up the course's stated goal of attending to the "role played by social and political issues in the evolution" of English Studies by tracing efforts over the past forty years to "recover," as per the essay's title, the writings of nineteenth-century American women writers. Topically, such a project is situated at a familiar disciplinary juncture, in its modest way emulating work like that by Vanderbilt or Shumway. It is "about" the process by which a certain set of writings, from a certain set of writers, has come to be afforded a measure of literary and historical significance by and for the academic enterprise of English Studies.

The essay follows the general formal and methodological patterns of such studies, as well. Certainly the textual format is familiar: sixteen pages (typed, double-spaced) divided into six sections, each section headed by a roman numeral, citation and quotation in accordance with the *MLA Style Manual,* and so on. Though still a "school" paper, it has the look of a prepublication manuscript for a journal such as *College English.* And much the same sort of comparison can be made concerning its method. In what we earlier called the behavioral sense of that term, the mode of inquiry as represented might be considered slightly unusual in that it includes (and duly cites) an interview with Judith Fetterley, a member of the Albany faculty who is also afforded a significant role in the essay's recounting of the recovery movement. As a practical matter, however, whatever research utility this interview might have had—as a source of leads, for instance—it turns out to have little evidentiary impact.[3] Rather, and in keeping with the tradition of literary historians (one grounded in what is imagined to be a corpus of essentially stable, and therefore crucially reexaminable, texts) the essay relies primarily on what people have published, or caused to be published, in written form. In other words, the essay operates in the context of and therefore exercises whatever disciplinary authority it may wield in relation to published writings that variously comment on, constitute the results of, or otherwise contribute to what it figures as the long-term, large-scale, collective enterprise of recovery. These writings include Florence Howe's "A Report on Women and the Profession," an address-turned-journal article featured here as an early call for recovery; Fetterley's *Provisions*, which is characterized as "granting the public access to stories long lost and virtually 'unheard of,'" (4) such as Catherine Sedgwick's "Cacoethes Scribendi"; Mary Kelley's *Private Women, Public Stage*, which examines "'domestic novelists' and their . . . publishing power" (Farnan 7); and so on.

Further, these sources are deployed in what still appears to be the dominant approach to writing history in U.S. culture, and certainly in English Studies, in which a rhetoric of unmediated observation renders as causally linked a series of "events" in what is understood to be the more or less coherent "life" of this recovery movement. Narrated throughout by the same dispassionate third person we read in the preceding excerpt from its opening pages—one closely related, it is worth noting, to the objectivist narrator we saw Jeff construct in his response to Pym's *Excellent Women* in the last chapter—the net result can be characterized as the creation of a corporate voice or, more accurately, a corporate voice-over (think Walter Cronkite on *The Twentieth Century* or David McCullough narrating Ken Burns's *Civil War*), a rhetorical strategy designed primarily to subsume or supplant individual and/or private experience. Section III, for instance, devotes three of its six pages to the publication of Fetterley's 1985 *Provisions* by way of illustrating the motives and the mechanics of recovery, but it does so in part by representing that year as *the* high point in the essay's recovery story: "The year *Provisions* was published, 1985, appears to be something of a banner year for both critical and publishing work on the women writers of the nineteenth century," the narrative claims.

> Joanne Dobson, Judith Fetterley and Elaine Showalter, in collaboration with the Rutgers University Press, launched the American Women Writers Series which "makes available for the first time in decades the work of the most significant, influential, and popular American women writers from the 1820s to the 1920s."

And there was more:

Also in 1985, Mary Kelley published *Private Women, Public Stage*, an examination of "domestic novelists" and their forceful publishing power. Jane Tompkins published *Sensational Designs: The Cultural Work of American Fiction*, a collection of essays that examines the social power of women writers such as Susan Warner and Harriet Beecher Stowe and which includes the frequently reprinted "Sentimental Power: *Uncle Tom's Cabin* and the Politics of Literary History." *The New Feminist Criticism*, a collection of essays concerning, among other things, the formation of, and exclusion of women from, the American canon, was edited by Elaine Showalter. Sandra Gilbert and Susan Gubar edited *The Norton Anthology of Literature by Women: The Traditions in English.* . . . (Farnan 6–7)

This bit of (em)plotting confirms what is in any case clear enough from the essay's opening description: while this narrative might be described as dispassionate, it is decidedly not disinterested. To be a cooperative member of the audience this essay constructs is to accept from the outset that the story line's current terminus—the situation whereby Cummins's novel "stands alone" on that library shelf—somehow represents an unhappy predicament, a less than satisfactory outcome to the recovery story. The essay's basic strategy, then, is to carry out something of a recovery of recovery in hopes of moving the plot along. It wants to offer enough (of what will be presented as) background— the "real" story—that readers will learn or be reminded of the means by which books like *The Lamplighter* came to be on library shelves in the first place, but also to do so in a way that makes both the stakes *and* the price already paid seem very high indeed—too high, at any rate, to let those efforts go to waste. To that end, Sections II, III, IV, and V each offers an episode in the recovery saga, albeit not in strict chronological order: the galvanizing impact of Tillie Olsen's work, with special attention to her 1978 dedication in *Silences* ("bearing witness to what was (and still is) being lost and silenced,") (2); the development of Fetterley's *Provisions* and the aforementioned boom of 1985 (3–9); Florence Howe's 1971 "A Report on Women and the Profession," with a particular emphasis on how the rising demand of women's studies courses motivated recovery efforts in the first place (9–12); and the 1970 founding of the Feminist Press and its influence on publishing practices (12–15).

Section VI returns to the disciplinary present depicted in Section I to sound what is, given the method, the logically necessary and rhetorically inevitable alarm. Citing a fairly recent Fetterley article, the 1994 "Commentary: Nineteenth-Century American Women Writers and the Politics of Recovery," Christiane's narrator argues "that without critical literary histories based upon the primary texts" the movement has rescued so far, "the work done to recover them will have been for nothing" since it will, in words quoted from Fetterley's article, "'be all too easy for the texts we have recovered to disappear again from memory' (605)" (16). Indeed, the narrator suggests that in some instances it is too late already:

> In fact, several books already have "slipped away." Louisa May Alcott's *Work*, a book that was available and part of one of Elaine Showalter's Women's Studies courses in the late sixties, has since gone out of print, as has a collection of Alice Cary's short fiction reprinted by the American Women Writers Series in the mid-eighties. Critical work is imperative at this stage, lest the work of nineteenth-century women writers fall back into what Olsen refers to as "silence," and lest the shelves surrounding *The Lamplighter*, void of biographies and histories, eventually take over even the small space now allotted to Cummins. (Farnan 16)

In certain respects, the project we have chosen for our second example, Brenda-Lee Rabine and Lois Dellert Raskin's "Multivocalities: Writing in the Disciplines at SUNYA," is quite similar to Christiane's. It has the same general look of a prepublication manuscript: twenty-two typed, double-spaced pages of prose (not counting bibliography and appendices), parenthetical citations, longer quotations arranged in block form (here single-spaced)[4], and so on. More substantively, it features much the same sort of plot, telling the story of a collective enterprise—in this case, the first seventeen years of the Writing Intensive (WI) Program at SUNY–Albany—as that enterprise moves from humble beginnings through boom years, and then on down to what is represented as a similarly unsatisfactory, albeit not entirely hopeless, current scene. And, finally, although the essay does offer, as its title indicates, a number of voices that complicate its campus-specific narrative in ways we will describe, its framing account of the larger "Writing in the Disciplines (WID)"/ "Writing Across the Curriculum (WAC)" movement (1)—the macro-account, if you will, within which Albany's efforts stand as an idiosyncratic micro-instance—features the same sort of corporate voice-over we saw in Christiane's project:

> Writing and rhetoric theorists from [the 1960s] "gave to the WID/WAC movement its focus on the classroom as community; its student-centered pedagogy, often with a subversive tinge; and its neoromantic, expressivist assumptions" (Russell 273). In September 1966, the Dartmouth Seminar, a month-long conference bringing together NCTE [National Council of Teachers of English] leaders with Britain's National Association of Teachers of English [NATE], seriously challenged American models of composition pedagogy. The British had embraced earlier American "progressive" education theorists like Dewey, and were incorporating the cognitive behaviorists such as Piaget and Vygotski into their curricular reforms. James Britton, then a highly influential British educator, would stongly influence his American counterparts in "linking the development of writing in the disciplines with personal writing" (Russell 273). [Rabine and Raskin 3]

These similiarities notwithstanding, it is clear that, for the purposes of this course and in the context of this Ph.D. program, Brenda-Lee and Lois's project represents the perspective not of literary history or literary criticism but of rhetoric and composition. This association is most pointed in the way the project frames its topic. While this study might broadly be said, like Christiane's, to be "about" the institutional processes by which certain writings and/or writers have come to acquire significance for the enterprise of English Studies, the writings and writers in question—those produced by college undergraduates in disciplinary or "content" courses—have never been designated as "literary" in a way that has brought either them or any related institutional processes into the domain of literary studies. On the other hand, such writers, writings, and processes have long been among the central concerns of rhetoric and composition. In the same way that Christiane's project can be said to emulate the Vanderbilt or Shumway work represented on the course reading

list, this one might be said to emulate—again, in its modest way—
that of James Berlin or Susan Miller or, particularly given its
focus on a single institution, Robin Varnum. Or it might be useful to think of it this way: insofar as journals are illustrative of
the way English Studies marks off its intradisciplinary topical
boundaries, an article framed along these lines—i.e., an illustrative institutional case study of instructional practices in writing—
might have some remote chance of appearing in an eclectically
edited *College English,* but it could absolutely never turn up in
*PMLA* or *Philological Quarterly,* and would be a far more likely
candidate for outlets such as *WPA (Writing Program Administrators)* or *Language and Learning Across the Disciplines.*

But Brenda-Lee and Lois's project has methodological ties to
rhetoric and composition as well and in both the investigative
(i.e., behavioral) and evidentiary senses we have invoked. In terms
of the former, as a function of the field's long-standing preoccupation with student writers and school practices and, more recently, its interest in literacy even more broadly conceived,
researchers in rhetoric and composition have found it both useful and necessary to develop an investigative repertoire which,
while it includes many of the traditional techniques of literary
studies, is also considerably broader and more eclectic. Certainly
that breadth and eclecticism are reflected in this project. Thus, in
their inquiry into the general background of WID/WAC, Brenda-
Lee and Lois draw on the same sorts of text-based methods as
Christiane, and deal with an analogous mix of published documents that variously comment on, constitute the results of, or
otherwise contribute to what is figured (like the recovery movement) as a large-scale, collective academic enterprise: Emig's
"Writing as a Mode of Learning," the Russell book quoted previously (*Writing in the Academic Disciplines, 1870–1990*),
Herrington and Moran's *Writing and Learning in the Disciplines,*
Walvoord's "The Future of WAC," and so on. Even some of the
project's institution-specific information is derived by methodologically similar means from two sources which, if not actually
among any library's holdings, are nevertheless easily accessible
as official university documents: *The Graduate Teaching Assistant Handbook,* which includes a discussion of writing in the
disciplines, and the 1986 University Senate bill (No. 8586-10)

that instituted Albany's Writing Intensive requirement in the first place, the instrumental heart of which reads as follows:

> IT IS HEREBY PROPOSED:
> I. That for the B.A. and B.S. degrees, students must satisfactorily complete with grades of "C" or higher, or "S," two writing intensive courses, including at least one at or above the 300-level.
> II. That this degree requirement become effective for all students graduating in May 1990 and thereafter.
> III. That this proposal be referred to the President for approval. (Rabine and Raskin 14)

Far more of Brenda-Lee and Lois's institution-specific information, however, is not document-based in this sense at all, but derived from sources that did not exist in textual form prior to the investigation—sources that, insofar as they are now documentable at all, were actually created by (stand as artifacts of) the investigation: interviews (both face-to-face and telephone), e-mail exchanges, solicited student writing, and notes taken at a department meeting. In fact, the essay's account of Albany's Writing Intensive Program is based primarily on these sources, and in particular on the extended interviews and/or e-mail exchanges with four faculty members who had played various official roles in it. In this excerpt, for example, the recollections of Donald Reeb, an economics professor who directed the program for most of its first decade, are "compiled from [an] interview . . . [held on] 4 November 1997" and presented textually in a format similar to that for an extended quotation:

> Dr. Reeb's thought was that senior faculty in each department would be the ones who had been trained at a time when writing instruction was paramount and that therefore these senior department members would be likely to embrace the philosophy of the WID program. He believed that since senior faculty would be the most likely to teach these courses, and since senior faculty do not like teaching freshmen and do not like teaching large lecture classes, that WI courses in the various disciplines would tend to be the upper-level courses. He sought invitations to meetings with selected faculty in each department, drawing on his contacts from his many campus-wide political activities. . . . He refers to this series of departmental

explorations as his "chicken salad sandwich days." He was trying to get the entire curriculum and program in place by December 1987.

Having convinced many departments of the need to provide these WI courses, he then had to backtrack when he realized that he had not provided a formula that would let each department know how many such courses it needed to implement. He decided to mandate to each department that they provide sufficient WI spaces to permit all graduating students in that major to take two WI courses. He created the fiction, not spelled out in the Senate Proposal, that each department was responsible for taking care of their own WI needs. (Rabine and Raskin 15)

Moreover—to move to our second, evidentiary sense of method—the information derived by these diverse means and from these diverse sources is also deployed in a way characteristic of rhetoric and composition, or at least far more characteristic of rhetoric and composition than any branch of literary studies. As we suggested previously, literary history in particular is grounded in what is imagined to be an essentially stable and therefore reexaminable corpus of texts. This corpus can expand, of course, and does so all the time. But what enables literary research as a corporate enterprise is the possibility—the imperative, really—that one investigator can examine the same texts another has examined, so that through alternative interpretations the group can carry on the production of an intersubjective, hermeneutically based knowledge. Hence the sense of urgency implicit in Christiane's account of the recovery movement: to "lose" primary texts is, at least in principle, to lose potentially valuable objects of study and thereby diminish the possibilities for the enterprise overall.

Insofar as it focuses on student writing, however, rhetoric and composition research simply does not work that way. Clearly, there are plenty of texts available to be examined and interpreted. But the field has so far not required or even seemed to expect that most such texts would be *re*-examined or *re*-interpreted: it has not canonized them, commissioned definitive editions of them, engaged in a struggle for shelf space for them with the proponents of Hawthorne and Cummins, or anything of the sort. At least in part *because* key texts are generally not accessible, the chances that some subsequent investigator will cover anything like the same ground and offer an alternative interpretation are for all practical purposes nil—and nowhere more so than in case studies of the kind Brenda-Lee and Lois take on. The operative evidentiary standard for such studies might be characterized as illustrative plausibility. On the one hand, such a history seeks to offer enough information of the right kinds to represent plausibly the situation under study and, on the other, to resonate with—and thereby help illustrate something generalizable concerning —analogous institutional situations.

Obviously, there is no mechanical formula for achieving this balance. Generally speaking, however, it puts a premium on (a) drawing on a range and variety of sources in aid of what might be called, in a rough adaptation from other research paradigms, triangulation; and (b) featuring those sources rather prominently in the research report itself, since referring readers to consult them independently would be an essentially empty gesture. We have already said a good bit about Brenda-Lee and Lois's project in terms of (a): the fact that their informants included students, teachers, and administrators, and that their document base features official university documents, solicited student writing, interview tapes, e-mail, and so on. In terms of (b), as the essay proceeds— as it moves from its account of the WID/WAC movement in general to its specific account of Albany's version of such a program—these sources are afforded a greater and greater share of the available textual space. In fact, beginning with page 12, every page save the last features at least one block quotation from one or another such source, and a number of pages are dominated by them (so that the Reeb interview in the preceding excerpt occupies fully two-thirds of page 15 and one-third of page 16).

In this sense, finally, the project's methodological connections to rhetoric and composition can be said to exercise some formal influence as well. Thus, although the corporate voice-over we described earlier never disappears altogether, it does recede, giving way at a gradually accelerating pace to those other "voices" ("multivocalities") of the title. When the plot of this history reaches its narrative present, it also reaches a sort of multivocal climax, wherein the text is given over to an uninterrupted series of eight excerpts drawn from writings the investigators have solicited from current students and/or teachers in Albany's Writing Intensive Program. All of them offer testimony along the lines of this excerpt:

> "In the Women's Studies Introduction course I teach, when we've read a play at home, I've asked the students to write a response before our class discussion. I read the 2–3 page responses during the break and read from certain prompts, incorporating the responses into our group discussion. The students then can identify their work, extend their responses, etc. I like the idea of immediately integrating the students' work "as text" along with other critical/biographical/historical and visual materials in our discussion." (Rabine and Raskin 20)

The overall result is a melding of, or at least resonance between, form and argument, so that the gradual movement from voiced-over monologue to something close to a polylogue both presages and dramatizes the project's closing argument:

> The endless cycles [of the Writing Intensive Program] are wearisome, the sense of failure is present, but clearly the conversation has not ended. There are many voices at SUNYA to continue the multivocal dialogue—without voices, multiple voices, there can be no reform, no movement forward. (22)

Our third and final project from The History of English Studies course is Jennifer Beck's "The Poetry Workshop 'after' New Criticism," and we have chosen it to represent what the program proposal identifies as the perspective of "contemporary writers." As its title suggests, Jennifer's study deals with (is "about") the relationship between the New Criticism associated with Tate, Brooks, Warren, and others, and the cluster of practices in the teaching of creative writing grouped, for historical purposes, under the heading of the workshop. Topically, then, of the course's major readings the project is closest to D. G. Myers's *The Elephants Teach,* or even more, given its chronological range and what we shall see is its theoretical orientation, Jed Rasula's *The American Poetry Wax Museum,* R. M. Berry's "Theory, Creative Writing, and the Impertinence of History," and—a title Jennifer cites three times—Patrick Bizzaro's "Reading the Creative Writing Course: The Teacher's Many Selves." Jennifer's project can be said to trace developments in this mode of writing instruction over a roughly

seventy-year span (the 1920s through the 1990s), paying particular attention to the interaction between instructional models
and the modes of reading—the critical theories—that have been
the central preoccupation of the English departments by which
such instruction has nearly always been sponsored. Hence the
quotation marks around "after": as this interaction plays out,
the word takes on different shadings, from "chronologically subsequent to" and "in the manner of/as influenced by" all the way
to "targeting/out to get."

Formally and methodologically, however, Jennifer's approach
departs from these topically related studies, and indeed from any
of the course-related writings we have considered to this point,
in a number of ways. The most immediately striking of these
departures comes in terms of form, of genre: the project consists
of a series of four annotated poems and an accompanying text-
and-image collage. The poems are, in order, "Precursor: Expressionists"; "Room, subject, view"; "Pedagogy"; and "Collage."
By way of illustration, we will quote all of the first, which seeks
to characterize a strand of creative writing instruction that pre-
dates New Criticism, emerging shortly after World War I. It might
be called (though his name is not invoked) the Hughes Mearns
model:

> Radical, no; they did not turn
> to Greenwich but inward,[1]
> though perhaps some hoped to find
> the bohemia within. Break from
> factory progress, the money-machine, yes
> but not generally into tea rooms.[2]
> (And those too, saucers in hand, had their conversions:
> saw a light in the smooth-lettered text,
> did not see the syntax shift within themselves,[3]
> and raised up the reading souls of their keeping
> without irony, essentially enlightened.)
> Can the self be handled so,
> unwieldy for the geometry of desks?
> It breaks through leaf membrane to the word[4]
> but does not embarrass its dichotomous drives.[5]
> Empowered, the validated I sweeps a gesture,
> capes its hero shoulders, cloaking parts[6]
> in text(ured) cloth,
> one authentic moment at a time.[7]

1. As per Berlin, the liberal culture advanced by progressive education "helped create a climate in which expressionistic rhetoric could develop" (73). Lawrence Cremin, quoted by Berlin, explains that those interested in [radical expressionism] no longer "flocked to the Greenwich Villages of New York, Chicago, and San Francisco" as they had done before World War I, but rather turned to "a polyglot system of ideas that combined the doctrine of self-expression, liberty, and psychological adjustment into a confident, iconoclastic individualism that fought the constraints of Babbitry and the discipline of social reform as well" (73).

2. This meant to invoke the generalists, such as Norton, who saw training in literature as a guard against vulgarity and as part of the necessary training for a class born to rule (Graff 83).

3. Text as fixed, discernible.

4. Belief in "natural" expression of the self.

5. Per Kristeva's "Heterogeneity" in *Revolution in Poetic Language*; there was no discomfort with the singular, coherent Romantic narrator, which was usually equivalent to the "I" of the poem. Also, see quotes in collage.

6. Jed Rasula writes that "In the workshop, the anxiety occasioned by the conspicuous shadows of critical theory, literary history, and everything else convened in the university could be dispelled by waving the poem as the wand of selfhood—and appealing to the supreme validation of personal experience" (423). This stems from the Expressionism which rose in reaction to philological methods of textual analysis.

7. Looking back at the concept of a unified subject as an heroic past. Expressionism empowered students by encouraging the journey into the self, but without critical analysis of the problem of the self (or of linear time). This issue is still contentious due to the divide between those who want to incorporate post-modern theory in the classroom and those who wish to keep workshops as safe havens from such intrusions. (Beck)

Not all the poems are annotated at exactly this footnote-to-verse ratio, but the formal pattern is constant: a scene of sorts—an evocation of the workshop, if you will—offered in the verse, with the notes in the style of *The Wasteland* to direct "the reader to the sources of many of [the poem's] allusions and explaining certain phases of its plan" (Allison et al. 1034).

In ways that "Precursor: Expressionists" exemplifies quite effectively, this formal departure carries over into the orchestrating of narrators and the construction of audience. Like the other student projects, this one features a number of textually constituted "voices," but here there is a pronounced and consistent stereo (or perhaps contrapuntal) effect—two more or less equal voices in a constant interplay—neither found in, nor really available to, either of the others. The narrators constructed for the poems themselves—the textual main events presented in the larger typeface on the upper half of the page—are variable: in this first poem, there is an oblique or perhaps oracular alternative to the corporate third person, retrospectively characterizing two "theys", in each subsequent poem, one or another "we" speaks from or for the workshop of a given era.

At the same time, while the footnotes may be spatially subordinate—smaller typeface, lower on the page—they nevertheless constitute the larger body of text, and they also have the more consistent, if not necessarily more prominent, textual presence. With a single exception, the narrator constructed for the footnotes in all four poems is a version of that same corporate voice-over we saw in the other student projects, operating here to mediate (and presumably to regulate) the reader's experience of the verse in relation to the historical, theoretical, and critical texts on which it draws and with which it resonates. The net result is to invoke a fairly specialized audience on behalf of the poems, readers who are understood to be more than casually familiar with at least the general subject matter and, not infrequently, the footnoted sources. So, in "Precursor," the parenthetical sketch of "the generalists" (lines 6–11, notes 2 and 3) requires at least a general familiarity with the relevant critical/pedagogical debates, as in the contrastive nod to New Criticism's hallmark fondness for irony ("raised up the reading souls of their keeping without irony"), and in the play on the way in which more contemporary debates raise questions about the "essential" self ("essentially enlightened"). But the same sketch offers even more to a reader conversant with the argument and terminology of *Professing Literature,* for whom the otherwise rather elliptically mentioned "Norton" of note 2, for instance, is easily recognizable as the "splendidly imperious" Charles Eliot of Graff's chapter on "The Generalist Opposition."

Methodologically, meanwhile, Jennifer's project is not particularly exotic in what we have been calling that term's investigative sense. Even more than the other two projects we have considered, this one represents itself as drawing in a fairly traditional way on published texts treated as secondary sources.[5] The "Works Cited" (offered on a separate page and in MLA format) lists fourteen titles, all of them published: four with a predominantly historical focus (Berlin, Graff, Myers, Rasula); four in critical theory (e.g., Kristeva's *Revolution in Poetic Language,* Lacan's *Ecrits: A Selection*); and six devoted to institutional/pedagogical commentary (e.g., Bizzaro, Perloff's "'Theory' and/in the Creative Writing Classroom"). The only source in any sense comparable to the sorts of primary texts used in the other projects —Christiane's "recovered" fictions, say, or Brenda Lee and Lois's interviews—comes in the third poem, "Pedagogy," the first footnote to which claims (in the sole break from the corporate voice-over mentioned earlier) that the poem "is based in part on my experience in a poetry workshop with Gerald Stern, writer-in-residence at Bucknell, Spring 1994" (Beck 5). But, even here, that "experience" is not represented in any documentary way (e.g., syllabus, notes, letters, etc.).

However, in the other sense of method we have been invoking—the evidentiary system deployed—"The Poetry Workshop 'after' New Criticism" takes a tack quite different from those followed in the other two projects. Thus, whereas Christiane's grounded its authority in a hermeneutic intersubjectivity, and Brenda-Lee and Lois's aims to generate an illustrative plausibility, Jennifer's seeks what might be called dramatic integrity: to construct text-based "voices" that readers will accept as representing—as somehow "true to"—the contexts of time and place and culture from and for which they purport to speak. In the absence of the more conventional rhetoric of unmediated observation and its account of causally linked events, these poems are presented more as a sequence of discontinuous scenes-with-footnote-voice-over. Thus, while there is still a plotline of sorts—the four poems follow a rough before-during-after trajectory for New Critical influence in the poetry workshop—connections between and among these scenes are mostly implicit, a matter of cumulative resonance and recurring motifs. The most efficient way to illustrate the resulting dynamic is to quote a second poem—the aforementioned third, entitled "Pedagogy"—in full:

## Pedagogy[1]

The circle has a center which is not space;
take the poem, take the pen, take anything but
the A-train to meaning.
"I am here with this, born
of me, of feel, and really happened,"
says student C, while pupil A
though opaque with internal expression
has carried the image through,
consistently yet—a provocative last line shift—
and isn't-that-why-we're-here-folks.
He speaks, and we
Write down "image," good apprentices to his
unified genius.[2]
The craft contains the don'ts
long known, the danger of the
conditional tense.

We take our own voice for granted,
though we hear, distantly, female voices question
how the I has been choreographed into march.[3]
Still, we want the rightness of his answers,
not to face erasure
or negotiate our selves,[4]
having just come into the light of the forum
ourselves,[5] writing and not just **understanding poetry**.[6]
Want his sure appraisal and his stories about Auden,
Want his age-spotted hands
to nest us in the present on a first name basis
to place us here, plumbing depths, naturally,
fixed, and speaking.

1. This poem is based in part on my experience in a poetry workshop wth
Gerald Stern, writer-in-residence at Bucknell, Spring 1994. In his article
"Writing After Theory," Tom Andrews of Ohio University quotes Stern on
poets' reactions to literary theory: "As far as theory is concerned, or what is
called theory, I think the same criteria [as those used when deciding to read
'traditional' critics] should prevail: if the writing is interesting, and if the
ideas are provocative, it is worthwhile reading. . . . I don't know if poets are
troubled by the same thing in theorists as the traditional critic, say the liter-

ary critic, is. They are not upset if that critic is being displaced or challenged, nor are they terribly upset by the power or the dance of the theorist" (13 col 1). Andrews then criticizes Stern for his ultimately dismissive attitude toward theorists as not taking human life "seriously."

I should note that I very much enjoyed the workshop and still correspond with Stern, but my readings for this project have inspired a re-evaluation of that semester.

2. Patrick Bizzaro writes in his essay, "Rethinking, (Re)Vision, and Collaboration" that the master-apprentice pedagogical approach helps perpetuate the legacy of New Criticism and its emphasis on the interpretation of the text. The professor is assumed to have expertise. In this system, he continues, the professor is also expected to be able to know what the student originally intended to say and to be able to explain to the student how s/he failed in translating those thoughts into poetry. In addition, the practice of employing well-known, well-published poets to teach creative writing workshops is a "star" system which "reinforce[s] the belief that the best way to learn how to write is to do what the teacher says. In the master-classroom, where workshops are conducted by renowned writing stars, revision of a text is a matter of learning to read the poem . . . as the teacher has read it and manipulating the text to the teacher's satisfaction" (Bizzaro 242).

3. Gayle Elliott of the U of Wisconsin writes that "The creative writing workshop has served as a point of departure from traditionally hierarchical classroom power structures and has evolved its own pedagogy; feminist theory seeks also to delineate new pedagogical approaches and to critically engage the old" (109). She continues later in the essay "Pedagogy in Penumbra: Teaching, Writing, and Feminism in the Fiction Workshop": "Creative writing, as a discipline, comes late to the discussion of pedagogy. Perhaps this is because creative writing is not about the production of knowledge but the rendering of experience, the creation of art. And art and theory find themselves at odds . . . . Yet it was within the writing workshop that the shape of the classroom literally changed: once-regimented rows of desks rearranged into a single, inclusive circle, the peer dynamic between teacher and student altered accordingly." Elliott seems to discount the lingering effects of New Critics on the workshop learning environment. More to the point of the placement of this footnote, she writes that feminist literary studies have helped bring to the fore the practice of analyzing the rhetorical position of "I."

4. Bizzaro focuses on the need in workshops to negotiate student identity, to teach students to have identities in the classroom other than apprentice to the all-knowing master. The teacher is then responsible for encouraging other models of identity/behavior in the classroom, for becoming an expert not on how to read individual texts but on how to disperse authority. One way of accomplishing this would be to employ reader-response, feminist or Marxist criticism or deconstruction to encourage new models of identity or the teacher and student relationship.

5. "In their academic affiliation, the workshops were structurally positioned to cater to the young. Not surprisingly, the adolescent quest for selfhood would become the de facto theme of workshop verse" (Rasula 434).

6. Brooks, Cleanth and Robert Penn Warren. *Understanding Poetry: An Anthology for College Students.* New York: Henry Holt, 1938.

(Beck)

Among the various possible connections between this poem and "Precursor: Expressionists," two will serve to illustrate the evidentiary method at work. The most immediately visible, in that it comes in the first line, is the figuring of the workshop in spatial terms. The first poem was concerned with the challenge facing an "expressionist" pedagogy in a school setting, and its key formulation in this regard was a question about the fit between students and schools, between a "confident, iconoclastic individualism" and such institutional realities as furniture bolted to floors in neat rows, or the comparable efficiencies of a psychometric paradigm: "Can the self be handled so,/unwieldy for the geometry of desks?" This motif is picked up in the title of the series' second poem, "Room, subject, view," a poem which—temporally grounded in the 1960s and '70s—also opens with its own image of the workshop-as-space, this time introducing one version of a post-New Critical teacher as an agent therein:

> There are no rungs in this room
> it spreads horizontal;
> the voice at the head bids us to move
> not so much toward what was never so well
> as along the fissures, our discontents.

When "Pedagogy" begins by announcing that "The circle has a center which is not space," therefore, it does so pointedly *against* these first two configurations. The "geometry of desks" has been altered—no furniture bolted to the floor or neat rows here—and the room might still be said to "spread[s] horizontal." But "the voice" that "bids" has moved from someplace "at the head" to become the "unified genius" who fills (or even is) the circle's center, the poet/teacher/master through whom all writings must pass.[6]

And we can see the same sort of interplay in the different ways the poems characterize the students as poets, as writers. In the expressionist workshop of "Precursor," there was "no discomfort with the singular, coherent Romantic narrator" (n. 5).

On the contrary, the student-poet it "empowered" appears as an unabashedly Byronic figure, a "validated I" who most fully becomes him- or herself in the grand "gesture" of writing poetry, by virtue of which that "I" can "cape[s] its hero shoulders, cloaking parts/in text(ured) cloth,/one authentic moment at a time." By comparison, the situation of the student-poets in "Pedagogy"'s 1990's workshop is a good deal less glorious, if perhaps more poignant. As it happens, a version of that "validated I" is still on the scene, poetic powers much diminished, in the figure of the teacher: the "unified genius" who, "age-spotted hands" notwithstanding, has the "'star'" credentials (n. 2) to suggest that he may once have thus caped his own hero shoulders. And perhaps there are traces of that earlier "I," too, in the efforts of "student C," the one who hopes to derive *auth*ority from *auth*enticity: "'I am here with this, born/of me, of feel, and really happened.'"[7]

For the student-poets as a group, however—for that collectively apprenticed "we" who dutifully "write down 'image'" because the master says it—this workshop offers a rather different set of possibilities, one poised between a dangerous past and a threatening future. On the one hand, the unified transcendence of expressionism's "I" has begun to seem problematic: "we" might be able to take "our own voice for granted," but not unself-consciously enough to get swept up in Byronic poses; women in particular need to be wary about how donning that "cape" may result in them also being "choreographed into march." On the other hand, these writers are not yet ready to accede to the equally unnerving regime represented by such things as post-structuralist conceptions of the subject and/or the author: they are not yet prepared, as they put it, to "face erasure/or negotiate our selves,/ having just come into the light of the forum/ourselves, writing and not just **understanding poetry**."

What they want instead, and what this master-anchored, New Critically influenced workshop ultimately provides, is a kind of shelter, a developmental halfway house that allows them to be— in a more potent and perhaps less pejorative sense than usual— *self*-indulgent. There is still some choreographing involved, of course, but not into anything so regimented as a "march"; the choreographing appears in any case to be consensual. Thus, in addition to what are (for now) the comforting formalist "rightness of his answers" and "his sure appraisal," along with the ties to a tradition demonstrated in "his stories about Auden," the student-poets very much "want" the master to ground them in a shared here-and-now, however local and contingent they know it to be: they "[w]ant his age-spotted hands/to nest us in the present on a first name basis/to place us here, plumbing depths, natu-rally,/fixed, and speaking."

As with the renderings of the workshop as space, the series' representations of students as poets accumulates in this episodic way, reaching a climax of sorts in the closing lines of the final poem, "Collage." In the late 1990's workshop featured in this final piece, the validated I and its "nested" descendants have given way to "the personage, jigsaw,/parts remaining seamed . . . presenced multiply" (ll. 27–30); and the student-poets, growing restive under the New Critical order, are beginning to go "after" that order in a rather more pointed way:

> The mind sub-level drives forward,
> reacts to the breaking upheaval
> into violent language, into po
> > > etry.
> Suddenly, there is a she;
> Chloe likes Olivia and neither
> agrees to silence in the laboratory.
> Many others take seats in the shop circle;
> jouissance moves political and ontological loves.
> They can perhaps, but not often,
> break
> > > sud-den
> with delirious rain—you can't
> know—can't sleeve
> the engine
> of this
> all.
>
> > Can't sieve
> so fine but there will be
> the heteroglot in the midst of your
> flour(ing)[7] univers(ality). [lines 33–53]

7. white, sustaining

(Beck)

Thus, while this project, like the other two, ends by moving into a textual present that we are expected to understand as contemporary (although in this case it is not the *return* to that present it is in the other two projects), its suasory power does not derive from any comparable sort of sustained discursive argument. Rather, its sources are dramatic, and at this point at least figuratively genealogical. The narrator who addresses readers in this rather accusatory direct address is descended from, and carries on the work of, the series' other student-poet voices, this time (re)incarnated—reinvigorated—by forces generally collected under the heading of the postmodern ("the personage, jigsaw," the more inclusive academy, "jouissance"), and now figuring the New Critically dominated past as an oppressive regime that is beginning to crumble. In carrying out its historical work, then, Jennifer's project ends not with the relative comfort of the corporate voice-over (a promise that, if we mend our ways, the recovery movement or the WAC program will be all right) but with what amounts to an oracular threat to a whitebread, patriarchal tradition:

> . . . you can't
> know—can't sleeve
> the engine
> of this
> all.

> Can't sieve
> so fine but there will be
> the heteroglot in the midst of your
> flour(ing) univers(ality).

## "Every Classroom a Nexus of Discourses"

To this point, we have concentrated on the way the Albany program's predilection for extended work in a preferred mode operates within the boundaries of a single course: how it affects different students negotiating the same classroom at the same time. It is not hard to see, however, that the curricular imperative that gives rise to projects as varied as Christiane's, Brenda-Lee and Lois's, and Jennifer's in The History of English Studies course has implications for student writing that go beyond the boundaries of any specific course: that it has an effect on how the same student negotiates different courses over time. Since students are not only *not* obliged to conform to a predetermined discursive trajectory in each course they take, but are in fact expected to represent their various (intra)disciplinary perspectives—to make "every classroom," as Eugene Garber characterizes it in the title of an essay about the program, "a nexus of discourses"[8]—there is both considerable opportunity and considerable pressure for students to develop their own formal, topical, and methodological agendas as they move from course to course and on toward examinations and dissertations. Indeed, this dimension of the curricular imperative can be framed quite ominously: if students do not work to write themselves into a professional and disciplinary identity over their two or three years of coursework, no one else will either. In this longitudinal sense, the object of the curriculum, in Garber's phrasing, is "to give every student an opportunity in every course to advance his [or her] ongoing work" (3).

This notion of ongoing work should not be construed too narrowly. Garber suggests in his original formulation that a given student might be at work on "a book of poems, an examination of the hierarchies of academic discourse," or a study of "the tensions within contemporary feminist theory" (3), and certainly this can be the case. So, for example, Christiane's work on the recovery movement—begun in courses prior to her work in The History of English Studies course—subsequently fed directly into her qualifying examinations, and her dissertation will almost certainly consist of just the kind of scholarship her essay calls for. But experience also suggests that the nature of such ongoing work will often be less fully articulated, and even more often still evolving. While most students enter the program with a reasonably clear idea about where they hope to head in both the discipline and the profession, they frequently need the opportunity, especially during their first year, to carry out various test runs, as it were, as a way of gathering momentum; even when they have identified specific longer-term projects, their discursive trajectory through the program may still change, often in unpredictable ways. In short, curricular negotiations concerning such ongoing writing projects remain decidedly two-way: "the teacher says to the student," to cite Garber one last time, "let me see your ongoing work because my belief is that that work will enrich this class and be enriched by it. And, who knows, some class may give the student's work a whole new dimension or direction" (3).

As with our efforts to illustrate how the program's different perspectives might come together in one course, our best strategy here is to offer a detailed examination of this dynamic at work, in this instance by tracing the work of one student as he moves through a series of three courses. For this purpose, we have chosen Ron MacLean who, given the labels the program provides, would be considered a contemporary writer with a primary interest in prose fiction. Our account of his work begins in a course offered under the "Writing in History" rubric (the same paradigmatic branch that includes The History of English Studies, 1880–Present) called Theories and Practice of Creativity. The general catalogue copy characterizes this course as posing a series of questions:

> What theories of creativity, exceptional or ordinary, have been held in the past? How do they inform or contrast with modern educational theories and theories of poetry, music, and the like? Are these discussions simply ideologically and historically significant, rather than teaching us truths? While focusing on theories of creativity, this course additionally interrogates theory in the light of the experience and practice of course participants. (*English Graduate Study* 11)

Early on in the version of the course Ron enrolled in, students were assigned a two-part random writing experiment, drawing on the methods of Constantin Stanislavsky, John Cage, and Ethel Schwabacher, among others. For the first part of the assignment, MacLean composed a poem called "The Source of Streets," which included these lines: "It was a wrong number, a grid of/scorching streets, ringing/three times in the dead of night." The second stage of the assignment required students to expand on some image produced for these initial random compositions. MacLean chose this image of a grid of streets, and produced a narrative—also entitled "The Source of Streets"—that represented an effort to imagine what such a grid would look like, and where it would have come from.

On the day of the unveiling, Montiel wore a blue suit with a scarlet handkerchief sticking up out of the pocket. The crowd of hundreds of our citizens poised on the hillside outside the Bear mansion that early morning, waiting for the fog to lift so we could look down on our streets for the first time. As the sun parted the mist, the villagers gasped and Montiel smiled at the wonder of his creation, the grid of streets topped in red clay forming a geometrically perfect maze of interconnections and deceptions.

Montiel explained to us, as we watched in awe, how there were exactly seven routes from any one point in the city to any other, the shortest always exactly three blocks, the longest several hundred miles, so that you could vary the length of your trip according to how eager you were to reach your destination; he explained, his face lit in a broad grin, that in addition to the aesthetic and engineering beauty of the grid, this maze, there was a very practical beauty. And with a flourish of his arms he lifted a cloth of the same color as his handkerchief to reveal a giant iron lever of the sort once used for trains at switching yards. This, he said, was to be our city's defense against attack for, when pulled, it would change the pattern of the outer sector of streets so that they would all lead into one another, but none of them would enter the city proper. Montiel demonstrated, receiving help from both Edward Bears on the awkward lever, and we watched with amazement as the grid shifted and the city became protected by countless dead ends, surrounded by what seemed to be one endlessly meandering road that went all around us but never led anywhere. ("Structures" 24–25)

In the context of the specialty-based Magisterial tradition, Theories and Practice of Creativity—were it offered in an English graduate program at all—would likely have required argumentative academic prose research papers on one or another topic concerning creativity: "Gender-Based Differences in Paradigms for Creativity: John Cage and Virginia Woolf," say—writing, in short, that conformed formally, topically, and methodologically to a fairly standard "academic" trajectory. For Ron, however, the intersection between course and writing was obviously rather different. Certainly it was not a matter of form—neither the initial experiment nor the subsequent expansion imposed any formal constraints; nor was it a matter of topic—neither his poem nor the later narrative are "about" creativity in any usual sense of that term. Instead, their intersection—their interaction, if you will—is best understood as methodological, particularly in that term's more behavioral sense. With a refreshing openness which, as much as anything, calls needed attention to the generally more covert but equivalent means employed in other English doctoral courses, Theories and Practice of Creativity sought to alter—to engage, disrupt, challenge—Ron's composing practices.

Moreover, Ron argues that this challenge did affect his work as a fiction writer—gave it, as in Garber's intimation, a whole new direction. In his previous fiction, Ron reports, "I tended to know what I wanted to say before I said it, much like preparing the final draft of an analytical paper. The process of writing the story, then, was largely a matter of constructing a persuasive argument toward the thesis I had developed—demonstrating what I had come to know rather than continuing to explore it" ("Nexus" 8). For "The Source of Streets" and, as we shall see, for subsequent related stories, this was not the case. For the first time, he was "driving without a road map. Walking the high wire without a net"—a mode of composing that gave him, however paradoxically, "freedom from [his] own preordained ideas" (9).

The following semester, Ron enrolled in the core course of the program's "Literary History" branch, Models of History in Literary Criticism, explained in the (Spring 1991) course bulletin as follows:

> The controlling model of history in literary criticism in almost all of its diverse schools turns out to be Hegelian, and the first session [of the course] will examine not the Hegelian theory of history as such but the ways in which historical time pervades Hegelian thought on all levels. The next four sessions will focus [sequentially] on the relationship of Hegel to current Marxism, current post-structuralism, current psychoanalysis, and current feminism. The remainder of the course will be devoted to alternative conceptions of history and time which have appeared in radical Modernism. The following texts will be studied: Melville's *Moby-Dick* and Charles Olson's essays on

Melville; Linda Henderson's *Non-Euclidean and Four Dimen-
sional Geometry in Modern Art*; several texts by Gertrude Stein,
including *How to Write*; Donna Haraway's "Manifesto for
Cyborgs"; Attali's *Noise: Music and the Critique of Political
Economy*; and Greil Marcus' *Lipstick Traces* along with several texts relevant to it. The course will be directed toward the
production of a major essay or other writing project. ("Graduate Courses" Spring 1991 2)

Students wrote responses to these readings, to be shared with the
class, in whatever form seemed appropriate and relevant. For his
required writing project, Ron continued work on the narrative
that had begun with "The Source of Streets," which had evolved
into a novel-in-progress called *The Beet City Chronicles*. By this
time, he has come to conceive of the constitutive chapters as representing

> a series of fragmentary manuscripts unearthed in archaelogical
> digs around what was once the citadel of a ruler of that part of
> the world, called Khan. These manuscripts present varied, ulti-
> mately incomplete, and often contradictory versions of events
> of a world that had seemingly succeeded in writing itself out of
> existence. This book is an effort to piece together and present
> the history of this lost city, its development and ultimate con-
> flict with the Khan's empire, and an attempt to understand the
> desire of its residents to remove themselves from history. ("What
> My Book Is About" 1)

Models of History in Literary Criticism therefore presents him
with an interesting opportunity:

> I had a fairly definite agenda. I wanted to work on my novel,
> and get feedback on it. Since the novel is the attempt to re-
> count the history of a mythical city, pieced together from frag-
> mentary and contradictory accounts of this lost civilization,
> reading and talking about how literature has perceived history
> seemed relevant. I hoped the class would stimulate my think-
> ing about literary constructions of history, and provide an op-
> portunity for reactions to my novel—are the historical themes
> coming through? are they "working"? —from people who were
> reading and talking about the things I was writing about.
> ("Nexus" 13–14)

In keeping with that agenda, consider this excerpt from a chapter called "Letter from the Khan":

> My rule has become dominated by an aesthetic, my judgment and decisions guided by the colors and shapes of the movement beneath me, the panorama of human activity that reaches me only as a shifting of color and shape, patterns of fluidity that are more, or less, appealing to the eye. I lead based on these patterns of fluid motion. I make my decisions based on the shifting shapes below me, removed from considerations of individual humanity, of budgets and timetables and lunch hours. I watch out the small square window of my uppermost room for hours every day. You'd be surprised at the consistency of the movement, at the familiarity of the patterns. . . .
>
> How would I serve my people by going down among them? How could I better govern from seeing their problems, so many, so varied, so mutually contradictory, so that to help one group is to harm another? In the first place, it is not safe for me down there. Too many would like to see me dead, and not even out of a vision for leadership, a way to right the wrongs of this empire—for then, I like to think, I might give way—but out of a sheer hunger for power, to which I cannot succumb. If I were to go down, I would also shatter the delicate balance of daily life here. What right do I have to alter my people's image of me, whether that be of hero, tyrant, or even divinity? It takes all of these perceptions, does it not, to sustain the social, economic and political networks in all their dissonant harmony? An abstracted image of a leader is the best service to the populace, for they can create of me what they need. (2–3)

Here course and writing intersect along what we have been calling topical lines: in a readily defensible way, *The Beet City Chronicles* is a novel which, like the course, can be said to be "about" models of history, about the "problem" of history—or at least is so in a way in which MacLean's earlier course-sponsored version of it was not "about" creativity. Ron explains his experience of this intersection in terms of freedom and constraint:

> The class provided me with a healthy balance of freedom and constraint. The freedom not to have to make explicit connections every week between the reading and my responses allowed me to assimilate material that was significant to me at

my own pace and in my own way, which tends to be intuitive, relying more on pursuing a thread of emotional and subconscious connections than on "rational" argument, where connection must always be evident. The useful constraint came from knowing that I would be asked, "what does this have to do with the reading?" Or, the question one classmate asked about a character in my novel, "who *is* this Kahn guy?" I felt an obligation—and a desire—to articulate the connections that I knew existed. ("Nexus" 14)

MacLean established a third and final relationship between course and ongoing writing project the following semester in a class called Revisionary Poetics and Literary Practice, one of six courses listed under the program's "Writing Theory and Practice" rubric. The catalogue copy characterizes this course as a "study of the ways in which our notions of textuality, both within and beyond western cultures, have been challenged and refigured by, for instance, aleatory and performative practices, postnarrative conventions, and the ethnographic study of oral traditions" (*English Graduate Study* 13). Working within those general parameters, the version of the course MacLean took— offered, as it happens, by the same Eugene Garber quoted in this section—focused on certain post–World War II developments in American fiction. The reading list included novels (e.g., Djuna Barnes's *Nightwood*, Ishmael Reed's *Mumbo Jumbo*), shorter fiction (by such authors as John Barth, H. D., Clarence Major, and Gertrude Stein), and criticism (including Maurice Blanchot, Christine Brooke-Rose, Shoshana Felman, Marjorie Perloff, and so on), but the course also depended heavily on student writing:

> This course focuses on twentieth-century American avant-garde fiction, mostly post–WWII. The intentions and effects of this fiction will be studied from aesthetic, historical, philosophical, ideological, psychoanalytic and other perspectives. The course should be of interest to creative writers, rhetoricians, and literary scholars. Literary analyses, rhetorical analyses, and fictions are equally welcome. Each student will present to the class a work or work-in-progress for discussion. By the end of the semester, each student will have completed a substantial project, which may be in a single mode or mixed. ("Graduate Courses" Fall 1991 5)

As in the other two courses, the syllabus allows for a wide range of writing projects, including the more familiar forms of graduate school writing—i.e., for any number of argumentative academic prose studies *of* such fiction: a comparison between Robert Coover and Clarence Major, say, or a study of influence involving H. D. and Djuna Barnes. But it also allows, and indeed specifically invites, "fictions" as inquiries, fictions understood as fully legitimate explorations of the subject area. MacLean's response to the required substantial project was in two closely related parts. First and primarily, he continued work on *The Beet City Chronicles*. By the end of the course, and as a function of writing done over the intervening summer, he had completed drafts for some ten chapters: "Letter from the Khan," "Montiel's Revenge," "The Khan in the City of Streets," "Coming of Age," and so on. In addition to continuing work on specific chapters, Ron also composed a series of commentaries that dealt with both his general thinking about the novel and his ideas about its structure. His final project for the course involved a combination of these writings and was submitted under the title "Structures." The following excerpt is from Section Three, "The Models," which features a series of seven possible ways to organize the book:

1. The Mirror Model
In which the structure would mirror the grid of streets; a maze which, from within, at various moments seems to be leading somewhere, only to come to a dead end, or to a shift which leads somewhere entirely different, which eternally denies access to its center. The streets of Beet City are designed to keep the heart of the community protected; to defend against penetration. They allow access to the outskirts, to various supplementary roads toward the city, but a shift of the lever keeps those roads from leading to the center, and keeps the Khan always wandering a perimeter, convinced he is getting closer to the core. His desire sustains in him the hope which the structure of the system categorically frustrates: there is no way in.

So with the novel. Each story strand would progress for a time, moving toward a moment of revelation, toward Montiel's kitchen, toward the knowledge of what happened there, who died in the straight-backed hardwood chair, who won the war, why the story of this conflict and of these civilizations disappeared from world history—and then, in turn, each strand would be walled off by the impossibility of knowing, whether because of a myriad of contradictory possibilities, or due to an information gap where something is simply unaccounted for.

In an already complicated novel, however, I fear that such a structure, while true to the principles the book grows from, may render it incomprehensible. No, that's not entirely it. This approach leans too far to the side of deconstruction; it lacks sufficient drive of the desire to tell a story. (26–27)

In this third instance, the relationship between course and writing—one obviously encouraged by the course design—can best be characterized as formal, with some traces of a topical connection. MacLean explores the subject of avant-garde fiction mostly by working at length in a *form* that falls under that rubric. Meanwhile, his commentaries, although focused specifically on his own project, are—by virtue of that project's formal status—therefore also on the course's topic: they are, in other words, "about" (an) avant-garde American fiction, *The Beet City Chronicles.*

## "you can't/know—can't sleeve/the engine/of this/all"

Ultimately, we want to be careful about how much pressure we put on the student projects we have featured at length in this chapter. It is worth a reminder, for example, that The History of English Studies, 1880 to the Present is designed to be taught in the first term of the graduate curriculum's four-term cycle, so that most students take it early in their doctoral careers. Certainly that was the case here: Jennifer and Lois were in their first semester of doctoral work; Brenda-Lee was actually still in the M.A. program; while Christiane, somewhat unusually, was in her last semester of coursework.

Along similar lines, it is important to note that despite Ron's sustained investment in *The Beet City Chronicles,* that project did *not* finally turn out to be his dissertation. Rather, in keeping with what we characterized as the two-sided nature of these negotiations, he moved on to write a collection of short stories entitled "Who We Are," a project with clear structural ties to *Beet*

*City* (the stories are linked in various ways) and thematic connections as well (in that, like *Beet City,* it is preoccupied with a kind of "lost" history), but one that deals topically with a contemporary American family.

Finally, we need to acknowledge again what we have suggested often enough before: these projects are necessarily illustrative, not representative. And this is more than simply a logistical problem. Even if we multiplied examples here—offered six or eight projects from sections of The History of English Studies, say, or tracked the ongoing projects of a half-dozen students like Ron—past would not serve usefully as prologue. As we explained in Chapter 5, this program's decision to base curricular coherence on the integrated interests of those who take and teach the classes means that each cadre of doctoral students must do more than rehearse or study or witness this process of integration as it has played out in the past: they must *enact* it. Hence the importance of remembering that projects like these are a *public* feature of the courses in which they are written: they are made available through duplication, discussion, and presentation, and do not simply become part of a private correspondence between teacher and individual student. Hence, too, our heading's invocation of the lines from Jennifer's "Collage." In this program, neither students nor faculty can control the processes the curriculum is designed to set in motion, "can't/know—can't sleeve/the engine/of this/all."

These cautions notwithstanding, we obviously also believe that these projects illustrate reasonably well the most expected effect of Albany's curricular dynamic: that is, how the idea that every classroom might be a "nexus of discourses" creates the curricular possibility—indeed, the necessity—for extended work in a preferred mode along these lines. As it has turned out, however, that dynamic has come to operate in another sphere as well, with some students pursuing the possibility that it is not only the program's classrooms that might function as a nexus for its various discourses, but single pieces of their own writing. These efforts—we call them recombinatory writings—are the subject of the next chapter.

## CHAPTER EIGHT

# Charting Courses (2): (Re)Combinatory Writings

In the last chapter, we focused on how writing by Albany's doctoral students responded to the curricular imperative to explore each course's subject from the perspectives of creative writers, students of rhetoric and composition, and literary critics,
looking specifically at how the program's constituent discourses,
as represented in the work of different students, might converge
in a single course, and how one such discourse, as represented in
the work of a single student, might be negotiated through a series of different courses. In this chapter, we turn to what can be
best understood as a reciprocal effect of this curricular design.
That is, we will consider how, as a function of the classroom
dynamic this imperative engenders, two or more of these
constitutent discourses might converge in the writing of a single
student in a single course.

In thus shifting our focus, we obviously do not mean to suggest that the writings we have been featuring until now show no
signs whatever of such convergence. One of the most clearly articulated goals of the program—or at any rate, one of its charter
proposal's most prominent predictions—is that it will "make traditional distinctions between composition, creative writing, and
literary criticism difficult to maintain" (2); and our characterizations of writing-to-get-situated as a provisional lingua franca and
our characterizations of students doing extended work in a preferred mode as "negotiating" courses both acknowledge the in-
evitability and desirability of intramural influence. It is possible
to trace that influence in the individual projects we have already
featured, perhaps most pointedly in John Latta's work on
Coleridge or Jennifer Beck's on the poetry workshop. But the

same is true in others work as well: in Wilma Kahn's engagement of Louise Wetherbee Phelps, say, or Brenda-Lee Rabine and Lois Dellert Raskin edging toward collage as they close out their effort to represent writing across the curriculum. In short, any student text written for any course in this curriculum can be understood as having had to contend with, and therefore to have been shaped by—to have been attracted or repelled, challenged or supported, and so on—the program's other discourses.

Nevertheless, if we plot such challenges to the field's traditional distinctions along a continuum, with the far right, say, representing the preservation of such distinctions and the far left their utter disappearance, we would place the writings featured in this chapter further left than any of those featured in Chapters 6 and 7. They move beyond influence in this intramural sense into the realm of full-fledged merger, yoking two or more of the program's constituent discourses to create various hybrids, and in the process overtly re-fusing—the wordplay seems particularly apt—the traditional distinctions between those discourses. Hence our characterization of these writings as a reciprocal curricular effect. When motivated writers are forced into repeated contact with both one another and a variety of discourses, the writers are bound sooner or later to find ways (or, depending on how we want to construe agency in such a context, to be led or forced to find ways) to connect those discourses. Move among them. Mate them. Match them up. Merge them. Meld them. Hence, too, our use of the term *(re)combinatory.* Not only does it foreground our concern with the mechanics of this process, the sorts of structural arrangements by which such convergences come about, but its biological resonances—referring to the formation in offspring of genetic combinations not found in the parents—allow us to do so in a way that adds a usefully organic dimension to our prevailing nuclear metaphor. These writings are the microresults of the program's macroprocesses, (by)products of its ongoing fusion experiment. As such, they are often both unfamiliar and relatively unstable: strange, evanescent, short-lived creatures. But they are also—nevertheless and insistently—vital, evidence that the program is alive and well, and crucial to its staying that way.

# By Way of Example

For the most part, students seem to work their way into this realm of (re)combinatory work in one of two ways. The first, and the one we will be considering in this section, grows out of the practice of allowing students to treat their own writing as a kind of example in the context of a given course-based project. As we have said so often, participants in this program need to find ways to bring their various intradisciplinary perspectives into courses, and exemplification is nearly always the default mode. For new instructors and new students in particular, it is simply the most obvious choice. So, for instance, students in a regularly offered course such as Writing and Revision frequently turn one of their own projects—completed or ongoing—into an object of study: they use the multiple versions of an essay or a short story (and/or the process of actually producing those versions) to exemplify something about the process of revision as it is understood from a particular disciplinary perspective. Versions of this reflexive option are regularly available in other courses as well: Composition Theory, Poetics and Literary Practice, Gender, Race and Class in English Studies, and so on. We have already considered a variation on this practice at the end of the last chapter, where—in Revisionary Poetics and Literary Practice—Ron MacLean uses his own novel (*The Beet City Chronicles*) as the focus of a critical project (his paper called "Structures"), thereby responding in a second way (his work on the text of the novel being the first) to the course's invitation to examine the structural challenges that have been a preoccupation for twentieth-century avant-garde fiction.

Not surprisingly, however, this kind of exemplification evolves in some interesting ways. As a point of entry, after all, and intentions to the contrary notwithstanding, it tends to preserve the traditional academic order of things: to reflect a discounting of student writing—an effort to keep such writing in its place by objectifying it rather than engaging it—of precisely the kind that the program is intended to challenge. In choosing a project to help us illustrate the possibilities along this line, therefore, we have opted for one which, while it may not move all that far into the realm of (re)combinatory writing—it is not what anyone is likely to call seamless—nevertheless poses its challenges to this traditional discursive order of things in ways we think are usefully visible. It was written by Barbara Chepaitis for a special topics course called Constructions of Self in the Teaching of Writing, which the course bulletin described as follows:

> This course will focus on the ways in which the "self" has been or might be represented in the teaching of writing. It will consist of three major strands of inquiry. The first will examine the construction of self offered in a sampling of extant pedagogies, particularly those that might be called "self" centered: e.g., how is self understood in William Coles' *The Plural I*, or in the workshop models described in Joseph Moxley's *Creative Writing in America*? The second strand of inquiry will focus on the members of the class: on how, that is, we understand our selves as writers, and how this understanding affects the writing classrooms we try to create. The third strand will explore possible alternatives: i.e., we will read potentially provocative texts— e.g., Lester Faigley's "Judging Writing, Judging Selves"; Carol Gilligan's *In a Different Voice*; *When Rabbit Howls* (by the Troops for Truddi Chase—a book written by multiple personalities); Walker Percy's *Lost in the Cosmos*—as points of departure for experiments with other constructions of self and the ways of teaching they might engender. ("Graduate Courses" Fall 1992 5)

Barbara's project is probably best described as an extended version of the sort of response papers we looked at in Chapter 6: it runs about ten pages, seven double- and three single-spaced; has only an informal title, "Comp and the Self"; and relies heavily on an expressive/personal register which, especially given Barbara's primary identification as a fiction writer, is reminiscent of Wilma Kahn's prose in Chapter 6. Its somewhat unusual length is a function of two complicating factors. First, Barbara is preparing for a qualifying examination in the same general area the course will cover, so that all the writing she does for the latter serves double duty. The second complicating factor is more immediate and not academic at all: she has had, her opening sentence explains, "some fairly serious medical problems" that not only prevented her from completing the previous response (so that this one does double duty in that sense as well), but that turn out to play a significant role in the writing she does for this one. ("I'll be writing more about that in a bit," promises the second sentence.) After a short opening section dealing with the overall scope of her exam preparations, Barbara's narrator announces that this particular response paper will focus on some of the early course readings, most notably Coles's *The Plural I*, Robert Brooke's *Writing and Sense of Self: Identity Negotiation in Writing Workshops* (1991), and the rather exotic *When Rabbit Howls.*[1] In general terms, the project will be concerned with how writing as a kind of naming relates to the construction of self:

> I've been thinking a lot about that very brief sentence in Coles, where he says that someone writes about their experience in order to establish a relationship with it. I've been wondering how that works and thinking that it may be related to the importance of naming, and to Truddi Chase, in this way:
>     When something is unnamed in you, it invades the whole self internally without the self having any choice about it. When something is named/written, it then has an external manifestation and you can establish a relationship with that manifestation, and make choices as to the nature of that relationship. Is this part of the whole, and if so, how much of a part? Is this holistically part of me and do I like that?
>     Lale Davidson told me about the Leslie Marmon Silko story of two Native Americans whose families had been wiped out by consumption, and how careful they are not to speak any of their family members' names, because if they do then the family will return out of pity and live on their doorsteps. But not speaking their names creates a different problem—they spread and disperse like cracking ice.
>     So there seems to be something crucial, if frightening, about naming, being willing to establish that relationship. You are invoking some creation that will then have an existence outside the perceived boundaries of the self. (Chepaitis 3–4)

Even more specifically, however, the project focuses on the role that genre plays in this relationship-building process, reacting in particular to the seeming failure of the course's rhetoric and composition-based readings to account for fiction or poetry—their failure to deal with what might elsewhere be called poetics.

Thus Coles and Brooke, she notes, "mention 'stories' briefly and vaguely, as if there was no difference between writing a story and writing an essay" (2), a tendency Barbara's narrator finds problematic, especially as a teacher of writing: "The issue is, if I ask my students to deal with the self within the construct of a piece of fiction, how is that different from asking them to deal with the self in the construct of an essay?" (3)?

By way of answering this question, she announces that she will consider her own writing practices—"Maybe I should start with myself, then, and figure out the process for me" (4)—in aid of which undertaking she makes the first of a number of switches in what might be called discursive identification. This first time she shifts from the context of rhetoric and composition into the realm of nonacademic autobiography in order to offer an abbreviated version of the sort of reflective narrative frequently favored by writing teachers (see, e.g., Coles and Vopat's *What Makes Writing Good*):

> Okay. Back to the beginning of this (letter? essay? story? Pick one.) At the beginning of the semester, I found out I was expecting. Unexpectedly expecting. Still, we were pretty happy about it, except that I didn't feel right.
>
> It was very odd. I had no sense of a presence of any kind in me at first, and I did with my first pregnancy. I thought this was just me being crazy. Then I started having pain and cramping. One doctor told me that all women suffer during pregnancy, that will be a hundred dollars thank you very much. Another sent me for an ultrasound to see if it was ectopic. All the while I kept having pain, low-grade fever, and intensely disturbing images of what was going on inside me.
>
> When I started bleeding I decided to terminate the pregnancy, mostly because I had a great sense that something was horribly wrong—and I do mean horribly—even though all the while I thought I was crazy, too, for feeling this way. The doctor who examined me previous to the termination also had no doubts that something was wrong, which reassured me somewhat. But it was after the pregnancy was terminated, when he told me that I could not have carried to term, that the experience fell into place for me.
>
> What he said was "There was too much old blood among the products of conception." (Chepaitis 4–5)

This account represents one way a writer might handle the process of naming/writing, a familiar and surely defensible means of trying to share—and perhaps thereby also to gain some sense of relationship with, control over—a traumatic experience through language. Moreover, Barbara's narrator contends, such an account could easily be carried further:

> I could tell you that I had an incomplete miscarriage and was cleaned out good. That I was scared at what I was feeling and going through. That Lale and Cindy went with me through the whole procedure so my husband could stay home with my son and worry and fix my rocking chair because he had to do something. I could tell you that I have a family history of problems in pregnancy going back a few generations. I could tell you that I felt something sick inside me. I could tell you that I felt better almost immediately, and knew that I had done the right thing, and that the experience strengthened my connection to a sense of women's history and what that means. I could say all that in an essay, or in speech to friends, or pretty much as I have. (5)

Ultimately, however, this narrator makes it clear that these modes of telling are not sufficient: either they do not, as Coles would have it, allow her to establish a relationship with her experience, or else the relationships they do enable turn out to be somehow less than fully satisfying. She goes on to report that she felt compelled to produce an alternative account—"also had to write this poem/story"—a text which, switching discursive identification again, she presents in its full, three-page, single-spaced length. Picking up on the attending physician's closing comment on the terminated pregnancy, she gives it its own title—"Old Blood"— and because of its topic, its power, and its function in our own argument, we have followed her lead in presenting the complete text. The lines are arranged as nearly as possible to match the original format:

### Old Blood

"There is old blood among the products of conception," the doctor said before the pregnancy derailed. I have tasted this, and believe it to be true.

There is old blood
    among the products of conception.
Old Blood.
         Whose blood?
My grandmother's when,
        tall, broad, Lithuanian and
angry,
    she went with the witch
to open her own cervix and drain away
captivity.
         Blood red and Lithuanian and
old as eyes slanted by invasion.        Old as the language
of oppression, long since old.

There is Old Blood among
the products of conception.
   I believe this.
My grandmother DeRosa
    Maybe screaming,
        certainly afraid, in
pain, her
    sisters helpless as she
gives birth and then
      dies.

Her blood, old as a sea swamp,    old as wolves
suckling children,       Old as cat eyes
runs through mine and
gathers in my womb
a lake   my womb.

    So I go down
    I go down, Ereshkegel, Innana, Lilith woman
Old call me      and I
go down to them,      leaving behind
2 sisters, light and young
to wait on the edge of my return
    to stand and wait
tossing ladders, cats and gowns for my return
    2 sisters, light and young
to wait, holding the moon.     I go down.

    The swamp is thick with reeds all
reeds that bend, sway, whistle and wear my face.
    Thick with whistling reeds that wear
my face and wet rushes wrapping my arms.

Father, you cannot save me now.
Mother, perhaps you can hear me you
know
I have shared your blood here, too.

I swim, entangled, reeds
whistling,  my face   and    arms    wrapped   in
rushes
all whispering
here     here     here
    Swim to a
child old child sitting
on a mushroom,    wrinkled,
grizzled face
laughing at me with two teeth and
long nails
A cup    in her sharp old hand.

This
is no baby, pink and new.
This
is no cooing child of mine
    Here among the thick wet smell of swamp birth death and
birth again to death.
    This is an Old One, called me down til I invert,
fold and unfold redouble and collapse inside to
out to
    the swamp   I   came
from     hold     inside
    like a dream of primordial life.

Sisters,
    It is scary here.
    There are things you
    don't really want to know.
Better to be daily, daily coffee, daily prayers and
    bread than taste
How Old is Blood and
The Products of conception.

Sisters, throw ladders cats and gowns.
Wait, holding the moon for me.

    I have gone down.    Old
One laughing with grizzled face, two teeth, long nails and a
cup because
she knows the burden of a gift, the gift of a burden,

Blessing and fear, fear of blessing.
Yes.    I will.    I will.
   I know now.      Alright.
   That is all.

I have come to make the offering.
I have come called to take a gift.
   For my grandmothers
One just dead,     one dead of life
   born too hard.
This is the way of it.
   Grandmothers,
      Here,
Old Blood running through me,
   A gift of the Old One where the swamp is thick, and
necessary.

   Sisters,
   She has come with the taste of Old Blood in her mouth.
   She has come to give me yesterday.
Tomorrow I will have to find
for myself.

   I drink Old Blood.    Old Blood.      My own,
drunk and fertile,
   here   here    here
My throat accepts the offering of the knife and
   It is done.

Old One, I thank you.    I take the crown.
   I will know what to do with it as I go on.

Breathe.   Now Breathe.    Breathe.

Sisters,
   light and young,
you have waited on the edge of my return. You have
helped me up from Ereshkegel's journey
with ladders, cats and gowns.
Now wipe the rushes, reeds and water from my face. Listen for
a singing man.
Now walk with me into this night and
3 sisters, light and young are here.
3 sisters, light and young, return.
3 sisters stand and look, still with wonder,
at the ancient blessing
of the crescent moon. (6–8)

It hardly seems necessary for us to comment at any length on the differences between these two accounts of the terminated pregnancy. Barbara's narrator herself suggests—switching discursive identification back again to the rhetoric-and-composition-based commentary—that the first version might be considered "the external portion—this is what happened" (9), if not precisely in literal or clinical then in commonsensical or, to borrow the story/poem's adjective, "daily" terms. This is the experience, and hence the self, as it might be constructed in terms of the narratives available for secular, workaday, American middle-class life.

As per her earlier comments on naming, the second account, "Old Blood," represents "the way it existed inside me, which I made external and available for viewing by myself and others by writing it" (Chepaitis 9). In this latter rendering, the events are set in something closer to a mythopoetic context, and they make a very different kind of sense: the blood is now "old" in a much broader way that includes the idea of inheritance; and the ordeal of the termination itself is refigured as a distinctively female quest with ritualistic overtones—still enormously painful, still deeply disturbing, but now also featuring a far more active role for the protagonist/narrator, and meaningful in ways simply not available to the other modes of telling. Barbara's narrator calls this latter mode "imagic" and, for the purposes of a course on Constructions of Self and the Teaching of Writing, wants to make the case that it is worth both valuing and teaching:

> I happen to value this. I don't know to what extent the academy does. I'm not even sure to what extent my students do, except that they're invariably pleased when I tell them it's okay to write a piece of fiction for a final project.
>
> At any rate, my belief is that the writing and reading of fiction has a definite pull on that part of us which is the symbolizing creature, and I believe that's a fairly important part. We don't need to be taught to dream. It's a natural function of our mind. And I believe that working with fiction/poetry (or that combination of the two which I'll call imagic writing because I like the term) is one way into the self - sometimes the only way, because it allows students to bypass conscious blocks on what they mean, and deal with the language of dreams. (9)

As we suggested in introducing this project, we are not anxious to claim that it moves very far into (re)combinatory territory. Not only have other projects we have considered before now also involved two or more discourses in various configurations, but some of them were considerably more finished looking, more fully disciplined. Given this one's reliance on the personal/expressive register and its function as a kind of in-class/preexam correspondence, we might easily enough classify it as another example of writing-to-get-situated: a set of reflections which, while unusually far-ranging, might nevertheless be best understood as pre- or protodisciplinary.

Ultimately, however, what leads us to contend that this project finally does move into (re)combinatory territory—that it challenges the field's traditional distinctions in a different way than the others we have considered so far—is the *relationship* it establishes among its discursively differentiated parts, and in particular its reluctance to subordinate any one such part to any of the others. Thus, whereas Jennifer Beck's "The Poetry Workshop 'after' the New Criticism"—the most obvious candidate among our previously considered projects for inclusion under this (re)combinatory heading—definitely involves two of the program's constituent discourses, creative writing and literary criticism, it visibly subordinates the latter to the former. There is the textual main event—the verse; and then, off the page proper and in a smaller typeface, there is the contrapuntal commentary—the footnotes.

By contrast the three primary discourses featured in Barbara's project—rhetoric and composition, as represented in the discussion of naming and genre; creative writing, as represented by "Old Blood"; and, from "outside" the program, the personal/autobiographical represented in the account of the troubled pregnancy—all have what amounts to equal status: they are, in effect, coordinate. Certainly this is true in a spatial sense. All appear on the page proper, in the same font and typeface, and each takes up two to three pages of the ten-page total. But it is true conceptually and rhetorically as well. Strictly speaking, none of the three gets the first or the last word, since the piece actually ends, much as it begins, with a short paragraph on the overarching issue of exam preparation.[2] And even in a less literal sense, while the

argument about the value of story and the power of imagic writing obviously frames the two narrative accounts of the pregnancy,
it does not subject them to the usual academic/disciplinary treat-
ment—it does not render them as (re)sources located somehow
"outside" this text (and perhaps outside the academy altogether),
there to be mined for useful nuggets of excerpted, analyzed, or
otherwise processed "evidence."

Rather, these three discourses are equally present in this textual sense, and equally, if not indeed more forcefully, compelled.
Thus the narrator makes it quite clear that she "had to" write
the response paper dealing with these issues and the course readings; this was, after all, both the class assignment for the preceding two weeks and part of her exam preparations. The narrator
is no less clear, however, that during the same time period she
"had to" deal with "some serious medical problems"—her page-
4 account of which begins in a rhetorical gesture of considerable
significance in this context: "Okay. Back to the *beginning*" (emphasis added). And, finally, in response to still a third sort of
imperative, the narrator reports that she "had to" write "Old
Blood," and it too appears, in full and uninterrupted—undisciplined—by commentary of any kind.

In part, then, this project puts pressure on the field's traditional distinctions as a function of its explicit argument. It contends that, if Coles is correct and people do indeed write about
their experience to establish a relationship with it, there must be
something problematic about an institutional/professional division—the one between composition and creative writing—that
seems so ready to divvy up the forms that make establishing such
relationships possible, and in the process to deny a good many
students any formal opportunity to experience the power of imagic
forms. In other words, Barbara's project questions, among other
things, the prevailing segregation of instruction in textual modes
whereby what is imagined to be the "factual" or "literal" gets
situated in rhetoric and composition, while what tends to be labeled "imaginative" or "fictive" (or, at its most pejorative, "fan-
ciful") is ceded to creative writing, or excluded from the academy
altogether.

To an even greater extent, though, it is the overall configuration of Barbara's project, this text *as* a piece of writing, that puts

pressure on the field's traditional distinctions. It might be most usefully characterized in this sense as enacting a challenge to them, with its consistent first-person narrator not only moving the reader through a decidedly nontraditional (re)combination of forms, topics, and methods, but—precisely by virtue of *being* consistent—doing so in a way that denies that reader the opportunity to situate those forms, topics, and methods in familiar or comfortable arrangements. Thus, although the project can be said to be "about" the uses of story and the potential of imagic writing, a focus which—insofar as it also highlights certain formal features—gives the piece the feel of an essay; it can just as surely be said to be "about" the trauma of this one particular terminated pregnancy. And the project is "about" this particular pregnancy not in the distanced or abstracted way it might be if either the literal or imagic rendering were drawn from the work of some third party (a published poet, say, or one of Barbara's students), or even of Barbara herself in some more distant past, but rather in a more immediate sense, whereby these renderings are represented as being at least as urgent for the narrator as any academic argument about the uses of story. Read with these urgencies as its focal point, then—and, again, with a concomitant emphasis on certain of its formal features—the project takes on the feel of a letter, or a poem, or even a prayer.

The project's challenge to the traditional disciplinary order of things boils down to this: the "I" who shepherds us through its various sections—the one who describes preparing for her examinations; who takes issue with Coles and Brooke; who is told by the doctor that she "could not have carried to term"; whose "throat accepts the offering of the knife"—this "I" resists the fragmentation and the hierarchicization that those distinctions seek to impose on her. In a word—in *the* word—she refuses those distinctions, and she makes it difficult for her readers not to do so, as well.

## Considering the Source

The second means by which students most often move into (re)combinatory writing can be traced to that most fundamental of academic practices, working from sources. We have alluded in various ways to its centrality as a feature of English doctoral education—most notably, perhaps, in Chapter 6—but its status is obvious in any case. In order to participate in any of the field's ongoing inquiries, students need to master (or, to use the formulation that is probably even more apt than usual here, need to learn and submit to) the disciplinary protocols that govern how those ongoing inquiries, as embodied in the designated appropriate disciplinary sources, are textually represented. Not surprisingly, and as we saw was the case with exemplification, Albany's curriculum complicates this process, partly because it tends to bring together onto reading lists and into classrooms sources from across various intradisciplinary divides, and so puts a strain on extant protocols; but even more because, beyond bringing these sources together, it puts a premium on their interrelatedness, encouraging students to move beyond extant protocols—those traditional distinctions again—in search of alternative connections.

Efforts in aid of this latter enterprise have taken a variety of forms. For instance, students have taken advantage of techniques as simple as rearranging source materials in different ways—in adjacent columns, say, or in alternating lines—juxtapositions which inevitably complicate the process of reading by causing one text to be read "against" another. Some students, creating what Lori Anderson calls a "transcript of sight" (7), have assembled a text by transcribing, in order, those passages from two or more sources over which the reader's gaze has traveled. More overtly rule-governed processes have been called on to make these connections as well. This response to Jasper Neel's *Plato, Derrida, and Writing,* for example, pairs selected passages from the *Phaedrus* and "Structure, Sign, and Play in the Discourses of the Human Sciences" to create an interesting conversation:

> PLATO: Let this tribute, then, be paid to memory—yearning for what we once possessed, a remembering of what our soul once saw as it made its journey with a god, looking down upon what we now assert to be real and gazing upwards at what is Reality itself.
>
> DERRIDA: Ah, the logos-zoon—the pharmakon! A beginning, of course, that is forever fictional, and the scission, far from

being an inaugural act, is dictated by the absence of any decisive beginning, any pure event that would not divide and repeat itself and already refer back to some other "beginning," some other "origin."

PLATO: Perhaps. Never mind, let it pass and tell me this instead. If a man doesn't know the truth about any given point, will he ever be able to recognize any similarity, whether great or small, between other data and that which he does not know?

DERRIDA: Any *full, absolute* presence of what *is* is impossible; not only that any full intuition of truth, any truthfilled intuition, is impossible. In the openness of this question we no longer know. This does not mean that we know nothing, but that we are beyond absolute knowledge (and its ethical, aesthetic, or religious system), approaching that on the basis of which its closure is announced and decided. Such a question will legitimately be understood as *meaning* nothing, as no longer belonging to the system of meaning.

PLATO: You might think you speak as though you make sense, but if I ask you anything about what you are saying, you go on telling me the same thing, over and over forever. (Ramjerdi "Response" 1)

Amy Schoch's "Check-Out Time Is Always Already," written for the Models of History in Literary Criticism course, exercises even more license to specifically parodic ends by casting Frederic Jameson as Freddy J, operator ("He does not own it. He would never do that." [1]) of the Untranscendable Horizon Dude Ranch. According to the color brochures in its lobby, the ranch is a "collective spa for the healing of the 'bourgeois subject . . . and its schizophrenic disintegration in our own time'" (1), a project carried out through group sessions wherein "Freddy" holds forth for the ostensible benefit of such group members as a Cooperesque cowboy named Gary and his Allenesque partner Gracie ("Say goodnight, Gracie"), with the dialogue drawn from such sources as *The Political Unconscious*, Deleuze and Guattari's *Anti-Oedipus*, Gregory Ulmer's *Teletheory*, and the television show *Mr. Ed*.

The project we have chosen to feature at length here, however, illustrates a particularly broad range of the (re)combinatory possibilities along these lines. Entitled "Composition," it was written by Jan Ramjerdi as a final project in a course we have considered before, Composition Theory, which the program's literature describes as an "introduction to composition, the field whose primary concern is writing: what it is, how it is taught and learned, and how it has come to be an object of study" (*English Graduate Study* 13). Although Jan's project, like Barbara's, runs ten numbered pages (counting the two for its Works Cited), it is mostly single-spaced and in a rather small (8-point) font, so that in word count it may be the longest piece we have considered so far. The following excerpt (a bit more than its first three pages) does a good job of introducing its most salient topical, formal, and methodological features:

### Composition

Throughout a text, or a book, or an oeuvre, the anonymous horizon (already preparing the way out) contradicts the linear model of unique order: 'The golden mountain is in California.' Life and death, this network of references, these constellations nearest to oneself, are not, for archeology, obligatory domains. The possibilities of reinscription (rather than limited and perishable individualities) is the archive in which terminal unities link. ("Foucault on Foucault")

I am dreaming I am in school. I receive a notice mailed to me saying I am to participate in a dance performance. Wondering if there is some mistake, I appear at the appointed place at the appointed hour, willing to take the chance. There are a lot of people warming up. The instructor demonstrates one by one the steps we are to do but I know I am not doing as well as the others who seem to catch on to the movements right away. I speak to the instructor during a break. I ask him if he is going to choreograph a dance. The movements we are practicing are not united; they do not flow together.

I am supposing that in every society the production of discourse is at once controlled, selected, organised and redistributed according to a certain number of procedures, whose role is to avert its powers and its dangers, to cope with chance events, to evade its ponderous, awesome materiality. (Foucault, "The Discourse on Language" 149)

In other words, the discourse scrupulously keeps within a circle of 'solidarities,'

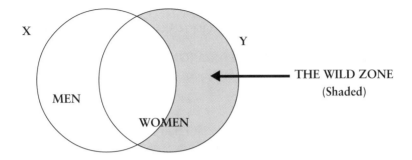

X

Y

THE WILD ZONE
(Shaded)

MEN

WOMEN

and this circle, in which "everything holds together," is that of
the readerly . . . . the solidarity of notations thus appears as a
kind of defensive weapon, it says in its way that meaning is a
force. (Barthes, *S/Z*, p. 156)

Mastery is Might, Craft, and Temperance by means of useful,
impressive principles of rhetoric like the arraying of soldiers in
battle. ("Cicero on Cicero")

HELLO, I'M ERICA JONG. ALL OF YOU LIKED MY
NOVEL *FEAR OF FLYING* BECAUSE IN IT

In a society such as our own we all know the rules of excluion.

YOU MET REAL PEOPLE. PEOPLE WHO LOVED AND
SUFFERED AND LIVED. THAT'S WHY YOU LIKED IT. MY
NEW NOVEL *HOW TO DIE SUCCESSFULLY* CONTAINS
THOSE SAME CHARACTERS. AND IT CONTAINS TWO
NEW CHARACTERS. YOU AND ME. ALL OF US ARE
REAL. GOODBYE. . . .

The most obvious and familiar of these concerns is what is
*prohibited*. We know perfectly well that we are not free to say
just anything, when we like or where we like, not just anyone,
finally, may speak of just anything. (Foucault, "The Discourse
on Language," p. 149)

WHAT WAS I SAYING? OH YES, MY NAME IS ERICA
JONG I WOULD RATHER BE A BABY THAN HAVE SEX. I
WOULD RATHER GO GOOGOO. I WOULD RATHER
WRITE: FUCK YOU UP YOUR CUNTS THAT'S WHO I AM
THE FUCK WITH YOUR MONEY I'M NOT CATERING

TO YOU ANY MORE I'M GETTING OUT I'M RIPPING UP MY SKIN I HURT PAIN OH HURT ME PAIN AT THIS POINT IS GOOD. ME ERICA JONG WHE WOO WOO I AM ERICA JONG I AM ERICA JONG. (Kathy Acker, *Hello, I'm Erica Jong*)

What was I saying? Oh yes.

What I was going to say was that I think writing must be formal; the art must be respected . . .

> I tell the instructor I have no formal training in dance and my receiving the notice must have been a mistake. He laughs noncommitally. The other students encourage me to stick with it—saying it doesn't make that much difference whether or not I've had training. I decide to stay with it for awhile. If shortly before the performance it becomes clear I will spoil their act, I'll drop out. I continue to practice with them—not doing very well but I keep trying to imitate the others.

for if one lets the mind run loose, it becomes egotistical; personal, which I detest. At the same time the irregular fire must be there; and perhaps to loose it one must begin by being chaotic, but not appear in public like that. (Virginia Woolf, *A Writer's Diary*, p. 67–68)

Let us take a simple example: In the early eighteenth century, a beating of wings designated from afar the tangled unity of mass discourse, a labyrinth in which I have no face. The difficult problem of location in all this fog, whether written or spoken, may, in fact, be regarded as the primitive (not entirely foreign) law of 'things' (effaced, or put in parentheses) anterior to discourse, or an animal in a field of possible forms or a residual (remanent) structure of embarrassed stability, or an initial region of twisted (or translated, or deformed, or travestied, or perhaps even repressed) play, where I am lying in wait for me, over here, laughing at you. ("Foucault on Foucault")

You only have to look at the Medusa straight on to see her. And she's not deadly. She's beautiful and she's laughing. (Helene Cixous, "The Laugh of the Medusa," p. 315)

Having naturally done this I naturally was a little troubled with it when I read it. I became like the others who read it. One does, you know, expecting that when I reread it myself I lost myself in it again. Then I said to myself this time it will be different and I began. I did not begin again I just began. In this beginning naturally since I at once went on and on very soon there were pages and pages and pages more and more elaborated creating a more and more continuous present including more and more using of everything and continuing more and more beginning and beginning and beginning. (Gertrude Stein, "Composition as Explanation," p. 518)

Why are we doing this? I ask the instructor. He says a woman has been condemned to death. We will perform the dance at her execution. We will wear black bands with bells on our wrists. Who is this woman? I ask.

This was a dream I was dreaming 12 years ago when I was trying to begin, beginning to try to begin to begin writing, but I didn't know how. I thought there was a WAY to begin, which I didn't know there wasn't in the beginning. I was thinking:

> 1. Now a whole is that which has a beginning, a middle and an end. A beginning is that which does not necessarily follow something else, but after which something else naturally is or follows. (Aristotle, *Poetics*, p. 418)

I didn't know

> Beginning again and again is a natural thing even when there is a series. (Stein, "Composition as Explanation" p. 516)

I was thinking:

> 2. One should construct plots that are dramatic and that involve a single action with a beginning, a middle and an end (an end is the opposite [of a beginning] it naturally follows something else, either necessarily or for the most part, and has nothing after it), so that it may produce the appropriate pleasure just as if it were a single and complete picture. (Aristotle, *Poetics*, p. 418 and 426)

And

> 3. Also a fine picture or any fine thing composed of parts should have these parts regulated and should also have an appropriate magnitude. (Aristotle, *Poetics*, p. 418)

But

> No one thinks these things when they are making when
> they are creating what is the composition, naturally no
> one thinks, that is no one formulates until what is to be
> formulated has been made. (Stein, "Composition as Ex-
> planation," p. 516) (Composition 1–4)

In explaining why we regarded Barbara's project as (re)combinatory, we emphasized the *relationship* it established among its discursively differentiated parts: the way it brought together, and in particular coordinated, topics, forms, and methods traditionally associated with rhetoric and composition, creative writing, and personal autobiography. As this three-page excerpt should begin to suggest, Jan's project involves a comparable kind of relationship-building carried out on a much more ambitious scale. In all, "Composition" comprises some seventy of these single-spaced entries, drawn from over twenty sources: Foucault, Barthes, Acker, Stein, Aristotle, and the others appearing in this section, but also Julia Kristeva, Patti Smith (*Babel*), Millicent Dillon ("Jane Bowles: Experiment as Character"), Jacques Derrida, Adrienne Rich, Hayden Herrera, Jenny Holzer, Elaine Showalter, and more of the author's own writings. And, as this list suggests, these sources represent a referential breadth that not only includes the categories the Albany program customarily uses to identify its constituent discourses, but also one that rather swamps them, renders them inadequate: yes, literary criticism (Barthes, Artistotle, and Dillon, say), rhetoric and composition (Cicero), and creative writing (Acker, Smith, Ramjerdi)—but also, or at least more accurately, critical theory, literary biography, autobiography, feminist theory, personal writing, and so on.

The result is a text that mounts an even more serious challenge to the maintenance of the field's traditional distinctions than did Barbara's. This challenge is not topical, as to some extent it was for Barbara's project. While "Composition" can be said to have a number of threads—to deal with the agency of the subject in discourse (e.g., Foucault, Barthes); the situation of the Euro-American woman-as-writer/artist in the twentieth century (e.g., Woolf, Stein); and the story of what the narrator of the "I am dreaming I am in school" piece has gone through in trying to become a woman writer[3]—it seems to us that these coalesce sufficiently that we can say the piece is "about" the agency of the female subject in discourse, with a special emphasis on that subject as a writer/artist in the twentieth century. In this sense, it represents a topic which—especially by contrast with the matter of a troubled pregnancy—would be reasonably workable and disciplinarily relevant for literary criticism, rhetoric and composition, or creative writing even as traditionally configured.

Still, if the project's handling of topic doesn't generate much (re)combinatory power—does not pose much of a challenge to the field's traditional distinctions—its approaches to form and method clearly do. Its spatially striking form, of course, is the most visible feature of this challenge. As with Barbara's project, we have no convenient generic label for it; even *collage*, which is probably the term most likely to be invoked, would seem to be less a generic categorization than an admission that we cannot actually provide one. In this instance, however, we do have something more in terms of an academic genealogy. An authorial endnote explains that the "idea for the form of this paper came from reading 'For the Etruscans' by Rachel Blau DuPlessis" (Ramjerdi, "Composition" 8). This lead turns out to be of limited value as far as generic labels go. Although DuPlessis offers a trio of influences—Robert Duncan's *H. D. Book,* Virginia Woolf's essays, and her own letters—the closest she comes to actually naming the form is to say that "many people have reinvented the essay" (288).

The DuPlessis lead is considerably more helpful, however, as a guide for how one might *read* "Composition." To some extent, this is simply a matter of gaining contrastive leverage. Seeing what kinds of sources DuPlessis assembles and how she deploys them makes comparable strategies in Jan's project relatively more visible and more comprehensible. In a far more fundamental way, though, "For the Etruscans" offers insight into the relationship between form and method that is central to both pieces. For DuPlessis, Etruscan functions as an emblem for what she refers to as "female aesthetic" (the absence of article is deliberate), the idea being that the latter finds itself in a cultural predicament that is comparable to the philological situation of the former:

represents, that is, an undeciphered language ("'the last of the important languages to require translating'" [Wellard qtd. in DuPlessis 272]) which—in the Latin-speaking world for the one, and a male-dominated universe of discourse for the other—"can be heard, if one chooses to mouth it, but not comprehended. Pondering is not to be expected, so why bother?" (DuPlessis 274). In announcing that this piece is *for* the Etruscans, then, DuPlessis is indicating that she will be operating in a textual mode that in fact *does* bother, one that bespeaks the female aesthetic. She *will* be mouthing it, in the hope that it will be recognized and comprehended as such by those in her audience—the culture's feminized Other, say—who will know it when they see it. In this sense, the form of "For the Etruscans" is integral to—maybe identical with—DuPlessis's method.

Jan's project represents a similar enterprise, carried out on behalf of ("for") the Euro-American female writer/artist as subject in discourse. One of her sources, as we indicated, is Millicent Dillon's "Jane Bowles: Experiment as Character," an essay (itself quite conventional) in which Dillon tries to account for Bowles's long-standing "anguish" at being unable to complete what would have been her last novel, *Out in the World*—"an anguish," suggests Dillon, "that she took to be a punishment for some nameless sin," and which "finally became punishment through the instrumentality of a stroke that afflicted her when she was forty" (140). In a section that begins near the end of page 4, "Composition" alternates between (what we eventually learn is) Dillon's account of Bowles's difficulties and passages from the notebooks and fiction of the "I" who dreamed she was in dance class, interrupted near the end with one very telling excerpt from Gertrude Stein:

> Notebook after notebook of uncompleted fragments testify to her trying to find her way, starting, breaking off
>
> > The last thing I saw before my head hit the sidewalk
> > The last thing I can describe with no doubt, no questions about
> > that imposed itself visually with no blurring
> > that imposed a lucid

last thing that I am sure of
last thing I can visually articulate

and beginning again,

Floating away from Molly like some page ripped out of a
kid's book
On an ultrafirm mattress lay
Rigorously adhering to my recollection of the incident
the last thing I recall seeing before my head hit the
sidewalk, the last clearly focussed image

sometimes with almost the same words, sometimes with a new
name for a character, or a new character, or a new set of characters.

Unnatural lights illuminate the blond child curled unconscious five stories
A child in pink pajamas
The image is the last
Faded, brown
The last thing she saw clearly before her head hit the sidewalk was the billboard above the brick mattress factory
on West Street flying away from her like a page torn from
a bedtime storybook. On the bare mattress a faded child
with blond curls and pink pajamas browning in the city
grime, unphased, sleeping, tucked safely five stories above
the sidewalk where Marie's head hit cracking her glasses.
("Credible Accounts")

Each time it was as if she had to take a flying leap to get started.
It would start, it would break off, it would start again. (Millicent
Dillon, "Jane Bowles: Experiment as Character," p. 140)

The last thing she saw before her head hit the sidewalk
was the billboard suspended over the mattress factory.
There was the sleeping child, a child in pajamas, a child
with blond curls, a child torn from the pages of a
bedtime story, an angel, her guardian angel asleep,
sleeping, her eyes closed. The sidewalk cracked. ("Credible Accounts")

Since the publication of the biography in 1981, . . . . I have
come to look at those fragments in another way, as a mode of
expression that was attempting to manifest itself through her

but that she could not accept. The cast of her mind and feelings was expressing its intention through this form—through fragmentation and repetition—

> As I was saying every one always is repeating the whole of them. As I was saying sometimes it takes many years of hearing the repeating in one before the whole being is clear to the understanding of one who has it as a being to love repeating, to know that always every one is repeating the whole of them. (Stein, *The Making of Americans*, p. 267)

but she took the result to be only failure. (Millicent Dillon, "Jane Bowles: Experiment as Character," p. 140)

I was considering myself a dancer at my own execution.

I was considering myself a dancer at my own execution. (Ramjerdi "Composition" 4–5)

You can see how this works. The "I" of the dream, the would-be writer, is represented as reenacting in her notebooks and fiction the pattern Dillon ascribes to Bowles, trying again and again to get it (somehow) right, but always seeing her efforts—particularly her affinity for the textual strategies conventionally derided as fragmentation or repetition—as "only failure." Hence the school dream: for a woman who wants to write, acceding to the master in the dance of discourse is likely to be—is designed to be—fatal, to make her a dancer at her own execution, to rub her out. In one sense, then, "Composition" is a preventive against or an antidote for the kind of discursive toxicity that poisoned Bowles: it represents "a mode of expression that was attempting to manifest itself through" the "I am dreaming" narrator, an approach to (auto)biography that simultaneously tells her story and saves her (discursive) life. At the same time, however, it is—like "For the Etruscans"—a public performance in that mode: a sustained discourse in a similarly encrypted language and—especially in the somewhat narrower context of Albany's programmatic ambitions—something of a (wo)manifesto concerning the possibilities of (re)combinatory writing.

## Challenging the Primacy of Print

We do not want to end this chapter without at least mentioning, however briefly, two other modes of student work—or, to be more accurate, student *composing*—that have demonstrated considerable promise as outlets for the program's recombinatory energies. Both of them involve media other than, or at least in addition to, the typed or typeset page.

The first we will call, for want of a more adequate term, performance: projects students take on that give primacy to the body—usually but not always including the voice—operating in some space. It is one of the peculiarities of English Studies that despite the central role teaching has played in its institutional survival (despite the fact, that is, that the primary means by which nearly all of its members have made their living has depended heavily on their ability to operate their bodies and voices in the class- and conference-room space), such ability has rarely been considered an important dimension of either the discipline or its doctoral training. This is not to say that the field and its doctoral programs have had no performative dimension whatever. Take a stroll past the windows of any series of college English classrooms, or take a peek into any series of MLA or AWP or CCCC convention sessions, and you will be able to discern various permutations of what might be called the field's performative parameters: the acceptable physical postures, ranges of movement, modes of dress, pitches and paces and tones of speaking voices, and so on. For the most part, you will be witnessing the operation of default parameters, limits set far more by an unarticulated pattern of socialization than any overt or explicit disciplinary training. Nevertheless—and especially in their variation—they serve as a good reminder of what is logically obvious: that English doctoral students compose their professional identities, and have those identities composed, in this more behavioral sense, too, along lines that reflect the field's internal divisions.

What a number of students in the Albany program have found (what the program's dynamic has encouraged them to find) is that performance is a useful medium for fusion experiments, a largely unpoliced arena in which to (re)combine elements from across intradisciplinary lines. We are at a serious technical disadvantage here in trying to represent such experiments (which is one of the reasons we have opted not to feature them at length). Still, it is not hard to imagine how techniques derived from English's own past or imported from the performing arts, the pulpit, various countercultural movements, and any number of other sources can be brought to bear in a doctoral classroom, and we have seen quite a range. In The History of English Studies course, for example, members of the class are cast in roles drawn from accounts of how the reservation schools sought to "civilize" Native American children—they have to speak the parts, say the words; in Theories and Practice of Creativity, a class takes over the basement of a house to work out the dynamics of various creation myths; in Constructions of Self and the Teaching of Writing, the class as a whole offers a public performance that juxtaposes texts borrowed or adapted from such divergent sources as Dr. Seuss ("I am Sam. Sam I am."), Donald Morton and Mas'ud Zavarzadeh ("This time, the pressure is so radical that the 'individual' has been rendered historically obsolete"), and Whitman ("I dote on myself, there is that lot of me and all so luscious") variously spoken, sung, and chanted (with audience participation) as a way of putting pressure on competing conceptions of "self." The list could go on and on: marionette and puppet shows, room-sized floor puzzles, poems performed in multiple voices, multimedia presentations (e.g., video- and audiotape supplemented with PowerPoint), in-class presentations for voice and saxophone, installations—you get the idea.

In our experience, many faculty (and some students, too) are at a loss in the face of such activities—at best bemused, at worst hostile—and we expect this will be true for many of our readers, as well. For all the field's recent critical preoccupation with materiality and the body, and despite a longstanding admiration among many of its members for certain kinds of performance, most of the disciplinary pressure in English Studies seems to be directed toward something like disembodied practice. If we absolutely cannot have the text-that-speaks-itself ("I'll read it when it comes out"), we are inclined to want only the most limited reminder of the body whose physical energies make the words appear: the talking-head-behind-the-podium is perhaps the best emblem (and even then we often prefer to "read along"). Given this context, the sorts of performance practices we have alluded to here are generally regarded as unserious/gimmicky/not what one expects from "real intellectuals." Indeed, even at Albany—where the willingness to tolerate experiment has had to be considerable—no student to date has completed a dissertation with a substantial performative component. (Jonathan Post's "The Container of Collective Performance" [1994], an argument that draws on some of these curricular activities, probably comes closest.) But this does not mean no one ever should or will. While the performative in this sense clearly represents territory into which the vast majority of graduate professors are not equipped, eager, or even willing to go—perhaps *because* it represents such territory—it may well prove in the end to be a disciplinary space wherein the field's otherwise seemingly intractable tensions can play out in fruitful new (re)combinations.

The other mode of student work we need to acknowledge here—the program's other major challenge to the primacy of print to date—we can label electronic or, perhaps, digital: projects students take on using technologies made available by the computer revolution. Developments in this area are hardly unique to the Albany program; a quick check of the Web for sites dealing with graduate courses in English Studies makes that clear enough. And, at Albany—again, as elsewhere—students always face constraints imposed by the limits of infrastructure and support. Nevertheless, the program has spawned a range of projects: Web pages of various kinds and any number of course-based listserves, but also multi- or hypermedia projects (featuring, for example, scanned-in manuscripts of Dickinson poems along with various print texts, audio readings, visuals, and music); so-called hypertext fictions using software such as StorySpace (along with experiments to see what happens to other kinds of writing—such as argumentative academic prose—when deployed through such software); collaborative large-group compositions composed in real-time using synchronous networking software; and so on.

There is no simple or direct way to compare student work in this area with those based in performance; the two do not even represent mutually exclusive categories. Still, we are inclined to say that, if only for generational reasons, the students tend to be even further ahead of the faculty in this electronic realm. More and more of the former enroll with fluencies the latter will simply never have. Thus, while it remains to be seen, both locally and nationally, exactly how the graduate professors of English Studies will come to terms with these media, and while no Albany student has yet submitted a dissertation grounded in this mode, we have no doubt whatever that these technologies will play a crucial role in the future of the field's doctoral education. And this will be all the more true in a fusion curriculum, in which the virtual space they make available—again, a space largely untrammeled by the extant professoriate—provides considerable opportunity for (re)combining elements from across otherwise troubled intradisciplinary lines.

## CHAPTER NINE

# Writing beyond Coursework: The Qualifying Examination and the Dissertation

At the very heart of our account of the Albany program in Chapter 5 was a section called "Be Sure to Get It in Writing." Its argument was pretty straightforward: given the program's ambitions, students enrolled in its courses must be invited to work from their perspectives as creative writers, students of rhetoric and composition, and literary scholars not only in terms of how and what they read, think, and say, but also—and most crucially—in how and what they write. In this chapter, we follow that line of reasoning to its postcoursework conclusion. Again, the argument is simple enough. If students are consistently invited to write from their various intradisciplinary perspectives during seventy-plus hours of required and elective classes, it only makes sense that they be given the same opportunity for the purposes of their two major post-coursework writing projects, the qualifying examination and the dissertation. From the students' point of view, no other policy makes sense. What good would all those prior invitations to advance their ongoing work be if in the end, when the degree and not just a grade was on the line, such work was disqualified?

But of course such a policy makes curricular sense, too, and for essentially the same reason. By rights, and indeed by definition, the most significant results of the program's fusion experiment—or at least its most significant results in terms of what students will write while they are still officially enrolled—will show up in the texts they produce for these two final, formalized occasions. It is therefore in the interests of the program and its sponsoring faculty that these occasions be handled in ways that are consonant with the curriculum out of which they emerge.

## An Integrated Structure

Ultimately—which is to say, for the purposes of this book, in real academic life—qualifying examinations and dissertations are governed less by policies than by faculty practices; this was true in the Magisterial tradition, and it is true for "Writing, Teaching, and Criticism," too. Thus, just as Albany students have to negotiate with individual professors regarding the writing they do in courses, so they have to negotiate with a faculty committee regarding the writing they do for the qualifying examination and the dissertation. In both contexts, obviously, faculty have the final say on what is and what is not acceptable.

What policies *can* do, however, is establish a context for those negotiations: express, in principles and procedures, the agreed-upon spirit of the enterprise. In this sense, two features of Albany's examination and dissertation policy are most important. The first has to do with the way the proposal describes the options available for the dissertation, a description entirely consistent in its flexibility with the curricular dynamic we have been tracing over the last four chapters:

> Dissertations may take a variety of forms and display a variety of focuses. They may be prose fiction, poetry, drama, criticism, empirical research, or some mixture. They may focus on the imaginary, the theoretical, the historical, the interpretive, the pedagogical, the linguistic, etc. (8–9)

The second feature has to do with the relationship between this open-ended policy on what the dissertation can be and the qualifying examination students need to pass before they can officially begin that final project. Like its counterpart in the Magisterial tradition, Albany's qualifying examination is intended to serve as both an important emblem and the penultimate rite of passage: to be, as the proposal puts it, "a microcosm of the program," a "site for integration" that "brings into play the various focuses of the program: composition, rhetoric, poetics, theory, pedagogy, language, and history" (7–8). In the context of this particular program, this means that the qualifying serves more as a bridge than a hurdle: it is intended to make the candidates' transition from coursework through to dissertation as seamless—as fully integrated—as possible.

To that end, candidates begin the examination process by working with a three-member faculty committee to identify what the proposal characterizes as "a specific area of study," a focus that "grows out of work done in the context of courses" but that also "looks forward to the dissertation" (7). Next, this committee and student consult on the design and administration of the three-part exam itself. Part one must be a three-hour written test in which the student is asked to analyze "the issues and questions that currently define the area of study" (7). Parts two and three, by contrast, are orals (in practice about one hour long). The first has a historical focus—must be concerned with the "issues and questions that have defined the area of study in the past"—while the second explores "a specific problem for research" (7) in the student's area of study.

It is crucial to note, however, that these orals are based on a pair of what are called "working papers," prepared by the student and submitted to the committee some two weeks in advance of the corresponding oral examination sessions. And these texts turn out to be a crucial link between examination and dissertation, the instruments most responsible for realizing the idea of the former "look[ing] forward" to the latter. It might be more accurate to say that students are urged to construct these working papers in a kind of dialectic with their dissertation plans. That is, when the proposal declares that the working papers may turn out to "serve as a draft of a dissertation prospectus", and that, in fact, "[s]uccessful completion of the examination insures that the dissertation is under way" (8), it is also clearly implying that a student must have a good idea what that dissertation is likely to be—how else would it be possible to thus assess its progress?

## The Qualifying Examination

As a function of this integrated structure, the qualifying examination as an occasion for writing enjoys a range of variation considerably greater than would have been typical in the Magisterial tradition. Since the exam is linked so closely with the dissertation, and since the dissertation is defined so flexibly, the possible range of variation on the former as an occasion for writing is also substantial. This is least true for part one, the three-hour written test which, while it makes an important contribution to the examination and dissertation process overall, does so far less as a formalized occasion for writing than as a framework for shaping preparation, especially in terms of the latitude it affords students in constituting a current scene for their specific area of study. Because students have a considerable hand not only in choosing the area of study but in determining how that area will be constructed, they are able to bring together in their preparatory reading lists texts from across the full spectrum of the program's constituent discourses. So, for example, Joanne Tangorra's examination—which we will rely on most heavily for illustrative purposes here—can be characterized, at least by way of brief introduction, as examining the "I" of women's poetry (including her own) and the "I" of students' autobiographical writings in the context of feminist and postmodern/poststructuralist theories, and of doing so in aid of (re)considering her own practices as a writer, reader, and teacher. The two hundred or so titles she assembles on her preparatory lists, therefore— from some portion of which she will construct a current scene— represent a concomitantly wide range of sources: feminist theory/ women('s) writing (e.g., Deborah Cameron's *The Feminist Critique of Language,* Trinh Minh-ha's *Woman, Native, Other,* Monique Wittig's *The Straight Mind*); women poets/women's poetry (e.g., Helen Barolini's *The Dream Book: An Anthology of Writings by Italian American Women*); autobiography, with a particular concern for gender (e.g., Shari Benstock's *The Private Self: The Theory and Practice of Women's Autobiographical Writings,* William Spengemann's *The Forms of Autobiography*); twentieth-century poetry and poetics (e.g., Tess Gallagher's *A Concert of Tenses,* Robert Hass's *Human Wishes,* Marjorie Perloff's *Poetic License*); and, finally, the teaching of writing (e.g., Wendy Bishop's *Released into Language: Options for Teaching Creative Writing,* Peter Elbow's *Writing without Teachers,* Susan Miller's *Textual Carnivals*).

As even this brief sampling should make clear, however, the actual writing of this portion of the exam is almost inevitably anticlimactic: three hours of on-the-spot composing—even in answer to a single question (and the number of such questions is determined by each examining committee)—clearly will not allow a student to get very far in working with such a range of materials. Between the rhetorical situation and the constraints imposed on time and resources (i.e., no texts or notes allowed), and despite whatever advantages word processing might offer for what has traditionally been a longhand exercise, the writing *as* writing tends toward a performance not unlike the compulsories once so crucial in figure skating: everyone involved knows that the performer needs to cover a certain agreed-upon ground, and do so in a way that allows her or him also to display an acceptable range of recognizably disciplined movements.[1] Thus Joanne's effort runs a game six single-spaced typed pages (in an 8-point font). In the following passage from a section called "Feminist Theory," the rhetorical stance, the mode of argument, and the forms of evidence are all fairly typical not only of Joanne's overall performance but also of the kind of writing this portion of the qualifying exam evokes for most examinees most of the time:

> The humanist/postmodern debate over the subject is raging within feminist circles as in the humanities in general. This debate has largely been coded as Anglo-American vs. French theory and has centered since the 1970s on issues of language, identity and sexual difference. Gilbert and Gubar, for example, on the "humanist" side, posit two poles: the mirror critics and the "vamps." Mirror critics, of which they are a part, assume that there is a "knowable history" and that texts are authored by people whose lives are affected by material and social conditions. They work within established categories of race, class, gender and literary culture. On the other side (French theorists such as Kristeva, Irigaray, and their American followers like Toril Moi and Peggy Kamuf) are those critics who reject the "hegemony" of such categories. Moi, for example, claims that we must proclaim with Barthes the "death of the author" if we are not to reinscribe patriarchal formulations and keep the binary opposition of man/woman intact. Similarly, Kamuf rejects what she perceives to be the patriarchal "mask of the proper name" and the biological determinism that goes along

with assumptions of a distinctly "female" signature. ("Qualifying" 2)

The working papers, however, present a very different sort of opportunity, providing students not only with more time (typically six to twelve months) and textual space (typically thirty to fifty pages, typed, double-spaced), but also with considerably more topical, formal, and methodological license as well. Much of the greater topical flexibility results from the shift in format, in particular the relocation of the interrogatory dynamic that pervades part one from the actual composing to the subsequent oral sessions. Thus, while the intradisciplinary intersections that are so important in constituting Joanne's area of study are certainly referred to in part one of the exam, their interaction is both more visible and more pointed in her first, historically oriented working paper. Indeed, the difference is apparent even before the text proper begins, in the title and epigraphs—devices not practically available for part one—and carries on from there:

**Changing "Subjects": The Shift from Expressivist
to Social/Critical Perspectives in Feminist Criticism
and Composition Theory**
"The new tradition exists. . . . It is a poetry whose poet speaks
as a woman, so that the form of her poem is an extension of
herself. . . . A poetry that is real, because the voice that speaks
it is as real as the poet can be about herself"
—Susan Juhasz
*Naked and Fiery Forms* (205)

". . . Gradually, a new and mysterious standard began to emerge.
That writing was most fun and rewarding to read that somehow felt most 'real.' It had what I am now calling voice. At the
time I said things like, 'It felt real, it had a kind of resonance, it
somehow rang true.'"
—Peter Elbow
*Writing With Power* (283)

Voice. Truth. The "real." Admittedly, I take the two quotes out of their respective contexts, erasing for the moment the myriad and critical differences between American feminist criticism and composition theory in order to foreground, at least provisionally, a "common" strain in their respective histories of the last two decades. Both Juhasz and Elbow have emerged as representative "voices" of an expressivist tradition in American feminism and composition, respectively, committed to the view of writing as self-expression—an extension of the speaking subject's consciousness which ultimately, via her inscription on the page, leads to individual and even collective empowerment. To be sure, American feminism and composition theory are not theoretical "unities," and neither are their respective expressivist traditions. Nevertheless, this view of writing (and its corresponding trope of "process") has been pronounced in American feminist readings of 20th-century women's poetry and in expressivist pedagogies that similarly privilege a poetics/rhetoric . . . of "self-revelation," whether in the autobiographical poem or personal essay. This privileging extends to teaching and writing practices in creative writing— particularly in the injunction to student writers to "write about what you know" (Hampl 24).

Increasingly, this view has been challenged by theorists in each field of study whose investigations of the "subject" of writing have come to be informed (rather than "transformed," as I will discuss later) by "critical theory" (and I use the term generally as a referent for theories of a destabilized "I" in which the subject is not perceived to be a unified, stable, transcendent entity, whose self is expressed by language, but rather a contradicted "self" constituted in/by discourse). The expressivist strain in each field has been challenged on the grounds that its "subversiveness" is perhaps "more apparent than real" (Berlin, "Rhetoric," 487) and that it harbors an "unrecognized romanticism" (Montefiore 11). Based as it is on paradigms of a universal (ostensibly male) subject, at best it is seen to replace a male-centered tradition with a female-centered/student-centered tradition without challenging the tradition itself and its underlying patriarchal assumptions. (Tangorra, "Qualifying" 1–2)

The greater license in terms of formal and methodological options, meanwhile, tends to be exercised even more fully in the second working paper, the one in which the candidate lays out a specific problem for research. Certainly this was the case for Joanne. Her effort, entitled "Autobiographical Acts: On Poetry, Poetics and Pedagogy," is a thirty-eight-page project (typed, double-spaced, with four pages of Works Cited) organized into eight sections, each marked by a Roman numeral. Its aim—to borrow from the title of a Susan Miller book she cites in both working papers—is to help find a way to rescue the subject of writing: specifically, to work toward a feminist poetics and a feminist writing pedagogy that, on the one hand, "reject[s] the notion of the self-in-writing as a pure writing effect—a fiction," but that also, on the other hand, "acknowledge[s] the 'fictiveness' of the enterprise" of writing such a self (17). In an effort to suggest how form and method are integrated toward this purpose, we will present nearly all of the project's first three sections, a total of about eight pages. This is a lot of excerpting, but it represents the only way to really get at this integration.

To begin with, pages one through three of the first section (it is four pages overall) comprise a segment of what Joanne will later call "narrative criticism" (7). Centered on what is ordinarily considered a disciplined/disciplinary activity—that is, the narrator's reading of the Nancy Miller book from which the title of this project has been adapted (*Getting Personal: Feminist Occasions and Other Autobiographical Acts*)—the writing is nevertheless constructed as a sort of dated diary entry, and cast in a progressive present tense. Here are approximately its first three pages:

### I. Hot Coffee, Apple Pie and Shopping in the Bronx
### 26 June 1994

I have been thinking about how to theorize the "I" of women's poetry (including my own) and students' autobiographical writings; the intersections between my writing, reading and teaching practices. This, I think, will be the subject of an essay on my poetics and pedagogy. Today, I come across a chapter entitled "Teaching Autobiography" in Nancy Miller's *Getting Personal: Feminist Occasion and Other Autobigraphical Acts*. In a Coda to the chapter, Miller tells a "story" about going shopping with her mother at the "old" Loehmann's on Jerome Ave. and 183rd Street in the Bronx (139–141). The occasion for the story is Miller's account of a pilgrimage she makes to Loehmann's at the end of her first semester of teaching at Lehman College (to which she had come by way of Barnard, Columbia, and Manhattan) after reading in *The New York Times* that the store would soon be closing its doors. Miller's pilgrimage to this "site of archaic female bonding rituals" fails to evoke the Proustian experience she hopes for when she "hits the racks"; nothing magical happens—in part because Loehmann's wasn't really her mother's "store" (she preferred

Klein's and May's where you could return things). But reading Vivian Gornick's *Fierce Attachments*—the autobiography that made Miller want to teach autobiography and also to write one (138), an autobiography that she has come to think of as her own—captures the heart of what going shopping with her mother really meant. What "got to" her "by its unnerving proximity to my own experience is a detail in the staging of the mother's need (demand is closer to the truth of it) for hot coffee" (140). . . .

As I read Miller's Coda about shopping with her mother, I am overwhelmed by its "unnerving proximity" to my own experience. Suddenly, I am thrown back in time, remember shopping excursions to Loehmann's with my own mother, leaving City Island mid-morning, driving up Pelham Parkway past the Bronx Zoo, the Botanical Gardens, the Italian neighborhood where my grandparents had lived, to Fordham Road, crossing Jerome Avenue in search of a bargain (though Loehmann's was not my "mother's" store either—she preferred Klein's or Bloomingdale's, in Westchester); then stopping for lunch at a coffee shop, occasionally Schraft's, where women of all ages sat in red vinyl booths with crisp new shopping bags bulging in the seats beside them like overstuffed luncheon guests. I am particularly struck by Miller's description of her mother's need/demand for hot coffee (as Miller was with Gornick's) and remember my own embarrassment when my mother sent waiters and waitresses scuttling back and forth to the kitchen until her soup or coffee was hot enough—so hot it "almost burned the tongue." (I think, too, of all the times my husband has expressed amazement at how I can drink my soup or coffee when it's "so hot.")

In fact, I identify so thoroughly with the details of Miller's Coda that the many differences between us are erased. To cite just a few: I am Italian not Jewish, and even though I spent a large part of my adult life living in Manhattan, I did not grow up there as Miller did . . . I am a poet and a teacher of writing; Miller is not. As Miller says of her relationship to Gornick, "the ways in which, according to the checkpoints of locational identity, I am like her are also ways in which I'm not like her at all . . . and yet despite these important differences, I felt written by this book," as I feel written by Miller's Coda.

Location: I read Miller's book in a rented house in Albany—to which I have come by way of the Bronx, Manhattan, Maryland and Virginia. I am overcome by nostalgia, the slippage between one "life" and another. In fact, Miller's Coda does provide something of a Proustian experience for me. I am dizzy with identification, with recognition, with the sheer "untheorized" joy of shared experience. How to contain it? How to "write" it? How to "situate" myself as a (woman) reader/writer in relation to Miller, Gornick, their texts? How to situate my reading of these texts [in regard] to my writing of them—about autobiography? ("Qualifying" 1–4)

However, this meditation on the relationship between discourse and identity—on what it feels like, but also what it might mean, to be thus "written by" stories (within stories within stories)—does not close out section I. Instead, the fourth page, a single long paragraph, is set off from what has come before and is marked, following Nancy Miller, as a coda. In it, the narrator tells still another story, this one concerning her efforts to recount for her own mother her experience of Miller's mother-oriented story (which of course includes Miller's experience of Gornick's mother-oriented story), a telling that in turn prompts the narrator's mother to tell a story about her experience with *her* mother (i.e., the narrator's grandmother). This shift in context expands the scope of the narrator's investigation of this particular manifestation of the discourse/identity dynamic, but it also raises new complications. Notice, for example, how the narrator is unable to control her mother's reaction—is unable, that is, to communicate directly, to induce in her mother her own "dizzy . . . identification," her "sheer 'untheorized' joy of shared experience"; and notice, too, the roles that marriage and language play in this new (story of a) story (which is also, at its chronological base, the oldest of these stories so far):

> Coda: I call my mother, who still lives with my father on City Island, to tell her about Miller's essay, wanting her to experience the same sense of identification, to say, yes, someone has written "our" story. But Miller's story—which I have co-opted and re-told through the lens of my own life—generates my mother's own autobiographical act, one that converges with and diverges from my own (and Miller's and Gornick's) intersecting at some points but not at others. My mother is white, middle-class, and "ethnic," as is Miller, but she is not Jewish; yet in some ways she is perhaps more like Gornick than like me—her Italian-American daughter. Like Gornick, my mother is the child of immigrants. I am not. I often forget this difference between us. Over the phone, my mother tells me a story

about taking my grandmother, an Italian immigrant who never learned to speak English (though I remember many conversations with her despite the fact that I didn't speak Italian at the time) to a podiatrist on Jerome Avenue. My grandmother was having trouble walking and though there were podiatrists on 187th Street (where my grandfather owned *latterie*—dairy stores) all of their offices had too many steps for my grandmother to negotiate. After doing some "research," my mother found a podiatrist whose office had an elevator. She suggested to my grandmother that after the appointment, they would go out for lunch, something they never did together. At first my grandmother protested—what would my grandfather have for lunch?—but then agreed after my mother promised they would leave "something for Pappa to eat." This outing remains one of my mother's "best" memories. Mainly, she remembers the image of my grandmother sitting across from her at Schraft's, a small hat perched on her head, eating apple pie, amazed at her good fortune: "Who would ever have thought I would come to be *here*?" she said, in her dialect. Just before we hang up, my mother says she wishes that she could remember her mother's exact words. (4–5)

The pattern thus established, however, undergoes a distinct formal transformation in Section II of this working paper. Marked this time as an "Interlude," this section consists entirely of the following poem, which—surprise, surprise—features its own "I" telling yet another autobiographical story (and, for that matter, another epigraph introducing yet another "I," this time from Elizabeth Bishop). Here, the context shifts again, moving from the immediate mother-daughter relationship to that between the grandaughter and grandmother. In doing so, it complicates still further the connections among language and body, memory and identity:

### II. Interlude: "My Grandmother's Leaving"

Of course, I may be remembering it all wrong
after, after—how many years?
    "Santerem"/Elizabeth Bishop

I gave her my room, the narrow bed
and crocheted cover stitched
with coral ribbon.   I gave her

my dresser carved of oak, a chair
to sit in afternoons. Three months
a widow, she looked out to the bay.
In her lap, a string of rosaries,
her fingers moving quickly
over each smooth bead. From a distance,
her hands were the hands
of a woman mending.

Each morning, I dressed her,
Kneeling on the floor
to slide the heavy stockings up
her swollen legs. Some days
she didn't even know my name.
*And who's your mother?* she would ask
in *her* language,
bending to me, balancing
her weight with one hand
on my shoulder. She kept
two black dresses hanging
in the closet: one silk,
one cotton, between my summer
clothes. They took on
the smell of cedar.
I took the one she chose
and held it up above
her head—she knew to lift
her arms—and then I pulled it
slowly down around her, smoothing
first the gathered slip and then
her hair, the blacker strands
insisting through the white.

Her other things—the hand-rolled
handkerchiefs, hats with veils
and feathers—were packed away
in the leather suitcase she kept
behind the bedroom door. She gave me
her silver cross to wear
around my neck, a book of prayers.
Those months before she died,
I slept downstairs
with just the things I needed. (Tangorra, "Qualifying" 5–6)

Finally, in Section III the project makes yet another set of shifts: in form, in time, and in level of abstraction. The narrator returns formally to the sort of prose featured in the first portion of Section I, and also shifts temporally to a related present—another textual here-and-now, as it were—this time in the moment of composing as opposed to the moment of reading. At the same time, this same narrator moves to a different level of abstraction in order to reflect on the rhetoric/poetics being enacted in the working paper itself, and in particular on the agency of the narrative "I"—the subject—as it is operating in the text we (are constructed to) have read so far:

### III. Border Crossings

I am writing autobiographically about autobiography—as a woman, a poet, a critic and teacher. My grandmother's question has resonance: "Who would ever have thought I would come to be <u>here</u>?" Here: Albany, New York. Here: As a "creative writer" theorizing about writing and teaching. Here: As a poet and a critic. Here: As a woman writing about women's writing.

The various subject positions I occupy (and the list is still only partial) lead me to cross borders of genre, discourse, profession, practice and theory. Such is the work of many feminist poet/critics described by Diane Freedman in *An Alchemy of Genres*, a study of the border-crossings made by women writer/ critics as they experiment with a self-conscious blending of traditional genres (poetry and autobiography, for example), subgenres (free verse, lyrics, fables, diaries) and disciplinary discourses (5). The "I" of this essay will be similarly transgressive, similarly self-conscious, opting for what Miller calls "narrative criticism," a (feminist) mode of analysis that displays a self-consciousness about its own processes of theorization (xii)—a material, personal writing that theorizes the stakes of its own performance (24). *Autocoscienza*: selfconsciousness. This is how Italian feminist Manuela Fraire describes it: "the practice of self consciousness is the way in which women reflect politically on their own condition" ([qtd. in] de Lauretis, *Alice* 185). I hear the seeds of this self-consciousness in my grandmother's question: Who would have thought I would come to be *here*? Implicitly, it asks how, as a woman (worrying about her role as wife, care-taker), an immigrant, an outsider on the margins of a dominant culture, would she (could she) come to have this slice of the proverbial "apple pie"? (Might my grandmother be asking now, from wherever she is, how her granddaughter came to be a poet, how she came to be the subject of her granddaughter's poem?) (7)

The rest of the project, Sections IV through VIII, proceeds in the spirit that this passage promises, with the narrator moving in comparably various ways through a range of linked topics: an analysis of the scholarship on autobiography (with a particular focus on the challenges posed by feminist and postmodern/poststructuralist theories); a somewhat more overtly autobiographical examination of the problematics of the "I" for women writing poetry, with an emphasis on situating her own work vis-à-vis other women poets;[2] the presentation of a poem she had submitted to a workshop "several years ago," followed by a prose reading of the old reading of that poem, and then a re-reading of it; and an exploration of how this emerging approach to the autobiographical "I" might play out in the writing classroom. The narrator tells us that the genre thus produced can be characterized, following Liz Stanley's *The auto/biographical I, The theory and practice of feminist auto/biography*, as "at least provisionally a feminist autobiography," a border-crossing mode that traverses the conventional boundaries between different forms of writing, "blurring the lines between autobiographical and academic discourse, between poetry and autobiography," and so on ("Qualifying" 8). As such, it is designed on the one hand to allow us to feel—or to *induce* us to feel—much the way the narrator says she felt after her encounter with Miller's Coda: that is, it seeks again and again to provide us with "I"-based moments that we can believe we recognize, and to invite us—it is our turn—to experience being "dizzy with identification, with the sheer 'untheorized' joy of shared experience." On the other hand, its relentless self-consciousness has a counterbalancing function, serving to remind us—also again and again—that there is something fictive about all of this: as the narrator's mother emblematically suggests after reading "My Grandmother's Leaving," it seems likely that the narrator was "conflating memories" in constructing what is ostensibly a painstakingly "true" story to offer what might better be understood as a "composite 'sketch' of her two 'nonnas'" (10).

The narrator makes it clear, however, that the ultimate purpose of moving us back and forth between these poles is not to force us to choose between them—to deny one and embrace the other—but to write us into a third kind of agency, one that "acknowledge[s] the (self-) fictions of any autobiographical account yet make[s] a claim for the pleasure and necessity of remembering" (9). From the feminist perspective represented here, at least, to do otherwise is to fall prey to a false choice, to give in to (be [mis]written by) a misleading and ultimately dangerous binary. A couple of lines from Elizabeth Spires's "Globe"—quoted in Joanne's project more than once—might serve as an appropriate summary of the articulated position: "Memory's false as anything, spliced in the wrong parts,/queerly jumping. But better than forgetting" (9).

As usefully illustrative as Joanne's project is in terms of both the format and the possibilities of the qualifying examination, it obviously cannot be considered typical or representative in any more substantive sense. We want to close this discussion of the qualifying examination, therefore, by sketching in just enough of two other efforts to provide some basic contrastive leverage. Our first choice for this purpose was written by Catherine Sustana; her examination operates at the intersection of what would likely be identified in the program as nineteenth-century American literature (with a particular focus on women writers), critical theory, and creative writing, and does so in order to consider what is represented as the "problem" of the sentimental. Part one, accordingly, deals with our "current understanding of sentimentality and of 19th-century women writers in general." The preparatory list features titles like Eva Cherniavsky's *That Pale Mother Rising: Sentimental Discourses and the Imitation of Motherhood in 19th Century America*, Mary Kelley's *Private Woman, Public Stage*, and Jane Tompkins' *Sensational Designs*; a representative selection of mid-nineteenth century sentimental novels (e.g., *The Lamplighter, Uncle Tom's Cabin*); and specialized sections of the scholarship concerning Harriet Beecher Stowe, Susan Warner, Maria Cummins, Fanny Fern, and Herman Melville. On the three-hour written test (eight pages, typed, double-spaced), she deals with two questions. The first concerns the relationship between "sentimentalism as a genre (or as an institution) and sentimentality as a characteristic that influences or surfaces in a work" (1); the second offers an assessment of the strategies critics have employed in addressing the absence of women writers from the canon of nineteenth-century American literature. As this opening passage from the latter suggests, the general pattern of argument is not much different from Joanne's:

> Some of the most valuable strategies that have been used to address the systemic exclusion of women from the canon of 19th-century American literature have been analyses of the misogyny inherent in much literary criticism, the disruption of the myth of universality and timelessness that has long been associated with canonical texts, and the redefinition of evaluative criteria. Although these strategies have been immensely important in helping to establish the validity of women's writing, they have all (necessarily, I might add) had to respond to an already-established canon in a way that seems to give that canon too much authority over the terms of the argument. It is my hope that these strategies can be implemented and expanded in such a way that we can truly restructure (or, preferably, destructure) our concept of American literature. (Sustana, "Qualifying" 1)

The working papers, however, give her a good deal more room to operate. The first is called "In Search of the Sentimental: Definitions and Denigrations." Taking its cue from Joanne Dobson's argument that "*Sentimental* is perhaps the most overworked, imprecise, misapplied, emotionally loaded, inadequately understood term in American literary classification" (1), this paper traces the process by which American literary criticism has arrived at the understanding sketched out in the first part of the exam: how the "sentimental" has come to be regarded as a kind of ugly excess in the tradition of American literature. However, the presentation is not limited to a dutiful or disinterested retrospective. Rather, it is a pointed argument that the recuperation of the sentimental is crucial in moving the American literary tradition and its operative hermeneutic toward what the narrator contends will be a much healthier condition: i.e., one in which "altruism, sympathy, empathy, pity, sorrow, and human connectedness" might be "taken seriously"; in which we might be able to "read about kindness as comfortably as we have learned to read about selfishness"; and in which "our understanding of emotion" would not be as "cynical and impoverished" as the denigration of the sentimental has led it to become (25).

This argument is then used to set up the second working paper, "Sentimentality and the Outsides of Language," in which Catherine's narrator postulates—and seeks, albeit on a limited scale, to enact—ways of writing that might help set such a recuperation in motion. Its thirty-five pages cover a lot of territory and draw on an interesting mix of sources: Deleuze and Guattari's *A Thousand Plateaus* figures prominently, for example, as do George Kalamaras's *Reclaiming the Tacit Tradition: Symbolic Form in the Rhetoric of Silence,* Helene Cixous's "Laugh of the Medusa," and Carolyn Heilbrun's *Writing a Woman's Life*; and there are lengthy sections dealing with *Uncle Tom's Cabin, The Wide, Wide World, Queechy,* and *Ruth Hall.* Even in the following brief excerpt from this project's opening pages, however—one featuring references to Rachel Blau DuPlessis, Robert Solomon's "In Defense of Sentimentality" (1990), and Suzanne Clark's 1991 *Sentimental Modernism*—it is possible to get a sense of its trajectory. Note especially the narrator's introduction of "Ellen" in the final paragraph. The name is the same as the protagonist's in Warner's *The Wide, Wide World,* and she/it will appear recurrently in this text as an emblem of, or perhaps an agent for, something like the sentimental as it is being recuperated here:

> "Further, an expository, 'semi-objective' voice is hardly the only mode of feminist critical discourse."
> —RACHEL BLAU DUPLESSIS,
> *Writing Beyond the Ending*

**The limits of excess**
If there were questions I could ask, they would be these: How do you move outside of where you are? Outside of what you're saying, or what you're supposed to be saying? Is the *outside* a place you can inhabit, or is it simply something to look for, think about, gesture toward? How do you demand recognition for something that has no name . . . or worse, how do you demand recognition for something that has already been rec-

ognized as something else? Do these questions make any sense to you? Do they make any sense?

Sentimentality implies excess—excess of emotion, of language, of emotional language. Robert Solomon writes, "It is as if the very word, 'sentimentality,' has been loaded with the connotations of 'too much'—too much feeling and too little common sense and rationality, as if these were opposed instead of mutually supportive" (305). To label something as excessive without qualifying *what it is in excess of* is to attempt to naturalize limits (limits of emotion or language, in the case of sentimentality) that may actually be constructed and/or changing. As Suzanne Clark comments on the word *sentimental*, "The word does not mean just emotional fakery. It marks the limits of critical discourse as if they were natural" (11). Such labeling implies that whatever is excessive could be eliminated without altering the effect or meaning of "enough," but in fact sentimentality is absolutely necessary in order to constitute enough *as* enough. . . .

The accusation of excess implies irrelevance—something is excessive if we already have everything we need. But to call something irrelevant is to acknowledge its otherness, to see it, and so we say it is redundant, already-been-done, too-much-of-the-same. I want to consider the possibility that excess might not be an unnecessary doubling, a repetition, a redundancy *within* language, but rather that it might possibly point to something *outside* the limits of language. Say there is a girl . . . let's call her Ellen, for no other reason than that I like the name. Does she belong here? Now? I introduce her because I wonder if she can tell you something that I cannot. I introduce her because I wonder about the spaces she can move in. (1–2)

These considerations—the possibility that excess might "point to something *outside* the limits of language," and that Ellen might be just the "girl" to guide our explorations thereof—will be given full play in Catherine's subsequent dissertation, as we shall see shortly.

Our second featured examination writer is Chris Gallagher, and he operates at the intersection of still another trio of programmatic constituents: the teaching of writing, the teaching of American literature, and the debates concerning what is usually called critical pedagogy. For the first exam—the three-hour written affair in which he is expected to characterize the current status of the issues he plans to address—the more literary side of his reading list features such writers as Nina Baym, David Downing,

Stanley Fish, Richard Ohmann, Robert Scholes, Mary Louise Pratt, Maria-Regina Kecht, Gerald Graff, and (perhaps most influentially) Gregory Jay ("The End of 'American' Literature: Toward a Multicultural Practice" and "Taking Multiculturalism Personally: Ethnos and Ethos in the Classroom"); their more rhetoric-and-composition-oriented counterparts include James Berlin, Ann Berthoff, C. H. Knoblauch and Lil Brannon, Susan Miller, John Schilb, Joseph Harris, and John Trimbur. As it turns out, he ends up writing about critical pedagogy as it currently functions in these two domains of English Studies, and especially about claims in the professional literature that work in these domains has taken important social or political "turns" in recent years. Basing his analysis in particular on Jennifer Gore's *The Struggle for Pedagogies,* Chris's essay demonstrates that while some such "turns" may indeed have taken place at the level of (announced) social vision, there has been far less successful enactment of them in the more instrumental arena of classroom practice. And the reason for this impotence, he contends, is that "the ways in which English studies has constructed *pedagogy* (and therefore students and teachers) has also forestalled the development of a critical civic project" (Question 1, p. 2). If the field hopes to move ahead with any such project, therefore, it must begin by reconstructing pedagogy, a challenge posed in the closing paragraph of his answer to the first (of two) questions:

> [W]e must all ask ourselves what Kurt Spellmeyer asks Composition specialists: are we willing to recognize "nonspecialists" as collaborators in the process of knowledge production ("Inventing")? I would ask this of all in English Studies, and propose that the "nonspecialist" knowledges of students must become part of our (post)disciplinary inquiry. This will mean—especially for those in literary study—giving up some of the privileges derived from the present scientistic disciplinary model, but I also believe it is necessary if we are to provide students with the critical civic education/pedagogies that so many of us seem to envision. We must move pedagogy to the "center" of our projects, and we must move students' knowledges to the center of our pedagogies. In this way, we may help the "objects" of our pedagogies become the "subjects" of their own experience, and—for once—we and our pedagogies can become the "object" of students' own scrutiny. (11)

Pursuant to the logic required by the examination process, Chris's task in the next part of the exam—his first working paper—is to examine the history of this situation; to try to explain where these impulses to foster a critical civic project in English education come from, and why they seem to be stymied:

> I want to inspect a particular line of thinking that has informed the work of progressive educators in English studies: the assumption, as Adam Katz puts it, that in order to "expand" democracy, we need only "produc[e] more democratic subjects" (211). In Katz's "oppositional" framework, this "liberal" thinking is dangerous because it fails to provide a model for abstraction from and confrontation with the ruling class (211); here, I want to inspect this "liberal" line of thinking for how it constructs students, teachers, pedagogy, and education. I am particularly interested in how "democratic" education and pedagogy in English studies have been complicit in perpetuating the teacher-as-producer, student-as-commodity model that Horace Mann and his cadre of industrialists put in place in the 1840s (see Bowles and Gintis, Trimbur "Literacy"). My hope is that in elaborating the limits as well as the radical reforms and still-unrealized possibilities of progressive education in English studies, I can contribute to debates over the value and significance of selectively reclaiming and reconstituting "progressive" work as we turn, once again, to "the social." (2–3)

To this end, this essay examines two prior periods in the history of English studies—"moments," as they are called—when "many English educators perceived the need to take a 'social turn'" in a way that is related to, or at least relevant for, contemporary educators with similar ambitions (6). The first of these periods covers the 1920s, and focuses on efforts made by the authors of articles in *English Journal* to enact the progressivism of John Dewey's "middle period" (e.g., *The School and Society, Democracy and Education*) in the English curriculum. The second period runs from 1937 through 1942 and focuses in particular on the Institute for Propaganda Analysis (IPA), a New York City–based group whose activities and influence can be said to have "enlisted" a good many English teachers in the uses of propaganda analysis as a particularly patriotic—even chauvinistic—but nonetheless still "critical" civic project. In neither instance, however, does Chris's narrator accept that the Dewey-inspired progressive impulse was effectively implemented: "I . . . agree with Bowles and Gintis," says this narrator, "that American education has never really witnessed the implementation of 'progressive education'. . . . [In both instances] when translated into pedagogical practice (and then back into pedagogical discourse), Dewey's brand of progressivism was transformed into a far *less* progressive set of reforms" (41–2). And in these failures, he suggests, lies a lesson for our own time about what a more successful transformation might entail:

> Perhaps this unfortunate eventuality was determined by the educational philosophy that Cubberly described in 1916: schools were factories designed to manufacture student-products to the specifications of "modern civilization." Unlike Dewey, many of the teachers who wrote in both periods—often including those who aligned themselves with Dewey—assumed that their pedagogy would unproblematically "produce" a certain kind of citizen or soldier or American or worker or leader. Perhaps more than anything else, this historical material points to the need to reflect on our constructions of students as "democratic subjects." We need to work toward new understandings of students as *already* social agents as they enter our classrooms, and not simply as material to be shaped and fashioned in our image. We need not—we should not—sacrifice our social visions, but we do need to have humility, to gain a sense of the limits of our formative powers. Moreover, Dewey teaches that we need not only to espouse those social visions, but to *enact* them in our pedagogies, in our curricula, and in our scholarship. (42)

Finally, the aim of the examination's third and final segment—the second working paper—is basically to apply this lesson. In part, it does so by reviewing and then extending existing critiques of critical pedagogy, especially those based in the work of poststructuralist feminists (e.g., Jennifer Gore, Elizabeth Ellsworth, Patti Lather) with regard to how the movement's scholarship (as distinct from any observed classroom practices) "has fallen victim to the same unfortunate overestimation of teachers'—and schooling's—formative power over students as had the mechanistic pedagogies against which critical pedagogy was posed in the first place" (1). The first twenty pages or so, therefore, are devoted to arguing that the seemingly unreflective belief in the possibility of "transmitting, transferring, or conferring 'critical knowledge' or 'critical skills'" that seems to characterize the writings of Henry Giroux, Ira Shor, Michael Apple, Peter McLaren, and so on is in fact "no more 'empowering' than transmitting, transferring, or conferring the 'Western tradition' or 'basic skills'" (1).

Perhaps more important, however, the latter half of the essay takes a step toward avoiding this trap by "work[ing] toward" what gets labeled, tentatively, as "'reflexive inquiry'": a range of pedagogical practices, the hallmark of which "is consistent and constant attention to the situatedness of learners and learning" by all present, "individual self-reflexivity by teachers and students *and* collective reflexivity by groups" (26). It issues here in the form of "'telling representations'" of those practices: "narrative theorizations which seek to read and reread, write and rewrite, the classroom—and pedagogy generally—as a site in which theory and practice interact and interanimate each other" (2). The idea is that enacting critical pedagogy as "reflexive inquiry" also (necessarily) involves attempts to recount it, but with the proviso that such recounting is itself also, as far as possible, reflexive. In this instance, the teaching in question took place over a two-year period at a college in the Boston area. This excerpt concerns a spring term course in "Writing I," taught in the aftermath of a disappointing fall course in Writing about Literature, and inspired partly by a midterm break spent reading Freire and Shor. Groups of students have been asked to research and write about topics of their own choosing:

> Nicole, Joan, and Mary have written about multicultural education. Nicole has written about her Asian-American heritage and specifically about Japanese internment during World War II; Joan has written about the need for white women such as herself to "connect" with women of other cultures under the banner of feminism; Mary, an exchange student from Greece, has written about how the battles over multicultural education mirror the struggles over immigration, concluding that neither is reflective enough about the value of diversity to the vitality of culture. Each has situated herself, em-bodied herself in her discourse (or been em-bodied by it). Each has begun where she is.

> *What about the article about illiteracy and lack of literacy*
> *skills in the paper this morning?* they are asked.
> *What about grammar, mechanics—WRITING?* they are
> asked. *How about letting us up with all this PC shit?* they are
> asked.
> The three writers begin again, patiently, to explain their
> positions.
> *How about my Writing About Literature class?* I ask, de-
> scribing it to them.
> *What did you DO with the material?* Nicole asks.
> *Did you just treat them like any other texts?* Mary wants
> to know.
> *That's not multicultural,* Joan points out.
> Here, I think, is my New Year's revelation, arrived at in no
> time at all—and by *students*. How could they know so easily
> what I must work to even begin to appreciate? (32–3,
> Gallagher's emphases)

This mode of storytelling, Chris's narrator contends, is at least
part of what the more successful enactment of a critical pedagogy must involve. Not success stories, or once-and-for-all stories, but stories "without endings, stories without self-evident
'lessons,'" stories which, in their resistance to closure, give teller
and audience alike "always more to think about, to theorize *out
of*" as opposed to onto—stories told, in short, to keep alive the
kind of humility described in the second working paper as one of
the key missing ingredients in critical pedagogies past. We will
see shortly that Chris, like Catherine, would return to explore
these issues much more fully in his dissertation.

## From Examination to Dissertation

With the examination providing a considerable momentum, candidates set about the task of moving from working papers to
dissertation.[3] There is no set formula for making this transition,
and our capacity to illustrate the possibilities is constrained even
more than for the examinations by the length of the documents
involved. Still, we want to extend this account of Joanne's,
Catherine's, and Chris's work at least far enough to flesh out
what are in any case the obvious procedural possibilities. We will

begin with Joanne Tangorra: For her the dissertation turned out to be a fairly straightforward extension of the examination process. Entitled "Waterborne: Poems, Poetics, and Pedagogy," her dissertation is made up of two major sections. The first consists of thirty-eight poems (arranged into three groups) under the heading "Waterborne: Poems"; the second, called "Autobiographical Acts: Poetics and Pedagogy," features revised but still recognizable versions of the two working papers. In essence the project as a whole enacts for official (and officially public) purposes—and on a larger scale—the examination's effort to "rescue the [writing] subject" of women's poetry and students' writing. According to the Abstract, this version, like the exam as a rehearsal, is "[p]rovisionally . . . a feminist autobiography in its self-conscious blending" of a variety of forms; indeed, with these thirty-seven additional poems ("Grandmother's Leaving" is still included), it is now more than ever a "cross-genre collection," and in that sense better equipped to carry out its mission:

At issue are the debates concerning the "I" of discourse within feminist criticism, composition and creative writing (specifically between expressivist and critical/social pedagogical perspectives), and the parallels and intersections between these fields as they relate to reading, writing and teaching practices. Within a theoretical framework that acknowledges the importance of life/lived experience in various autobiographical discourses, and at the same time encourages the examination of the role of social and historical practices in the shaping of these discourses, many of the poems in this collection are first-person lyric narratives whose speaker tells of lived (often, but not always, specifically female) experience, childhood memories and concrete occasions of the self in its engagement with the real world. These poems (and essays), positioned as provisional moments of self-presence and identity, foreground an "I" engaged in a constant re-writing of self in relation to shifting interpersonal, social and political contexts; it is through the interpretive act of re-writing that the subject's personal history and experience acquire materiality. Extending this framework to considerations of women's and student's writing, this dissertation argues for reading, writing and teaching practices informed by feminist poststructuralist theories which consider each woman/student writing subject [as] in process, constructed in/by language and through the dialectical relationship between the autobiographical act and the materiality of everyday life. (Tangorra, "Waterborne" Abstract)

For Catherine Sustana, by contrast, the exam could more accurately be characterized as point of departure for the dissertation—a means of leading up to a clearly related but also distinctly different writing project. The examination focused on what was represented as the unfortunate history of sentimentality in the American literary tradition, and its ultimate aim was to find ways of reading and writing that might make it possible to recuperate the sentimental—an ambition most fully articulated, and to a limited extent enacted, in her second working paper. The dissertation takes up similar themes; its official title, in fact, is "Letters in Excess: Cross-Genre Investigations in Sentimentality, Feminist Poetics, and Counterhistory." It even features excerpts from a half-dozen of the examination's sources (e.g., Clark's *Sentimental Modernism*, Deleuze and Guattari's *A Thousand Plateaus*, and Stowe's *Uncle Tom's Cabin*). But the project itself takes a form barely hinted at in that second working paper:

> *Letters in Excess* is a novel that combines creative and critical work to address theoretical issues regarding sentimentality, nineteenth-century American fiction, and feminist narrative strategies. The primary action . . . revolves around a set of letters bequeathed from a group of nineteenth-century women to their respective descendants. The novel focuses on one of the twentieth-century inheritors of the letters and the ways in which the letters change her understanding of her familial and social history. (Sustana, "Letters" Abstract)

We cannot do the project's structure anything like complete justice here; it runs some 220 pages and includes at least four key characters—two from the nineteenth century, two from the twentieth—whose lives as narrated are connected in ways that are complicated both in terms of story and structure. In addition, there are a dozen or so only slightly lesser characters, the aforementioned letters, e-mail correspondence, and more. By way of summary, however, we can say that the "Ellen" introduced in the second working paper emerges here as the focal twentieth-century inheritor of the letters mentioned in the Abstract. As the plot unfolds, we learn that Ellen is a member of the English department at the small liberal arts college in her childhood hometown that her parents had "always held out to her as the embodiment of educational achievement, a fortress of intellectual integrity," but which has now become simply "her routine place of employment" (15). She has qualified for this position—in which she has yet to earn tenure—by earning a Ph.D. in American literature, and by publishing "a narrow, narrow book" on "an obscure manuscript" by "an obscure writer named Lucy Elizabeth Bird," and in fact on "a particular piece of punctuation that was inadvertently added when the manuscript" for that book was typeset. Hence its "narrow, narrow title" (chosen, as Ellen laments, by the "marketing people"): "*Lucy Elizabeth Bird's 'Story of a Lady.' Period.*" (15).

As this sketch might suggest, Ellen is also not a happy person. Thus, while the primary action of the novel may, as the Abstract tells us, revolve around the letters, the *effects* of that action are measured most powerfully in terms of changes in Ellen's emotional state: her gradual coming to terms with, and to some extent gaining relief from, the sense of unhappiness—the "narrowness of her life" (14)—that preoccupies her throughout the narrative. When we learn of this unhappiness during her first scene, she is sitting on a bridge

> surrounded by the relics of her life—a black-and-white photograph of her and her father and brother holding up the fish they've caught while her sister sulks in the background, a stack of diplomas and awards taking her from the fourth-grade spelling bee all the way through her doctorate, a first edition of *Uncle Tom's Cabin*. (13)

The bridge itself doesn't amount to much—has, in fact, been taken out of use for cars, has barricades at both ends, and runs over a river that "isn't much more than a trickle, [so that] if Ellen threw herself in, she'd be more likely to break her collarbone than drown" (14)—but in its painfully ordinary, dead-end way it serves as a particularly apt emblem for the powerlessness she feels in the face of a very real malaise:

She has a hole in her heart—she is sure of it. Not an ordinary heart-murmur kind of hole, either, but a hole so big there might as well not be any heart left at all. The way Ellen sees it, she's got two choices: throw herself in, or throw in everything else and start from scratch. (14)

As it happens, Ellen manages to throw only a copy of her book over the edge—a "merely symbolic" act, we are told she would admit if we asked her, since "she has hundreds of remainders stacked in a closet in her house"; but symbolic, too, in its predictable futility, since even this semigrand gesture has a pathetic result: "The book lands with a sort of slapping sound and doesn't wash downstream. Instead it just lies across some rocks, its pages soggy and swollen and soft" (14).

In this fairly literal sense, then, the novel is about how this character's subsequent encounter with the preserved letters of some members of a circle of nineteenth-century correspondents, combined with a variety of other influences—including both an image-shattering letter from her own deceased mother, and her experience in teaching an undergraduate course in American literature—alters Ellen's understanding of who she is; in what alternative ways she might see or construct the story of her life; and so how she learns, or at least begins to learn, to repair this hole in her heart.

In another sense, though, the novel can be said to be "about" the similarly sorry state of emotional health faced by an American literary tradition which, at least as represented in Catherine's examination of it, has operated with an impossibly perverse understanding of the sentimental. Hence the dissertation's designation as a critical project. We do not want to be reductive about this; certainly the novel itself is not. But it is not a stretch at all to suggest that Ellen's malaise is at least partly a function of her "narrow, narrow" disciplinary training, and not much of a stretch to see in Ellen's gradual restoration to health some significance for the larger enterprise. Near the end of the dissertation, Ellen reflects on the letters she has been bequeathed, and she does so in terms that surely resonate for all of American women's writing. Her moment of revelation here—feeling "suddenly overwhelmed by the immediacy of books she has read a hundred times"—represents a kind of awakening we are given every reason to believe would be salutary for the American literary tradition as well:

> Ellen thinks about what these letter-writing women hoped to accomplish. At times, it seems like a tremendously selfish act, as if they wanted to monopolize history, as if they wanted to sneak up on their own daughters. At other times, it looks tremendously selfless, as if they were trying to save their heirs, trying to help their descendant daughters accumulate some kind of strength or wisdom that would be greater than their own individual store. She sees them reaching out, one at a time, trying to connect over the space of death. They are reaching out like Nancy's [her sister and vigilant social activist's] pleas for flood victims, like Harriet Beecher Stowe's entreaties to her readers, like eye contact from a woman in trouble. They are placing the responsibility for these stories in the hands of one woman at a time, and they are telling women, one at a time, that there is a precedent for a bravery and resourcefulness that is never written into history books or magazine articles.
>
> Too often Ellen has allowed the words on a page, their shape in black and white, to insulate her from what those words might actually say to her. The page is as flat as her prior one-dimensional view of her mother. Or, if not flat, then remarkably monotonous, one identical dinner plate stacked on top of the next, no variation, all symmetry. How could she have kept herself so distant? What her mother understood all along is that Lucy Elizabeth Bird was a woman, not an artifact. Ellen is suddenly overwhelmed by the immediacy of books she has read a hundred times. She feels that all-consuming struggle for faith in *The Wide, Wide World*; she feels Stowe's heart breaking at the thought of a child being sold away from his mother. Think about it: the child is lost forever. This is more than words on a page.
>
> There is, perhaps, something noble about the letters, Ellen thinks, because the women who wrote them were trying the impossible, trying to set down in words what there were never enough words to say. They must have known how much was missing from their letters; they had to feel the gaps and inadequacies. . . . Yet they kept writing—for themselves, for the women who came before them, and for the women who would come after. It is a gesture; even if their letters cannot tell the whole story, they testify that there is a story to tell. (Sustana, "Letters" 200–202)

Finally, while Joanne's dissertation can be said to be an extension of her examination writings, and while in Catherine's case those examinations serve as the point of departure for her dissertation's topically related but formally very different project, Chris Gallagher's final project falls somewhere between these procedural extremes. Although the dissertation retains both the basic form and general method of the examination writings, it introduces a fair amount of new material—makes considerably more of a topical shift, at any rate, than that by either of the other writers. Entitled "Reflexive Inquiry: Rethinking Pedagogy and Literacy" (1998), its Abstract offers the following overview and chapter outline:

Drawing on work in Composition and Education, this study inquires into historical and contemporary struggles between "functionalist" and "critical" visions of *pedagogy* and *literacy,* and argues that neither "side" has done justice to the complexity of these processes. The former tends to reduce pedagogy to skills-training and literacy to decoding and encoding skills. The latter often neglects to explore how sites of practice enable and constrain these processes. In this dissertation, I seek to counter these tendencies by weaving teacher narratives with historical and theoretical inquiry.

The first three chapters delineate past and present struggles between "progressives" and "functionalists." In Chapter One, I chronicle the emergence of progressive education and modern composition during the Age of Efficiency, contending that although many of their proponents viewed these initiatives as socially "progressive," they served to consolidate, rather than resist, conservative and functionalist views of pedagogy and literacy. Chapters Two and Three set out the current educational context. The former considers the reconsolidation of functionalism in the recent accountability movement, specifically in the drive for standardized assessment. The latter takes up how Critical Pedagogy and Composition—descendants of progressive education and modern composition—have sought to resist this development by constructing models of "critical" pedagogy and literacy, which, although useful, tend to favor broadly-conceived social and educational visions over inquiry into how students and teachers practice pedagogy and literacy.

The final three chapters seek to avoid this tendency by putting my vision of pedagogy and literacy as *reflexive inquiry* in dialogue with classroom and institutional narratives. In

Chapter Four, I consider community-building as reflexive practice by focusing on the work of students in a writing workshop. In Chapter Five, I explore evaluation as reflexive practice by continuing to reflect on the work of these students. I contend that in lieu of objectivist, standardized assessments, teachers and students should be encouraged to compose "reflexive representations" in order to "go public" with their work. Chapter Six offers such a representation, in the form of a narrative drawn from a Short Story course. I construct an alternative mode of narrating classroom work so as to theorize the complexity of these complicated human interchanges, pedagogy and literacy. (Abstract)

The six-chapter, 300-page dissertation follows roughly the same argumentative trajectory as did the 110-page examination, but the case being made has been both modified and expanded. So, for example, while some of the historical material from the first working paper makes it into Chapter One, "Pedagogy and Literacy in the Age of Efficiency"—most notably that dealing with *English Journal* articles during the 1920s—other material, such as the exam's account of the IPA project, disappears altogether. More to the point, the retained episode gets recast in a way that focuses it much more specifically on the interaction between literacy education—particularly as enacted by progressivists—and the principles of scientific management, with the dynamic now associated much more closely with what is here called (following Alan Trachtenberg) the "incorporation" of American education.

Chapters Two and Three are then recast accordingly. The contemporary proponents of functional literacy who are the focus of the former—"Pedagogy and Literacy in a Second Age of Efficiency"—are now represented as exercising their influence particularly in terms of a pressure for accountability, a kind of pressure that does not appear at all in the examination, and one that, for the purposes of composition studies, translates into a constant demand for the "objective" assessment of writing abilities, as if schooling were indeed a kind of factory in which teachers/workers cranked out students/products easily amenable to quality control. And these functionalists' contemporary critical-literacy/critical-pedagogy counterparts offered in Chapter Three— "Critical Pedagogy, Critical Literacy"—tend to be represented and evaluated in the same context: as if, that is, their efforts can be most usefully understood as a reaction to such pressure, and therefore judged in terms of their ability to combat this objectification:

> Those who advocate critical pedagogy and critical literacy [e.g. Ira Shor, James Berlin, Henry Giroux, etc.] worry about what "the system" and conservative reformers are doing to teachers, but they need to look more closely at the effects of **their** challenges and at **their** constructions of teachers, as well. . . . [In the least effective versions of such challenges and constructions,] [e]xpert theorists **envision** pedagogical and literacy projects, and teachers **enact** them. In this way, teachers, like students, are imagined as objects of "critical" projects. Amy Lee asks, "how can [students] be 'cultural workers' or 'empowered learners' in a discourse which theorizes pedagogical possibilities *around* them rather than considering students as central to the enterprise of pedagogy?" (8) I would expand the question to include teachers as well, for they, too, are at times theorized out of the pedagogical equation as mere transmitters of "critical knowledges." And in this way, those who advocate critical pedagogy and critical literacy, like the administrative progressives of the Age of Efficiency, and like the conservative reformers of today, take the power to engage and to construct pedagogical and literacy projects out of the hands of teachers and students. (150–51, Gallagher's emphasis)

Last, but also most important, this way of reframing the "problem" that faces the now twinned enterprises of critical pedagogy and critical literacy also helps to define what the dissertation's last three chapters are able to offer by way of a "solution." As indicated earlier, the second working paper made some initial moves in this direction, devoting perhaps a dozen pages to recounting a year of Gallagher's experience teaching in Boston, and thereby seeking to illustrate both a pedagogy—"reflexive inquiry"—and a mode of representing it—a "telling representation." In the dissertation, the parallel effort has been expanded logistically to upwards of seventy-five pages, and conceptually refined so that "reflexive inquiry" is now understood as comprising two separable activities: a disciplined pattern of classroom interaction called "reflexive practice," and a fairly specialized mode of writing about that practice called "reflexive representation" (253).

Chapters Four and Five are devoted to the former—i.e., reflexive practice—and each focuses on one key concept that critical literacy/critical pedagogy's objectivist leanings have tended to ignore or distort for instrumental purposes. Hence Chapter Four, "Community as Reflexive Practice," contends that a number of prominent critical scholars in composition, particularly, have "argued either for a radical restriction of our uses of this concept [of community] or for a wholesale rejection of it" (172), a campaign challenged here by an account of Gallagher's own teaching that emphasizes community-*building* as a practice. And Chapter Five, "Evaluation as Reflexive Practice," does much the same with evaluation. It begins by seeking to demonstrate the inadequacies of critical scholarship on the issue, emphasizing in particular that scholarship's often too uncritical reliance on portfolio assessment as a kind of panacea. It then responds to those inadequacies by describing at length (twenty pages), and with considerable patience for the "messiness" of the exchanges involved, the evaluation of a specific piece of student writing, an evaluation based—as a *practice*—on "constructivist" (as opposed to objectivist) principles: how that piece of writing was read not as a stand-alone textual performance to be measured against abstracted criteria, but as a situated communication in a specific context, "a means of coming to terms with other members of this [classroom and programmatic] community, of building social relationships with other teachers, learners, writers, and readers" (242).

This leaves Chapter Six to deal with reflexive representation: how such practices might best be made available for the subsequent consideration that reflexive inquiry requires—what it might mean, as Chris's narrator puts it, "to represent and to **enact** reflexive inquiry **from**" (as opposed to "in" or "on") a classroom, to move outward toward "public engagement" (253–54, Gallagher's emphasis). In other words, part of what it will take to fend off the objectivist forces at work in education on the one hand, and to encourage reflexive inquiry on the other, are ways of "captur[ing] the messiness of . . . pedagogy and literacy" as "human exchanges" (254). Therefore this last chapter, "Writers Writing Writing," employs a range of textual devices in an effort to construct a twenty-five-page narrative/commentary about a short story course in order to "dramatize the need to reimagine the possibilities for narrating and evaluating our pedagogical and literacy work" (253). We have reproduced approximately the first three pages of Chapter Six to illustrate the method involved.

## Chapter Six
### Writers Writing Writing

Students have arranged themselves—slowly, slowly—into four groups ranging in size from three to six students each. It is just after 8 a.m. and it shows on their faces. Bored already? Tired? Hung over? (It is, after all, March 18, 1996: the day after St. Patrick's Day.) Still thawing from long walks across campus in the brisk March air? I should care, but I don't—today, I simply want them to do their work. They look at me as if they expect great things but know they won't get them. I wonder if I look the same to them. Almost hostile this morning. Bad morning to ask this question.

*Will one group volunteer to be recorded for a project I'm working on?*

Silence.[1]

*No one?* No one. I am surprised, disappointed, even—slightly—angry.[2]

I look at Michael, and those two scenes—with which I will perhaps always associate him—replay themselves in my head:

**Scene 1:** last month in the gym. Michael thanks me—actually thanks me—for "raising these questions." Questions about how we read, how we write, how we make and are made by culture. Textual and cultural authority, perspective, entitlements: these are important to him, a history major. I am glad to hear it, of course, and I say so. We smile. Off in search of the weight room, Michael adds a final thought: "Too bad it's an English class."

**Scene 2:** last week in class. After a reasonably spirited conversation about gender and canonicity, we struggle, sputter, and finally fall silent when the discussion turns to sexuality and canonicity. Eve Sedgwick's *Epistemology of the Closet* has apparently left them cold. I ask why, what's going on. More silence.[3] A minute passes.

---

1. I mean *silence*.
2. Teachers don't get angry. I was *frustrated*.
3. I don't mean *silence* this time. Now I mean the kind of silence through which you can hear tiny non-silences: the intake of breath, the shifting of weight, the chewing of gum, the scratching of heads, the tapping of pencils, the cracking of knuckles—the kind of silence that waits impatiently for its own death. That kind of silence.

Two minutes. Maybe three pass before Michael, head down, says, very quietly, *We aren't accustomed to talking about these things.* Relieved, I thank him, ask him to elaborate. *We just aren't.*

\* \* \*

Judy:
    [T]he two things that have [a]ffected my readings the most are being white [and a] woman. Basically so far we have been reading short stories by the author Richard Wright. He is an Afro-American male from down South. Being a white women, I have never really encountered the pain that he was writing about. His writings have let me look at things in a different perspective, almost trying to place myself in his shoes. . . "They" say there is a battered women's syndrome, but the whole concept seems unreal to me. Reading about this bothered me more than most of the other things he wrote of, probably because I am a woman and that is something that still occurs regularly, even if it is more private now. I know that black men are still discriminated against, some are still beaten, such as Rodney King, but to me those situations are so much less involved in my life, because I am a white woman, that they don't [a]ffect me the same way that the would [a]ffect another black male who could read the same exact stories.
    —Feb. 2, 1996

\* \* \*

All student writing presented in this chapter is excerpted from letters written to students in another section of The Short Story. (As in previous chapters, students have given permission to use their work, and I have changed their names to protect their privacy.) In the first set of letters, writers were asked to introduce themselves to each other by reflecting on how their social locations and the ways they constructed themselves affected their reading practices. In the second set of letters, they were asked to communicate to their writing partner their early ideas about the short stories they would write for the course. For both letters, writers were doing exploratory writing in an informal rhetorical context. I've chosen to focus on these texts, and not, say, students' more formal essays, because I want to call attention to the status of writing that students produce when they are at their most self-reflexive—that is, when they are writing by what Kurt Spellmeyer calls "constructive indirection," when it is most clear that (as Foucault teaches) "we speak first, and then learn what we have said and whom we have become" (Spellmeyer 80). I also want to call attention to the status of student texts as knowledge (another concern of Spellmeyer's). So rarely, in my experience and reading, do we think *with* students, alongside their texts. So often, instead, we use them simply for purposes of diagnosis or illustration. If, as I have suggested, students are active producers of knowledge and are integral to the pedagogical process, then we need new ways of reading and representing student texts, new ways of valorizing them as knowledge.

\* \* \*

Deidre:

I'M CAUCASIAN. however un-P.C. it may sound, i'd be lying if i said this didn't affect how i read. when reading stories by minority writers i have to TRY to understand where they come from. it takes a conscious effort for a westchester white girl to IMAGINE being the victim of racism. i lack the background. i have to rely on the author's words. a perfect example of this is Richard Wright's short story, "Fire and Cloud." in the story, the pillar of a 1930's, southern, black community is threatened and severely beaten by a group of white men, for peacefully expressing his beliefs. i deeply sympathized with this character. my heart bled. i cried. yes, i know that what happened in the plot is WRONG. no question. but because i have never been in a situation this severe, i had to rely on Wright's details and descriptions.
—Feb. 2, 1996

Joe:

I can't actually relate to these stories. The major issue is that I am not black. I cannot relate to the time period. It's set in the late 19th century, and in the south. I am from New York and am growing up in the 90s. I like 90s clothes, 90s music, 90s movies, 90s technology. It's just not my style.
—Feb. 2, 1996

Derek:

if I read a novel by a black female writer, I would tend to believe everything that she says, because I have not had the knowledge or experiences that she holds.
—Feb. 2, 1996

## A Family Resemblance

Even on the basis of only these three dissertations, it seems reasonable to assert that Albany's version of a fusion-based curriculum has made it possible—at least so far—for students to write dissertations that reflect the curricular dynamic out of which they emerge. Obviously, this does not mean that all such dissertations will reflect that dynamic in precisely the same ways. Part of what is so interesting about the three projects reviewed here is just how striking and significant their differences really are. Topically speaking, for instance, it is surely still possible—although by no means unproblematic—to identify each with one of the program's constituent discourses: Joanne's with creative writing, Catherine's with literary history, and Chris's with rhetoric and composition. These identifications are not absolute, by any means, but they are certainly not imaginary, either. Chris's concern with literacy and pedagogy is much more characteristic of work published in *CCC* than in *American Quarterly,* while the latter journal—formal issues aside for the moment—would be a far more likely home for Catherine's efforts to recuperate a tradition of sentiment in American literature than the *AWP Chronicle* or the *Little Magazine,* which in their turn would surely provide better ready-made audiences for what Joanne's writing is attempting to do. And these ties are also signaled to some extent by the range of sources cited for each project. Thus not a single common title appears in the Works Cited of all three projects, and in fact only a half-dozen titles were common even to two. (For that matter, even if we go back to the more expansive preparatory reading lists for the examinations—since in Catherine's dissertation, particularly, the list of Works Cited consists of only thirteen items— only one title is shared by all three lists,[4] and only a dozen or so appear on two.) Insofar as such references are a measure of disciplinary and professional location, these three projects have staked out distinctly different domains.

And their formal and methodological differences are, if anything, even more obvious, although again no simple matter to sort out. On the formal front, more than half of Joanne's dissertation follows the print conventions of poetry, while neither of the other two has any such passages at all. On the other hand, Catherine's project consists entirely of what is represented as a fictional prose narrative; but while Joanne's and Chris's projects offer lots of prose narrative, and raise a good many questions about what might be called the truth-value of such accounts, neither ever goes so far as to claim to be offering prose fiction as such.

In methodological terms, Chris's project places a heavy evidentiary emphasis on texts his students have written; their authenticity matters so much, in fact, that the narrator assures us more than once that these have been handled in ways that meet both legal and ethical standards. Catherine's novel gives what is surely a comparable kind of weight to letters written by women who, according to the plot, have all died before the novel's contemporary action begins. Here again pains are taken in the story to assure us that such texts are both authentic and properly handled. In this case, however, according to the textual conventions invoked (this is, after all, a novel) there is a further implication that these documents were actually written by the same person who wrote the rest of the text. Joanne's dissertation, meanwhile, makes no presentation whatever of comparably "unpublished" documents by other writers in its prose sections—no student papers, no letters from anyone's mother, no diaries, etc.—but a few of the poems do claim a related sort of status: "Unrecorded Entries in Mary Shelley's Journal," for example, is dated "12 July 1822, San Terenzo" (7)[5]; and "Veronica Franco" is headed "Venice, 1575" and begins "I wear the veil like a virgin bride/given to mysterious ecstasies" (33).

In short, the program's influence over the dissertations Joanne, Catherine, and Chris wrote was clearly not a matter of producing formal or methodological uniformity along these lines. These are not projects anyone would be inclined to characterize as lookalikes or clones. Yet we would nevertheless contend that there really is such influence, that all three projects are connected to the program's eponymous concerns in important ways, and are therefore connected to one another as well. Thus, while Chris's project may foreground teaching more than the others, both Joanne's and Catherine's give that activity considerable space, as in the former's prose section called "Thoughts on Teaching Writing," and in the latter as a recurring element in protagonist Ellen's life. Likewise with criticism: if it figures most prominently in Catherine's project—all the more so if we are willing to accept her examination and dissertation as of a piece—Joanne's engages frequently in activities that fall under precisely such a heading (e.g., "Reading [Re-Reading] 'Leda,'" a section centered on the interpretation of one of her poems and its prior reception); Chris's obviously turns a comparably critical gaze on classroom interaction, student writing, and institutional practices. For all three, of course, writing is not only one concern among many, but the paramount concern. As all of them indicate unequivocally at one point or another, the dissertation constitutes not merely an argument for but an enactment of their respective disciplinary and professional commitments.

For programmatic purposes, the result is what we are inclined to call a family resemblance. It isn't that every Albany dissertation is marked by the program in such a powerful way that any reader of one in any context will be moved to say "Ah—another graduate of 'Writing, Teaching, and Criticism.'" As we have seen just with these three projects, there is no requirement imposing the kind of topical, formal, or methodological uniformity that would make such identifications possible. Seen side by side by side, however—or, to extend the image to include all the program's dissertations to date, assembled for a large group shot—it becomes possible to see that Catherine's project has things in common with Chris's and still others in common with Joanne's, and that Chris's and Joanne's have still other things in common that they do not share with Catherine's, but that they might well share with (fellow dissertation writer) Alex Reid's "Virtual Prognosis: Writing and the State," say, or Steve Ferruci's "A Critical Promise: Composition's Professional Identity and the Teacher of Writing," or Margaret Ervin's "Re-Placing Genius: Reconciling the Aesthetic and the Politics in Margaret Fuller's Writing," and so on. Taken together, these dissertations by the program's candidates constitute a body of work that the sponsoring faculty could never have written themselves; they also therefore mark, in a modest but very real sense, the enterprise's first fully public steps in helping to figure a new future for English Studies.

# REFIGURING THE PH.D.
# IN ENGLISH STUDIES

This third and final section turns from the specifics of Albany's doctoral curriculum and the writings of its students back toward the larger context of English Studies that was the focus of Section I. In doing so—and please note that the narration will revert to the first-person singular of Section I—I obviously do not mean to suggest that my collaborators and I have somehow exhausted the possibilities of "Writing, Teaching, and Criticism." Hardly. Even in just these first eight years or so of its existence—four times through the two-year curricular cycle—I would estimate that the students enrolled in the Albany program have turned out something on the order of two thousand formal writing projects, and even more less formal ones, as well. In all doctoral programs, and perhaps especially one like Albany's, writing is what graduate students *do*. Thus, although these last four chapters almost certainly devote more textual space to the presentation and analysis of doctoral student writing than any single publication in the history of English Studies; and while we tried to supplement our featured pieces by at least mentioning alternative topics, forms, and methods; we are nevertheless acutely aware of having passed too lightly over not only any number of terrific individual writing projects, but whole areas of composing that have enjoyed considerable student attention—work in electronic media, for example, and performance-oriented projects of all kinds.

As we tried to make clear from the outset, however, it is not the purpose of this book to offer an authoritative case study of the Albany program: to claim, for example, that this sampling of student writings was comprehensive or representative in such a way that it could be used to prove—in some quasi-empirical sense of that term—that "Writing, Teaching, and Criticism" was a success. Obviously, those of us involved with this project have made a substantial investment in this particular doctoral program *as* a program—rather more of an investment, in fact, than we ever could have made had it been more traditional or better established. And we also have a good deal at stake in its eventual success. We know from painful experience that we already face substantial difficulties making our various career ways, especially in the academic world, as holders of D.A. degrees, Ph.D.'s from an experimental curriculum, or—the double whammy—D.A. degrees from that experimental curriculum, without also having to explain that the program that conferred those degrees, never all that prestigious, had subsequently been dismantled and/or replaced.

It is for precisely the same reasons, however, that this final section needs to emphasize the program's basic principles—this whole idea of what I have insisted on calling, despite its neologistic awkwardness, the fusion-based curriculum—over Albany's particular attempt to enact them. Should the specific program we have been at such pains to describe here not survive, it becomes all the more important to us, at least, that those principles should not be buried with it. Think of it this way. If it turns out that we absolutely have to spend the rest of our working lives explaining that the experimental program that conferred our degrees is gone—and given our recounting of the Albany English Department's unhappy history with the business of doctoral education, you will understand why we know that this is always a possibility—we are determined to do all we can to ensure that it will have been an experiment that made a difference: had a lasting and positive impact on both how English Studies goes about preparing each new generation of doctoral candidates and—thereby—on the nature of the discipline itself. A grand hope, perhaps, but nevertheless the one in aid of which this final chapter considers what the fusion option might offer to English Studies as it enters the next century.

## CHAPTER TEN

# The Fusion-Based Curriculum for an English Studies in Transition

The dozen or so years that have passed since the conferences at Wye and Wayzata have not been particularly good ones for either English Studies or its corporate alter ego, the enterprise I have dubbed College English Teaching, Inc. This is not to say, of course, that absolutely nothing good has happened. To take two genuinely bottom-line figures in this context—only one of which seems to get much public play—the number of B.A.'s and Ph.D.'s conferred in English both seem to be climbing steadily. The figure for the former has gradually gone from a mid-1980s low of around 3.5/hundred (and raw totals in the low thirty thousands) back up toward 5/hundred (with higher overall enrollments pushing the raw totals over the one-million mark);[1] the latter figure has climbed steadily from its 1986–87 low of 668 back up to well over 1,000. And in neither case—this despite considerable furor over the increase in Ph.D. production (and even instances of particular programs cutting back at that level)[2]—does there seem to be any serious overall downturn in sight.

Unfortunately, these at least potentially positive developments have been overshadowed by the steadily diminishing status of English Studies in the academy overall: the stock of College English Teaching, Inc., if you will, has fallen rather sharply. The trends that signal this shift make up a familiar and fairly lengthy list—the continuing erosion in the number of full-time tenure-track faculty lines, the concomitant increase in non-tenure track and part-time appointments, incremental growth in teaching loads, salary compression, and so on—but what it boils down to is that colleges and universities are returning to English departments fewer and fewer of the tuition dollars (or the subsidized equivalent) that undergraduates pay to buy whatever it is those departments are selling . . . and finding out, so far at least, that it is possible to get away with doing so. I argued in Section I that English had been by far the most successful discipline in the U.S. academy at using tuition dollars to fund its broader professional and disciplinary agenda—i.e., it figured out fairly early on how to run a credit-hour factory staffed by instructors, TAs, part-timers, and so on, the surplus from which bought time (in the form of lower teaching loads) for the professors—and it has done an excellent job of modernizing this system during the post–World War II growth of higher education. What has happened now, in essence (and in some perverse way, perhaps, English might take this as a compliment), is that the institutions that used to spon-sor this arrangement have decided to move in on the operation, to take a bigger cut. Thus, as the numbers for B.A. and Ph.D. production make clear, the operation itself is still under way and—given in particular the increased use of part-time appointments—has been cranked up to turn a greater profit than ever. It's just that more and more of the proceeds are being distributed to units other than the English departments in which they are generated.

This evolving form of the old arrangement—the academy's version of what the rest of the U.S. economy has experienced as "downsizing," "contracting out," "outsourcing," and so on—obviously has had implications for every activity that takes place under the rubric of English Studies. For doctoral education, those implications have consistently been represented as a structural matter, a "crisis" in the "job market." That is, when colleges and universities hire fewer full-time, tenure-track faculty in English, the chances of any new degree-holder landing such a position obviously diminish; and of course those chances diminish fur-ther when, as has tended to be the case over the past ten years, Ph.D. production increases as well. In response to this standard rendering of the situation, two basic courses of action are gener-ally prescribed: first, full-time tenure-track English faculty at all institutions are urged to combat the use of any lesser sorts of appointments by whatever means might be available; and sec-ond, doctorate-granting programs are urged to exercise restraint in producing new Ph.D.'s.

From my perspective, neither this account of the problem nor these proposed solutions are sufficient. Granted, there are too many English Ph.D.'s—not to mention D.A.'s, M.F.A.'s, ABDs, and whatever else—chasing too few full-time, tenure-track positions. Granted, too, that Ph.D. programs—along with D.A. and M.F.A. programs—are responsible for having created this oversized pool of highly credentialed candidates. And granted, finally, that those who have managed to land the most sought-after positions do wield at least some power and (though the ethical argument is a good deal harder to mount) may even bear some responsibility for making similar careers possible for others.

But none of this quite gets to the heart of what ails doctoral education in English, which is ultimately not a structural matter at all, but a disciplinary one; or, to put it a bit more sympathetically, what the profession has experienced as structural difficulties over these last twelve years and more are in fact better understood as the institutional expression of long-standing intradisciplinary inequities: the sins of the *Magister,* if you will, being visited upon subsequent generations. In ways I have suggested before, English Studies, operating as the insistently hierarchical College English Teaching, Inc., has long since functioned by systematically *discounting*—without ever quite fully disclaiming—certain of its institutional wares: most notably, of course, the teaching of first-year composition, but also the teaching of writing in general (e.g., advanced composition, creative writing, technical and professional writing, writing centers, etc.); and, to a lesser but still considerable extent, lower-division teaching of all kinds. What has always made the credit-generating factory possible was the understanding—often tacit, to be sure, but unmistakable—that such teaching could be turned over to the less-than-fully-compensated and/or less-than-fully-qualified since it was not itself directly tied to the discipline's core activities.

Of late, however, the colleges and universities that heretofore tended simply to tolerate the logic of such discounting—allowed the English departments to apply it—have shifted to embrace and extend it. Thus, goes the institutional reasoning, if first-year writing courses, writing courses in general, and even many lower-division English courses can indeed be taught by less-than-fully-compensated-because-less-than-fully-qualified TAs and ABDs (and English departments themselves, after all, *the* experts in dispensing such instruction, have long sanctioned precisely this practice), why waste full-time tenure-track faculty lines to staff them? And if it turns out that the fully qualified, the actual Ph.D.'s, apply for such work, so much the better. Again, if English departments deem such teaching as somehow less than fully disciplinary—so that even full-time employees with titles such as "lecturer" or "instructor" have traditionally been compensated at grossly discounted rates for doing it—why should anyone else pay the full disciplinary fare? If you hire a plumber to mop the floor under a leaky pipe, or an attorney to sort envelopes in a law firm's mailroom (and if these analogies seem too harsh, check the attitudes expressed in the relevant professional literature), would you expect to pay the worker standard plumbing or legal fees, or something closer to minimum wage?

What makes this trend toward an increased discounting of college English teaching even more alarming is that it can so easily be extended to cover the vast majority of courses English departments have traditionally peddled. According to the MLA's survey of undergraduate English course offerings for 1989–91, for example, "the figures indicate that, on average, two-thirds of the course sections offered by departments are in writing, and close to half in English composition. Literature course sections account for approximately a quarter of all course sections, on average" (Huber 1996, 47). In addition, since a substantial portion of those reported literature courses would have been of the multisection, lower-division, general-education variety frequently assigned to adjuncts, TAs, and so on—let's assume these would make up about 10 percent of the overall total—it seems safe to say that at least three-quarters of the undergraduate courses English departments offer thus qualify as potentially discountable. Obviously, this isn't to say that 75 percent of all undergraduate English courses currently are being taught by employees on TA, non-tenure-track, and/or part-time lines. But it is quite clear that a steadily increasing number and percentage of them are (witness, for example, both the "Statement from the Conference on the Growing Use of Part-Time and Adjunct Faculty" [1998] and the "Final Report of the MLA Committee on Professional Employment" [1998]) and that a lot more easily could be.

Hence my contention that the situation facing doctoral education in English Studies is best understood not as structural but as disciplinary—or, to stick with the term my collaborators and I used throughout Section II, intradisciplinary: a function not of how English Studies relates to its host institutions, but of how its own constituencies relate to one another. It is one of those wonderful Pogo-esque occasions: we have met the enemy, and it is us. Thus, so long as the discipline of English Studies continues to support the internal discounting that has been the corporate bread and butter of its professional operation, College English Teaching, Inc., this increasingly problematic relationship with host institutions *cannot* be dealt with on anything other than a superficial or symptomatic level. Unfortunately, this does not mean that as soon as English Studies takes steps to end such discounting, these host institutions will immediately follow suit. As much as we might wish that were true, the situation is clearly too far gone for that; there is far too much momentum involved and far too many other interests profiting from the practices that paid off so well for English all these years. It does mean, however, that unless and until English Studies takes such steps—fundamentally reinvents itself in a form that ends such internal discounting—it will be in no position even to *begin* the negotiations that might result in substantive change.

Which brings us back to where this book began nine chapters ago: refiguring the Ph.D. in English Studies. The project of reinventing the field in these ways will obviously involve a substantial and sustained effort on any number of fronts, but no efforts anywhere will be more important—or, frankly, even *as* important—as those concerning the preparation of the next generation of scholars and teachers. If it does not or cannot happen there—to the extent, that is, to which doctoral education serves mainly to replicate the extant professoriate and thereby perpetuate the intradisciplinary relationships they professionally embody—the prospects for any significant or lasting change are severely diminished, if not extinguished altogether. Ideas for how such changes might best be effected will need to come from a variety of sources, and it seems unlikely that any one approach, any single plan, can, will, or even should prevail. Nevertheless, I want to close this chapter, and the argument of this book overall, by explaining why the fusion-based curriculum seems to me to be the best available means for moving doctoral education, and thereby English Studies as a whole, in a desperately needed new direction.

## On the Professoriate's Record of Futility

While my usage so far in this chapter has gone along with the field's professional literature in referring to its most recent round of Ph.D. placement difficulties as a "crisis," it would be far more accurate to characterize that situation—present and past—as part of a chronic condition: for English Studies, this is in fact business as usual. Various of the key numbers are familiar by now, but in the context of the argument I am even now engaged in making, they always—*always*—bear rehearsing. Thus, according to the surveys the MLA began conducting in 1976–77, the highest annual percentage of new Ph.D.'s "with known employment status" ever to report finding full-time, tenure-track, academic positions was 51.1 percent in 1991–92. *In no other year surveyed has that number risen above 50 percent.* Moreover, if we shift to the category called "Percentage of all PhDs with Tenure-track appointment[s]," the news is worse: the 41.6 percent rate reported for 1993–94—the year that seems to have justified the most recent invocation of "crisis"—falls exactly in the middle of the eight previously reported rates. Four were better, four were worse, and 41.6 percent turns out to be almost exactly the same as the surveys' overall average of 41.4 percent (Huber 1995, 48).

So, for at least twenty years (and indeed longer, if we want to include the unhappy effort represented by Cameron Allen's *The Ph.D. in English and American Literature*) the professoriate in English Studies can be said to have held firm: it has consistently failed to do whatever it could to significantly alter this oft-decried situation. Nor is it all that hard to see why. First, there is, as always, the matter of self-interest. As we saw in reviewing both the Magisterial tradition and the Wayzata proceedings, it has proved consistently difficult for this group to do anything that might interrupt the laying ability of the College English Teaching, Inc. goose while it was still producing a reasonable number of golden eggs. Thus, for the members of that fortunate 41 percent or so of English Ph.D. holders who have managed to land full-fledged academic positions over these past twenty years—or, to be generous, let's say the number is more like 50 percent—the system has seemed to work reasonably well. Moreover, thanks in particular to the protections afforded by the institution of tenure, the system has promised, and mostly still does promise, to continue doing so for the rest of their increasingly long careers. This has been all the more true, obviously, for those who have managed to become graduate professors in the field's tiny percentage of Ph.D.-granting departments. Given the nature of the system, the graduate professors—those who have been in what is by far the best position to effect any fundamental change in the enterprise—have also been the least likely to see, let alone feel, any pressing material need to do so.

But there is a second, more fundamental reason for this record of inaction, as well: the professoriate, and here even more particularly its graduate hierarchy, has genuinely not known what to do. Thus, when the editors of the Wayzata proceedings declare that the conference was radically inconclusive—i.e., that while the conferees could agree that the mode of doctoral education they understood the field to have been offering should be discontinued, but that they had no clear idea what ought to take its place—I believe them. In retrospect I wonder whether it could have been otherwise. After all, those conferees, most of them associate and full professors from doctorate-granting institutions, would by definition have been the system's most highly refined products; this also means they would have been the most likely to embody its internal divisions in their purest form: to have been most fully "in" literary history, or rhetoric and composition, or critical theory, and so on. (Check the MLA's *Job Information List* for the past twenty years. How many of the associate or full professor positions advertised ever call for a "generalist"—a term which, rather like "utility player," has long since acquired pejorative overtones?) Disciplinarily as well as professionally, such people would have gotten to where they were primarily by honoring, if not indeed overtly emphasizing, the intradisciplinary divisions upon which the field's discounting practices have been based. In this systemic sense, then—apart from the actual abilities or propensities of any given individual—they would have been among the field's *least* qualified members to lead any reform movement, the primary aim of which was to do away with precisely those divisions.

# But That Was Then, and This Is Now

As I suggested in opening this chapter, a lot has been happening to English Studies in recent years. Is it possible, then, that the current professoriate has changed significantly—enough so, at any rate, that the prospects for refiguring the Ph.D. have improved? On the issue of qualification, I believe the answer is unequivocally no. True, the disciplinary diversification that was one of the key factors in bringing the Wayzata conference into being in the first place has continued; there are by now, for example, not only graduate professors of rhetoric and composition teaching in doctoral programs around the country, but also at least a half-dozen endowed professorships: generously compensated research positions in an area of English Studies where such a thing would have been almost unimaginable for most of this century. But the emergence of these positions, along with parallel developments in other areas, has only added to the ranks of graduate professors who, precisely by virtue of their (hyper)specialization in an area demarcated by the field's extant divisions, are operating at a considerable remove from other such specializations. Again, this tendency is systemic, not individual, and as true for the compositionist as the medievalist, the novelist as the Emersonian: the same gesture by which the system anoints leading lights in any one of these "areas" necessarily creates the possibility for comparable expertise, and comparable experts, in other such areas as well—all of which and all of whom will tend by definition to be mutually exclusive.

On the count of the professoriate's self-interest, however, I believe that there has been some movement. In Chapter 4, I described the Wayzata conferees as representing a much chastened College English Teaching, Inc., and indeed they did. Between 1977 and 1987, the whole enterprise had really hit bottom, experiencing a twenty-year low in Ph.D.'s conferred and a more than thirty-year low in B.A.'s awarded to English majors. Nevertheless, those same conferees can also be said to have represented the field's hopefulness, a widespread belief that things were at long last looking up. Thus the Commission on Writing and Literature, out of whose deliberations the conference evolved, is reported to have completed its work "'in a spirit of cautious optimism,'" buoyed by the sense that at decade's end "the environment of English studies had changed dramatically: dire demographic projections had proved excessive, college enrollments were increasing, graduate programs expanding, new jobs proliferating" (Lunsford, Moglen, and Slevin v).

No such corporate optimism appears to be warranted at the end of the 1990s. Enrollments may be doing reasonably well, and Ph.D. output may still be increasing, but new jobs are decidedly not proliferating. One of the more dramatic ways to illustrate the directional trend in Ph.D. placement would be to compare a graph depicting the number of Ph.D.'s granted in English by year with the number of positions advertised in the English edition of the MLA's *Job Information List* over the past decade or so. Beginning in 1987–88, the former line would climb slowly but steadily upward, moving from around 700 into the 1,100 range. The latter, meanwhile, would head the other way, plummeting from a 1989 peak of well over 1,400 down to a 1993 nadir well below 900; then, although gradually recovering, this second line would do so at a rate that merely kept pace with the increases in Ph.D. production. These numbers look even more grim if we figure in, as a kind of shadow, counts of definite tenure-track *junior* positions as posted in the October editions of the MLA's *Job Information List:* 291 in 1990, 197 in 1991, 207 in 1992, 217 in 1993, 249 in 1994, and so on. In short, while English Studies will surely end up producing an average of over 900 new English Ph.D.'s per year during the decade of the 1990s, the average annual number of these full-fledged, junior-level October postings has little chance of reaching even 300.

Nor are those dismal figures the worst of it. For however troublesome this mismatch between production and placement might be from a corporate perspective, it has been made a good deal worse by the pace at which the system's lower-echelon members—particularly the teaching assistants and part-time faculty— have been organizing for professional and political purposes. After all, College English Teaching, Inc. has always depended on some version of just this pattern to supply it with the TAs, ABDs, and underemployed Ph.D.'s needed to run its discounting operation.

Thus, while this current batch of statistics may represent too much of what used to be a good thing, they would not seem nearly so ominous if the discounted parties were not also exhibiting a considerable restiveness about their places in this scheme—but they have been and will surely continue to do so. This has not been a strictly discipline-based development, of course; neither the positions nor the general pattern of labor practices involved are exclusive to English departments. Nevertheless, the nature and extent of English's dependence on such employees make it extremely sensitive to any alterations in their status. Consider just one more set of numbers: a 1996–97 MLA sampling of Ph.D.-granting, M.A.-only, and B.A.-only departments found that even in the B.A.-only units—traditionally the least dependent on such staff— an average of 50 percent of all first-year writing courses were taught by part- and full-time non-tenure-track faculty, while in the other two types, the averages (which also include graduate-student instructors) were 64 percent (M.A.-only) and a stunning 96 percent (Ph.D.-granting) (MLA Committee 29).

Organizations representing such employees are in a position to wield considerable influence over how English departments conduct their business. This holds doubly true—almost literally, and certainly figuratively—for those departments housing doctoral programs, especially as graduate student organizations on campuses all over the country have been both seeking and winning the right to engage in collective bargaining. An organized job action by employees in any or all of these discounted positions—a TA strike, say—might not damage the larger institution in any serious or long-term way, but it could easily devastate an English department, with negative effects on morale, full-time equivalents (FTEs) (the department's claim on tuition fees), and graduate enrollments. Even less dramatic actions—as when, for example, TAs successfully negotiate reductions in teaching load— are bound to produce ripple effects for workload elsewhere in the English department. Ultimately, then, while no one can be certain just where these two developments—the downward spiral in placement and the organizing of nonfaculty labor—will lead in higher education overall, the message for doctoral education in English Studies seems clear: business as usual will no longer suffice.

More directly to my point about professorial self-interest, this message actually appears to be getting through. To some extent, the evidence for this comes from the work of individual commentators—Cary Nelson, for instance, or Michael Bérubé, or Robert Scholes, to name three of the most visible. Even more significant from a corporate perspective, however, is the afore-mentioned "Final Report of the MLA Committee on Professional Employment," published in the spring 1998 issue of the *ADE Bulletin*. I need to acknowledge up front that this is not a document devoted exclusively to English Studies. The committee was charged with addressing the situation faced by all the "modern languages" represented in the MLA, and eight of its eighteen members were from departments other than English. Neverthe-less, I believe the report can be construed quite plausibly as this decade's counterpart to Cameron Allen's *The Ph.D. in English and American Literature* (the 1960s) and Lunsford, Moglen, and Slevin's *The Future of Doctoral Studies in English* (the 1980s). This is as close as English Studies will have come in the 1990s to offering an official position on what ought to be happening in doctoral education. And while the MLA Committee's analysis is cast in somewhat different terms than mine has been here—there is no mention at all, for instance, of a threat posed by organized labor—they characterize the situation in terms no less dire:

> [W]e believe that only serious action on a number of fronts will enable progress toward resolution of the economic, social, and educational problems posed by the inequitable and insuf-ficient multitier job system that has developed in all too many institutions across the country. What we confront is therefore a crisis in the truest sense of the word: not just an "unstable condition" but a "turning point," which we hope will evoke significant transformations of the academic settings we inhabit. Our tenured and tenure-track colleagues in English and for-eign language departments will have to change their thinking about the nature of the work we do, its purposes and its struc-tures. More specifically, in many cases they will have to reimagine the size and shape of the graduate programs they offer and the directions in which those programs ought to evolve, given the range of needs our profession will have to meet in the twenty-first century. (MLA Committee 39)

Hence my belief that there may by now have been sufficient movement in the English professoriate's self-interest—in their understanding, if you will, of what might be good for them—to believe they might actually be ready to refigure the Ph.D. For while the Final Report's rhetoric of change is plenty familiar, this particular invocation of "crisis" combines with the passage's two imperatives to produce a corporate stance that is significantly different from those we read in the comparable pronouncements of 1968 and 1989—one best characterized, in fact, as threatening. It is fairly simple: the tenured and tenure-track faculty "will *have to* change their thinking" about the nature of their work, and "will *have to* reimagine" the way they train people to do it, or else—and surely the threat is there—or else that work and that training will be dramatically altered for them, and by parties who will have little regard for either their discipline or their customary mode of professional life.

## Getting Help

Admirable as such imperatives are, however, they also present an obvious problem. If I am right about all this—if the professoriate's revised understanding of its self-interest has rendered it more open to a refiguring of the Ph.D. in English Studies, but if its overall qualifications for carrying out such a project on its own are worse than ever—who is supposed to engineer this refiguring? Who can be in charge? As even the brief excerpt from their Final Report may have suggested, the MLA Committee on Professional Employment does not quite come to grips with this dilemma, although it certainly seems to like poking around its edges. Elsewhere in their report, for example, they quote approvingly from Cheryl Glenn's unpublished brief to the group (*Doctoral Education: Education? Vocation? Profession?*), which argues—much as I would—that since "'over 90% of English programs and most likely between one-half and two-thirds of the total number of professorial-rank appointments are located outside doctorate-granting research institutions. . . . the primary goal of graduate education should *not* be to replicate the graduate faculty'" (36–37, emphasis added). In its "Recommendations to Graduate

Programs" the Committee reiterates this argument by way of introducing, albeit in vague and limited terms, ways in which such a shift ought to translate into features of the students' curricular and programmatic experience, contending

♦ that doctoral programs offer students courses in pedagogy that will prepare them for a range of teaching situations

♦ that programs offer PhD students experiences designed to familiarize them with the complex system of postsecondary and secondary education in this country (comprising four-year liberal arts colleges, community colleges, universities, and private as well as public high schools) and the full range of job opportunities available in that system

♦ that such introductions to pedagogy and to the varieties of academic work involve not only colloquia, seminars, and conferences but also, for instance, mentored internships, residencies, and exchanges among institutions along with experiences outside teaching, such as involvement in institutional, administrative, governance, and editorial tasks (41)

As you can see, however, in neither of these passages—nor, for that matter, anywhere else in the report—does the committee explicitly tumble to the perversity of the proposed arrangement. Consider. If the graduate faculty's goal is *not* to replicate itself, but rather to prepare doctoral students for careers "doing the kind of lower-division teaching associated with the great experiment in social access that inspires American education" (MLA Committee 40), . . . how can the extant graduate professors hope to provide the training required? The simplest and harshest answer is that they cannot: they are, as I have been suggesting all along, unqualified to do so. In this context, in fact, they are unqualified by definition: that is, while they *are* the acknowledged experts in a kind of work that their trainees will *not* be doing, they are also—or so it seems safe to assume—*not* the acknowledged experts in the kind of work their trainees *will* be doing.

It would appear that the most direct way to deliver doctoral education from the horns of this dilemma would be simply to remove the extant graduate faculty altogether and appoint in their stead people whose backgrounds actually equipped them to provide the kind of training the Final Report says doctoral students really need. To be sure, it might not be desirable for this alternate group to replicate itself, either; there is finally something reductive about characterizing any educational process in such narrow terms. Still, it certainly would be possible to assemble, and in fairly short order, a graduate faculty for whom the demands of the situation did not run so severely counter to their training and instincts: one better equipped not only to carry out the Committee's rather minimal recommendations—offering courses in pedagogy, familiarizing students with the country's educational system, and so on; but also to devise the rest of a new doctoral curriculum without having to accept, as a point of departure, that it was by design *not* going to involve training students to do the kind of work that had been most responsible for their (the faculty's) own academic and professional success.

No such wholesale changing of the guard is likely to take place, however. Although I confess that imagining the scenes such a reformation might provoke holds a certain perverse entertainment appeal, I do not actually believe that such a change should take place even if it could. For while it would certainly move the graduate faculty's credentials more into line with the realities of the employment prospects English Ph.D.'s have long since faced, it would do so without significantly affecting the problematic intradisciplinary divisions that created this situation in the first place. In other words, while it might manage to make what has been the low high and the high low, it would also leave very much intact both the various factions involved and the principles underwriting their enmities, with the result that the entire operation would be vulnerable to similarly perilous situations in the future.

The remaining alternatives, therefore, are specifically limited. I count three. First, the extant graduate faculty could actually retool, reform themselves: not merely "change their *thinking* about the nature of the work [they] do, its purposes and structures," as the Final Report proposes, but actually *become* the sort of faculty with whom we imagined replacing them. Second, professionals other than the graduate faculty could be given a more significant role in doctoral training. This is, I presume, part of what the Committee on Professional Employment is getting at when it recommends such things as "mentored internships, residencies, and exchanges among institutions along with experiences outside teaching, such as involvement in institutional, administrative, governance, and editorial tasks": expanding the pool of available expertise by granting students some sort of credit for training (or at least "experience") that is beyond the capacity of the faculty to provide. And, finally, of course, the doctoral curriculum could be altered to take fuller advantage of, and give a more significant curricular role to, the students themselves.

Obviously, these alternatives need not be mutually exclusive. On the contrary: assuming that the members of English Studies really do want to keep the disciplinary and professional enterprises afloat, the project of refiguring doctoral education will need all the help it can get. Having said that, however, I need to add that in my estimation, at least, the first two of these alternatives have a rather limited viability. On the first, then: even if the graduate faculty were to become deeply invested in their own disciplinary and professional retooling—and that is hard enough to imagine—it is difficult to see exactly when or how they might go about doing so. What would be the mechanisms? NEH summer seminars? Sabbatical years spent enrolled in alternative doctoral programs, teaching in public four-year or community colleges, working as interns in prison literacy programs or in entirely noneducational institutions? Any of these might constitute a start—might nudge the process of self-education in a new direction—but how far? And what would sustain that momentum? Indeed, I wonder if perhaps the Committee on Professional Employment's wording on this score wasn't even more apt than they intended, for it seems to me that for the vast majority of graduate faculty, changing the nature of their "thinking" about the nature of their work, its purposes and its structures, is about all that can be reasonably asked or expected.

The second option faces a similar and not unrelated set of difficulties. Let us assume the graduate faculty decides (and again, such an assumption requires no small leap of faith) that it is willing to build into the doctoral curriculum training and/or "experiences" that would heretofore have been considered extra-curricular. Such a decision raises its own set of hard questions. For example, given (again) the limits of faculty expertise, how will they decide which venues are and are not appropriate? For that matter, how will they even generate a list of venues to be thus considered? Who will they know to consult, and on what basis? Even if they manage to locate a set of such venues, the questions only get harder: What status is to be afforded on-site experts? What work will be asked of them, will it be monitored, and if so by whom? Who will pay for all of this—i.e., compensate the on-site experts, the students, any monitors—and how much? And how will whatever it is the students do "out there" be meshed with whatever it is the faculty are teaching in the rest of the curriculum?

These kinds of questions are tough enough for English departments to handle under any circumstances—as when, for instance, they seek to mount undergraduate internship programs or have a hand in placing secondary school student teachers— but they are surely even more fraught here, where the educational stakes are as high as they can get. And, frankly, there is no evidence whatever that the 140-plus doctoral programs in English could answer them satisfactorily even if they wanted to. If graduate faculties actually have the kinds of expertise and the connections to the world outside the universities it would take to make such activities a systematic and substantive feature of doctoral training, why haven't they used them before now, if only to enhance placement opportunities? In short, while I certainly will not say that such activities cannot or should not be instituted— they seem like a good idea to me, too—I believe it would be wise to keep expectations concerning their contributions to any refiguring of the Ph.D. very modest indeed.

Ultimately, then, and not at all surprisingly, I rest most of my hopes for any help English Studies might get in refiguring the Ph.D. on the shoulders of the field's doctoral students. You will have observed, no doubt, that as a function of the way this argument has been structured I arrive at this conclusion at least partly by a process of elimination—the students are the only ones left. As I hope the account of the Albany program offered in Section II will have made clear, however, I am motivated here less by desperation (though it is not entirely absent as a motive) than by logic: doctoral students in English Studies, present and future, constitute the largest, best motivated, and most talented group of people the professoriate has any realistic chance of recruiting to help it reform the way it creates the field's future generations. Nor am I alone in recognizing the possibilities this line of reasoning presents. In Chapter 4, I reviewed the various ways in which Gary Waller, James Slevin, and Helene Moglen all argued that involving students in revamping doctoral programs was at the very least an obligation, and at most a terrific opportunity, with Moglen in particular proposing an entirely different set of relationships at the heart of the enterprise—one which, as she put it, allowed "individuals and groups that formerly viewed themselves as being in hierarchical and competitive relationships to redefine themselves genuinely as colleagues" (Moglen 90).

Even more important, perhaps, I also find a related, more contemporary form of support in the recommendations of the Committee on Professional Employment. Nothing as radical as Moglen's, to be sure (that would be expecting a lot from a group commissioned by any professional organization) but one I nonetheless find heartening. One argument they make—a third imperative, in fact, to go with the two quoted earlier—is that the faculty "will have to form alliances with . . . graduate students" (39). They do not elaborate on what such alliances might entail, and it is only fair to note that they make the same assertion regarding a number of other groups (part-time and adjunct lecturers, undergraduates, parents). Still, such a recommendation marks an important step. To insist that the professoriate must now cultivate an alliance with its graduate students is to acknowledge that the relationship between the two has already changed: that the faculty *needs* the students in a way it has not needed them before, and that—if only as a quid pro quo—the students will need to be afforded a more significant role in determining the form and substance of their own educations.

The Committee's subsequent recommendations also support this reading of their position. To begin with, they recommend that every doctoral program should "routinely" provide applicants with a good deal of information before they apply: data on the job market in general and the particular program's placement record in particular; on that program's past students' performance in terms of time to degree; on patterns of financial support; and on the kinds of placement services the institution provides. Again, these may not seem like terribly significant measures, and it does not reflect favorably on College English Teaching, Inc. that a blue-ribbon panel might be needed to shame it into taking them. But these too mark an important step and help to set a very different tone by implying, basically, that doctoral students are not the immature, undereducated, deluded professorial wannabes portrayed so often in Magisterial lore, but rather thoughtful, discriminating adults capable of making informed decisions about pursuing a professional career.

And this shift in tone carries over into the Committee's proposals for how applicants ought to be supported once they are admitted. Thus, when the Committee proposes that all full-time doctoral students should receive full funding—ideally for at least five years, and if possible without teaching duties in the first and last (MLA Committee 40)—they are also asserting, at least tacitly, that doctoral study is a serious business undertaken by serious, qualified people: people to whom the faculty is committed in a putting-our-money-where-our-mouth-is way as the future of English Studies, and who deserve to be treated accordingly.

Much the same can be said for the Committee's other two recommendations on funding, which are as follows: that during those years when students are assigned teaching, they "should have primary responsibility for no more than one course each term, and that teaching should never be so onerous as to interfere with the timely completion of the dissertation"; and that, in general, "remuneration of graduate student employees should recognize the professional nature of the services they render" (40). I find the language here a bit more problematic—there is a lot of room for bureaucratic fudging in a formulation like "should recognize"—but the point gets made just the same. As a matter of principle, these recommendations suggest, doctoral students are professionals-in-training. As such, any duties they take on must be understood as the rendering of professional services; be compensated at a professional rate; and be carried out under working conditions—with regard to teaching but also presumably research and service loads—befitting that status.[3]

Probably the clearest example of this Committee's willingness to grant doctoral students a greater role in shaping their education lies in its handling of what might be called career flexibility: its insistence that programs allow students as much room as possible to determine their own postdoctoral destinies. We have already gotten some sense of this in those very first curricular recommendations quoted. Whatever else the Final Report's proposals to familiarize students with as full a range of employment opportunities as possible might mean, they certainly imply that candidates will also be able to tailor their individual programs to suit a comparably full range of career goals—even if, as would have to be the case fairly often, none of the graduate faculty were themselves qualified for most such careers.

And in fact the Committee elsewhere casts this implied promise in even stronger terms, proposing as a general rule that programs "should be sufficiently flexible that the professional model and full-funding principle do not exclude fully prepared students who have other objectives," and, even more pointedly, that for "at least the next five years" it is "incumbent on departments and institutions to make every effort to help these [new] PhDs find employment outside the academy" (MLA Committee 40). Thus, while such proposals are always framed in terms of departmental and institutional duties, they also tacitly serve to expand the students' enfranchisement: to make room, in the long term, for all sorts of students who want to make of their education something other than what the faculty might otherwise or traditionally have planned; and, in the short term, to actually declare that students can *require* the faculty to do everything possible to assist them in realizing their ambitions.

None of these recommendations, of course, goes anywhere near as far in expanding the specifically curricular role students might play in shaping doctoral education as do those my collaborators and I have outlined in describing "Writing, Teaching, and Criticism." So, for instance, as radical as the Committee's Final Report truly is in many respects, no passage ever asserts that the coherence of doctoral curricula in English ought to derive from "the integrated interests of those who teach and take the classes." Nevertheless, I believe the seeds of such a proposal are there—the tendency, the inclination, even the desire. Consider the cumulative reasoning: if the graduate faculty are not to replicate themselves, and if the students are not only to be encouraged to prepare themselves for a wide range of postdoctoral employment opportunities, but to be actively aided by the faculty in subsequently making good on such opportunities, is it really possible or plausible to expect that the curriculum can remain unaffected? That the students either should or would say to the faculty, "You just go ahead teaching us *as though* you were replicating yourselves—same courses taught in the same ways to the same ends—and we will do all the work of transforming whatever you manage to offer into the broadly marketable abilities you insist you want us to have (if only so you can look better/ feel good about yourselves)"?

It simply doesn't wash, does it. Thus, while the Final Report certainly never says as much; and while indeed the furthest the Committee seems to go in pushing the profession toward specific curricular reform is to offer such modest injunctions as "each PhD program should carefully determine what constitutes good practice" (40); still, lurking in the document's logic are much the same impulses toward Ph.D. candidates we traced in Albany's program proposal. Whether by accident or design, then—and whether, for that matter, this rendering of their position might persuade them to demur—I count the MLA's Committee on Professional Employment as very much on our side in numbering doctoral students among the most likely stalwarts of reform in English Studies.

## The Fusion Option for an English Studies in Transition

At this point, my analysis of the challenge facing doctoral education in English Studies at the turn of the century can be summarized as follows:

1. The Ph.D. in English is being devalued as a credential for college teaching; more and more such teaching is either carried out by non-Ph.D.'s, or by Ph.D.-holders in non-tenure-track and/or part-time positions.

2. The pattern of such devaluation, if not the trend itself, is a direct extension of the field's own long-standing practice of discounting both teaching and research in certain of its own areas—most notably but by no means exclusively the teaching of writing— and is also therefore rooted in what have proven to be very durable intradisciplinary divisions.

3. The field's graduate faculty might now be willing to move toward reforming doctoral education in ways that respond to (1) and (2), but the evidence suggests that they lack the qualifications to do so.

4. While the graduate faculty can cover some of its shortcomings through the retraining of its own members and/or the involvement of outside experts, its most promising ally in any such endeavor is likely to be its own doctoral students.

The courses of action available to English Studies—what I called in Chapter 4 its major strategic options—are pretty much the same as they were in 1987: dissolution, corporate compromise, and fusion. Assuming that my take on the current situation is indeed correct, it is not very hard to determine which of the three holds the most strategic potential for the future of doctoral education. We can begin with the least promising, corporate compromise: that whole business of holding the now more than ever conflicted factions of English Studies together and then, for the purposes of the doctoral curriculum, finding ways to present while preserving their competing interests. As I suggested earlier, this approach has been by far the most popular among doctoral programs in the post-Wayzata era—which also means, it seems to me, that it is responsible for much of the predicament in which the profession/discipline currently finds itself.

More to the point, it is not a strategy that appears to hold much future promise, in that it fails miserably to address any of the key elements I have outlined; it seems ill-equipped to make the situation any better. Thus, because it deliberately perpetuates the intradisciplinary divisions described in point #2, and with them the field's discounting practices, it can offer almost no defense against point #1, the devaluation of the Ph.D. by employers. As for points #3 and #4 . . . as I have suggested, the most generous reading of post-Wayzata events would be that corporate compromise truly represents the best reform effort the professoriate could manage, and that they are both really, really sorry and innocently baffled that things haven't turned out better. Less generous readings are easy to imagine, but the point remains the same: given the situation, corporate compromise cannot continue to represent the best the professoriate can do. If nothing else, it is excruciatingly short-sighted as a business practice; a service-oriented profession that colludes in subverting the value of the services it renders—one that is willing to cannibalize its recruits both while they are training *and* after it has licensed them—surely does not have a bright future. To invoke my earlier image: this goose is not only likely to stop laying golden eggs, but it might well end up being cooked altogether.

Dissolution appears to hold somewhat more promise, mainly because it seeks to transform the intradisciplinary divisions of #2 into full-fledged disciplinary ones. This opens up at least some possibilities regarding #1 and #3, in particular. Thus regarding #3, it might well be that more tightly disciplined (and almost certainly smaller) faculties could do a better job of attuning curricula to their students' real career prospects. Certainly this seems to be one of the advantages associated with any proposed Ph.D. in rhetoric and composition. That is, since English composition is by far the most frequently taught course in U.S. higher education (it shows up on students' transcripts fully three times as often as the next most frequent English department offering), a faculty devoted exclusively to work in that area has a good chance of turning out appropriately trained and very marketable students. If this did indeed turn out to be the case, it might help ease the problem of discounting represented in #1: it is possible that separate Ph.D. programs in, say, British and American literature, rhetoric and composition, and cultural studies could be run in ways that allowed their graduates to fare better in the institutional marketplace than have recipients of the increasingly incoherent English Studies degree. Assuming that such good things as these really did come about, they would nearly obviate any need for the nonfaculty support referred to in #4.

Realistically speaking, however, I am not all that sanguine about these possible advantages, and for two reasons. First, there is the distinct possibility that employers simply will not care if English Studies breaks up: the institutions most responsible for devaluing the Ph.D. in English Studies will simply shift to devaluing Ph.D.'s in literature, rhetoric and composition, etc., staff discounted courses with whichever sort is most available, and divide among the two or three new disciplinary units the same number of faculty lines previously deployed in English departments. The second reason for my skepticism, and one I outlined in Chapter 4, is that dissolution will actually make the situation worse: it will water down still further any institutional clout the English professoriate might have left by dispersing it over two or more rival departments, making it less likely than ever that it will be able to take substantive action against those discounting practices.

Hence I arrive at what is my foregone conclusion: that the fusion option is the best strategy currently available for reforming doctoral education in English Studies. As you may recall from Chapter 4, this approach—at least as I defined it—features three key requirements: everyone involved must commit to locked-room negotiations; doctoral students must be afforded a major role in the deliberations as participants, not spectators; and the graduate faculty must be willing to renegotiate their disciplinary and professional status vis-à-vis one another *and* those doctoral students. Obviously, these match up rather well with my rendering of the field's predicament. Thus the first two commitments offer the graduate faculty a means of getting past the dilemma represented in point #3—their willingness to reform doctoral education on the one hand, and their lack of qualifications to do so on the other—while at the same time setting in motion a process that not only could but should end the field's internal discounting practices and the intradisciplinary divisions on which those practices are based. While such an approach obviously involves the risk of fomenting far more and fiercer short-term infighting than either corporate compromise or dissolution—Gary Waller's martial metaphors come to mind—it compensates by offering considerably more long-term promise of preserving the group's collective institutional power. Departments able to maintain a reasonable facade of unity while undergoing such a process (no mean feat, to be sure) have an excellent chance of emerging from the process with the institutional stature of English intact, or even, since its debilitating internal divisions may well have been eliminated, enhanced.

The real clincher for me, however, is the extent to which this option's third required commitment provides the graduate faculty with the help they so obviously need in carrying out any real reform of doctoral education. To be sure, a fusion-based curriculum need not preclude the other sources of support previously described. A program designed along lines anything like Albany's, for instance, would certainly allow for graduate faculty retooling, and might well even encourage it by routinely confronting faculty with the alternative perspectives, texts, and methodologies favored by their colleagues and students. And if such a program could not be as amenable to the use of outside expertise —locked-room negotiations, after all, make it harder to involve anyone not fully invested in their outcome—mentored internships, residencies, and the like could nevertheless enhance what students could bring to the curricular bargaining table. So, for example, a student interning in a prison literacy program or serving a residency as a Web-page designer for a major local corporation stands at least as good a chance, and maybe a better one, of usefully integrating such work with her other curricular activities in a fusion-based curriculum as in one based on either the compromise or dissolution options.

Where the fusion option really outstrips the other two, however, is in mandating that the faculty put its authority on the table as part of the process, so that doctoral students are negotiating the terms not only of their own educations but of the nature of English Studies—discipline and profession—as a whole. Throughout Section II and most recently in my review of the MLA Committee on Professional Employment's final report, my collaborators and I have explored in considerable detail the range of abilities students can bring to this process and the kinds of contributions they can make. Here I want to add only that a genuinely committed graduate faculty can easily enrich the value of their students as a resource by engaging in savvy recruiting and admission practices. The Committee on Professional Employment touches on this point, albeit briefly, urging that while the field needs to reduce the number of Ph.D.'s granted each year, "no cutbacks be undertaken that might compromise the diversity of the graduate student population" (39). My impression is that they are referring mainly to demographic concerns—i.e., diversity in terms of gender and race, and perhaps also class.

It is easy to see, however, how for the purposes of stoking a fusion-based program it would be possible to go a good deal further: to expand the scope of such a commitment so that it included what might be called disciplinary and professional diversity, and also to reframe it so that instead of representing a holding action—i.e., an effort not to compromise gains already made—it operated as a deliberate strategy, a front on which the program would make continued advances. A graduate admissions committee would be charged with building a cadre of doctoral students in much the same way that many colleges and universities now seek to build a first-year class, operating not on some abstracted notion of merit, but developing a mix of students who complemented both one another and the faculty. This would be partly a matter of demographics in its more usual sense, to be sure—with a special emphasis, perhaps, on seeking a blend of people with very different educational backgrounds—but it would take account of disciplinary identification and professional trajectories as well: it would seek some combination of people who conceived of themselves as novelists or rhetoricians, literary historians or playwrights, poets or critical theorists, and so on, but also of those who were current or aspiring four-year or two-year college teachers, writing program administrators or technical writers, communications officers or literacy researchers, etc. In fact, departments might want to concentrate their recruiting efforts on filling these needs: not to reserve their best fellowships for the Harvard or Oberlin undergraduate with the highest GPA in English, or the applicant with the best combination of transcript and GRE scores, but rather to seek out and offer such fellowships to one of the more effective M.A.-holding teachers at the local community college, or the assistant director of the regional prison literacy program, or a promising young rural or inner-city poet, and so on. Such people would likely need serious convincing before they would agree to enroll, and the program would have to keep adjusting to their needs throughout their time in it. But these are, quite honestly, the kinds of people English Studies is going to need to recruit—and learn from—if it is at all serious about reform.

I assume it is sufficiently clear by now that my support for the fusion option in general does not mean I believe that all 140-plus English doctoral programs in the United States ought to drop whatever they are currently offering and install Albany's "Writing, Teaching, and Criticism" program instead. In a narrowly literal sense, perhaps, such a thing might be possible: a given department could conceivably vote to follow Albany's original program proposal to the letter, right down to copying the course titles, the requirements, the examination and dissertation structures, and so on. What that department actually *offered,* however, would inevitably be another matter entirely—would turn out to be a program which, like Albany's own efforts, gained its coherence from the integrated interests of the particular set of faculty and students who participated in it, who taught and took its classes. Thus, while there are certainly plenty of useful lessons to be learned from Albany's experiment—many of them hard-earned—imitation in any real sense is simply not in the cards.

Nor do I mean to suggest that English Studies ought to pursue this fusion option indefinitely. Despite what I understand will be regarded as the more outrageous features of the proposals outlined in this book, I am not in favor of perpetual disciplinary and professional turmoil. Although my invocation of College English Teaching, Inc. has often had a pejorative ring to it, it is because the business practices sponsored by English Studies, especially with regard to its uses of doctoral students both before and after they have earned degrees, have deserved it—have often been, as they often are now, broadly objectionable. For all that, I am not (quite) yet in favor of its dissolution. Assuming that it undertakes a major overhaul, a radical restructuring, I believe that English Studies actually can operate as College English Teaching, Inc., and as such play an important and entirely honorable role in U.S. higher education.

With these two acknowledgments that my ambitions for the fusion option really do have some limits out of the way, however, I want to end on a note more in tune with the Introduction's hubris and offer three final, rather pointed recommendations on how the Ph.D. in English Studies ought to be refigured. First, although I do not believe that all doctorate-granting departments can or should simply adopt Albany's programmatic structures as paradigmatic, I do believe all of them ought to approximate some version of its disciplinary mix. All such programs should seek aggressively to include faculty and students with interests and expertise not only in English and American literature, cultural studies, critical theory, and so on, but also—and in more than token proportions—creative writing, rhetoric and composition, professional and technical writing, and other writing-related areas.

Obviously, this will present more of a challenge for some departments than for others. There are a number of institutions—including some of the most hoary—in which the field's discounting practices run so deep that no tenure-track lines whatever are devoted to scholars in these writing-related areas. However, if doctoral education is going to move English Studies toward anything like an intradisciplinary synthesis; or, to take even the Committee on Professional Employment's more limited ambition, if it is ever to prepare its graduates more directly for their real career prospects; then it will need in every instance to feature a full range of what the field actually includes. I might put it emblematically as follows: English Studies will prove itself serious about refiguring the Ph.D. when a good many doctoral students enrolling at the Harvards and Berkeleys—as well as those at the Albanys and the Indiana University of Pennsylvanias—can expect not only to be prepared for, but actively led to *aspire* to, careers as writing teachers at a Cal State, Northridge or a Hostos Community College; as communications officers for General Electric or the Legal Aid Society; as directors of literacy programs at major state correctional facilities or rural school districts; and so on. Not quiescent writing teachers or communications officers or program directors—not docile supporters of a given status quo—but savvy professionals who are committed to and trained for careers in just such institutional settings. And for that to happen, fairly dramatic changes will have to take place in all English Ph.D. programs, but definitely more in some than in others.

My second recommendation has to do with duration. Specifically, I believe that while this fusion strategy cannot go on indefinitely, the professoriate as a whole—and the graduate faculty in particular—must make a multigenerational commitment to it. And just how long is that? At an absolute minimum, until the last of the graduates of the Magisterial system have retired, which might be (to choose a rough number) somewhere around 2020. Or, to offer an alternative but rather more variable measure, until the faculties of Ph.D.-granting English departments are dominated by the graduates of fusion-based programs—something that could happen sooner than 2020, at least in principle. Do dates like these, or indeed the whole idea of a timetable for reform, seem somehow untoward in a discussion of an academic discipline? Indelicate? Un- or anti-intellectual? Open to critique from commentators who would locate themselves on both the "right" and the "left" in the field's debates? Probably so, but no matter. Whatever realm English Studies might occupy, or whatever mythologies we may promote about its "timeless" conversations, College English Teaching, Inc. rumbles along in real time, and much of what it needs has to do with getting itself and its constituents—however unworldly they sometimes fancy themselves to be—onto some kind of schedule. Target dates of any kind are therefore a step in the right direction.

My final recommendation—and here I know I definitely represent my collaborators as well—has to do with making doctoral student writing one of the primary means by which this refiguring of the Ph.D. will be brought about. I am aware of how odd this proposal sounds even now: of how peculiar it likely seems, even at the end of a book like this one, to place so much of the burden for the reform of a century-old disciplinary and professional enterprise on the as yet unwritten efforts of such a group; many of its members, after all, have yet to so much as identify with the enterprise in any serious way. I am aware, too, that this will be by far the most difficult of these proposals to enact. All sorts of commentators, graduate faculty in particular, will propose changes in just about everything else—different readings, different graduate classroom practices, different teacher-training programs, shorter time to degree, longer time to degree, and so on: anything, anything, anything other than giving doctoral students greater license in terms of what they might write.

For all the reasons I have outlined in this chapter, however, English Studies simply does not have a lot of options in terms of who might take the lead, and even fewer in terms of how. Thus, while other efforts at change will surely be both welcome and important—and there promise to be a good many—I will stick with our initial position. The key to power in English Studies—its conservative linchpin—is doctoral education; and the key to power in doctoral education in turn lies in what students (are allowed to) write: writing is the work most crucial to their earning the degree; the work that most powerfully determines who they are and/or can be in disciplinary and professional terms; and, in some collective and cumulative sense, the work that has the most to do with the nature, and the future, of English Studies itself.

# NOTES

## Introduction

1. See, e.g., Bowen and Rudenstine 77–79.

2. In fact, there were three name changes between 1959 and 1962: to the New York State University College of Education at Albany in 1959; to the New York State University College at Albany in 1961; and then in 1962 to the State University of New York at Albany. These days, after a couple more changes, it is called the University at Albany, State University of New York.

## Section I

1. There have been a few exceptions to this rule over the past few years, most notably Patricia Sullivan's "Writing in the Graduate Curriculum: Literary Criticism as Composition"; Carol Berkenkotter et al.'s "Conventions, Conversations, and the Writer: Case Study of a Student in a Rhetoric Ph.D. Program"; and Chapter 5 of Ruth Ray's *The Practice of Theory,* which deals with the writing of graduate students enrolled in a composition theory course at Wayne State University. Even here, though, only Sullivan's study focuses on the writing in what might be called a mainstream or traditional English Ph.D. program; the other two deal with students working specifically in rhetoric and composition.

## Chapter One

1. As I will explain later, however, far from all German students who enrolled in a university did so in order to gain a Ph.D. or, ultimately, a professorship. According to Daniel Fallon, some studied long enough to launch a career in civil service, while for others the goal "was to complete the *Staatsexamen,* which was a qualifying examination in a given discipline for teaching at a *Gymnasium,* or for entry into certain other civil service positions" (39).

2. It is important here to maintain the distinction between American conceptions of the German system—the ideals that were so influential—and that system's actual practices. The extraordinary enthusiasm of the

German system's U.S. promoters often makes it hard to tell just how fully they understood such things as the system's history (and particularly its ties to the fortunes of Prussia), its relationship to either the state or the country's class structures, the problems created by its pyramidal structure, and so on. The seemingly autonomous professor at the pinnacle of that pyramid could indeed cut an extraordinary figure and often exercised considerable disciplinary influence, not only in Germany, but in much of the Western world. But all sorts of prices were paid to keep him there. See, e.g., R. H. Samuel and R. Hinton Thomas, *Education and Society in Modern Germany* (1949), or Daniel Fallon's *The German University: A Heroic Ideal in Conflict with the Modern World* (1980).

3. Perry was far less enthusiastic about other lecturers, and he did not much like the settings, either. One of his mentors, a Professor Zupitza at Berlin,

> could make any subject dull; and so could Hoffory, a Dane who must have been related to Rosencrantz and Guildenstern. Rödiger was a little better, and I liked the *Nibelungen Lied*, but the air in those crowded Berlin lecture rooms was notorious for its foulness. (97)

4. However, there could be different levels of interaction. Perry, e.g., reports being admitted as an "attendant" to a Zupitza "Seminar of exercises in Gothic and Anglo-Saxon" rather than as a "member," which meant he did not have the right to speak (95–96).

5. Indeed, the drive to create such institutions has a long history. See, e.g., Storr's *The Beginnings of Graduate Education in America,* and especially chapters 6–8. I cannot resist noting—albeit with a sense of irony concerning the events sketched in our Introduction—that one of the first such institutions to be formally constituted, though it never actually enrolled anyone, was the University of Albany in 1851. According to remarks Storr quotes from Dr. T. Romeyn Beck, then secretary of the New York State Board of Regents, the idea was to "'have in Albany a university equal to European universities and become in time equal to the celebrated University of Berlin'" (69–70).

6. Writing in 1930, Howard Mumford Jones describes the situation as baldly as anyone, although he opts for a more military metaphor (reminiscent of the Jesuits):

> The only course universally required in American college life is Freshman English; and one of the courses commonly required

is a course in English literature during the Sophomore year. To officer these courses requires an army of instructors, so that the staff of English teachers in American universities is today the largest single element in university and college faculties. These instructors demand training; the university presses them to increase their professional equipment; and, were there no other reason, since no man worth his salt wishes to be kept forever at the grind of Freshman themes, pressure to escape into the upper levels of English teaching would draw an increasing number toward graduate degrees. (Part VII, 203)

Forty years later, Cameron Allen reports on an NEA study for 1958 to 1960. He argues that the "fidelity of English Ph.D.'s to the teaching profession is almost miraculous when it is viewed against the general infidelity of the other learned professions" (17). During the years he was considering, 91.2 percent of English Ph.D.'s entered or continued teaching, compared to 77.2 percent for History, and 19.3 percent for Chemistry.

7. Daniel Fallon points out that the *Staatsexamen* "was a qualifying examination in a given discipline for teaching at a *Gymnasium,* or for entry into certain other civil service positions" (39). While officially administered by the government, it became more and more the general practice to contract "with university professors to construct and supervise the examinations." For this reason, Fallon argues, "it came to assume the characteristics of a first degree at the university" (39).

8. One of the most visible figures in the field's originary mythology, Francis James Child of Harvard, has come to be something of an emblem in this regard—the patron saint, perhaps, of graduate professors of English. For while Child may have been both "the first American scholar in English literature" and the one who "train[ed] the first American Ph.D. in English," Robert Grant, in 1876 (Allen 7–8), he is more often invoked for the priorities he established in having been the unsuccessful object of what David Russell has called "perhaps the first case of faculty raiding" (184). From 1876 to 1877, or so the story goes, Johns Hopkins's president Daniel Coit Gilman launched a serious effort to lure Child away from Harvard, where Child had served for some twenty-seven years. It appears he might have gone, too, except that Harvard president Charles W. Eliot made Child the promise he most needed to hear: that he would be "'relieved at last from the burden of correcting undergraduate compositions'" (Russell 184, quoting from Henry James's 1930 *Charles W. Eliot,* Boston: Houghton-Mifflin, 14–15).

Cameron Allen gives both the episode and the priorities thus established even greater significance by noting, albeit wryly, that "[b]y this action Gilman established an English department at Harvard although thus far he had failed to do so at Johns Hopkins" (8). Others to feature Child in this role include Kitzhaber (33), Graff (40–41), and Phyllis Franklin. Franklin notes that even later in his career—after almost twenty years without those compositions (1895)—Child looked upon the beginning of the term, and thus the interruption of his work on English and Scottish ballads, "'with some aversion and this makes me think I had better retire after this year'" (368). As Franklin puts it a bit further on in her profile of Child, he "view[ed] earning a living by college teaching" as an obstacle to scholarship (368).

9. Estimates about this rate are necessarily very cautious. Cameron Allen, for example, reports that "[o]ur knowledge about dropouts is very vague. The educationists have made studies of the problem, but no one has any exact figures for English Departments for any period of time" (51). However, working with somewhat incomplete but strongly suggestive data for programs in all fields, Bowen and Rudenstine report that "only about *half* of all entering students in many Ph.D. programs eventually obtain doctorates (frequently after pursuing degrees for anywhere from six to twelve years)" (105, their emphasis). In addition, their data for a specific set of institutions over a specific time period—1967 to 1976— puts the completion rate for English right at that 50 percent mark (124).

10. Cameron Allen, seeking to dramatize the acute shortage of Ph.D. holders after 1950, claims that "[i]n the 1890s the supply of Ph.D.'s in English was undoubtedly smaller than the demand; in fact, it was only in the unhappy period between 1931 and 1940 that there was any reasonable relationship between what was wanted [by way of degree holders] and what was to be had [for open positions]" (16).

11. As Robert Connors argues so passionately in "Rhetoric in the Modern University: The Creation of an Underclass," a good many of the positions available would have been for composition teachers at the instructor level and therefore would also have entailed working conditions and pay scales ranging from dismal to horrific. In keeping with the general pattern I will shortly trace in more detail, Connors makes it clear that a disproportionate number of such positions were filled by women (see esp. 66–79).

12. To get a sense of these earlier outputs, consider Jones's report that during its first fifty years (1876–1926), Harvard granted 196 Ph.D.'s— about four per year, and that during its first thirty-three years, the University of Chicago granted 102 degrees (n. 465–66).

13. The U.S. Office of Education only began requesting racial data in its compliance surveys in 1965.

14. There is a slight discrepancy in totals because the total on the Racial/Ethnic Group measure does not include Native Americans or Ph.D. recipients "who did not answer the questions related to race and ethnicity" (Bowen and Rudenstine 379).

15. It is worth noting, however, that Bowen and Rudenstine's figures indicate that between 1982 and 1988 "the number of doctorates awarded to blacks in all fields declined, from 1,133 to 951; the group's share of all doctorates fell from 4.6 percent to 3.9 percent," with declines in English "if anything, slightly greater on a relative basis" (40). Moreover, what data on gender they have suggest that the percentage decline in all fields was three times greater for black men than for black women. Thus, while the 7 percent figure likely does represent a high-water mark for English, it does so as a function of gains by people in the Hispanic and Asian categories.

16. Bowen and Rudenstine offer this overview:

> In the 1920s and 1930s, about 15% of all doctorates were awarded to women. During the 1940s and the years following World War II, the share of doctorates awarded to women oscillated within the 11 to 20 percent range. As recently as the years between 1958 and 1966, the percentage of all doctorates awarded to women remained between 10 and 12 percent. (32).

In 1958, they suggest, just over 15 percent of all English doctorates were awarded to women.

17. In *Graduate Study in Universities and Colleges in the United States* (1935), for example, Walton C. John reports that in counts taken every ten years beginning with 1900, the percentage of women in graduate enrollments in all fields approached a high of 38 percent (in 1930). He also reports, however, that the number of doctorates awarded to women in proportion to the number of enrollments was strikingly smaller than for men. Thus, in the 1930 count there were 18,185 female graduate students, and the number of Ph.D.'s granted to females was 332, while on the male side, of 29,070 students, 1,692 Ph.D.'s were granted. As John expresses it (since these are not cadre-based analyses), it can be said to take 54 female graduate students to produce a single female Ph.D.; while it takes only 17 male graduate students to produce a male Ph.D.

18. Cameron Allen's survey offers indirect evidence that this was indeed the pattern. Of 1,784 respondents who were recent recipients of the Ph.D. (1955–1965), the average age was 33.9 years, with a median age

of 33. This group would have included a large number of GI Bill–funded graduate students, whose presence would have pushed that age sharply upward. Assuming, then, that before the war this average age would have been a good deal closer to 30, and that time to completion would have been in the six to eight year range, Jones's sketch of the beginning student is about right.

19. These rankings were generated by comparing the data from Part I of the monograph "Production of Doctorates" (6–27) with those from Part II, "Baccalaureate Origins" (28–121). For the record, Washington produced forty-eight Ph.D.'s during the span under study, coming in at fourteenth in the country. On the other side of the ledger, Cornell ranked seventeenth in producing baccaluareates who earned doctorates in English, NYU was twenty-first, and Iowa was twenty-fifth.

20. Cameron Allen's 1965 survey reports that 6.8 percent of those who reported doing graduate teaching did not themselves hold a Ph.D. (140, Table 3.28). Among this group, the average age was fifty-two (144, Table 3.34), and nearly all (87.5 percent) held the M.A. (144, Table 3.35).

Chapter Two

1. While no comprehensive analysis of these developments seems possible, Bowen and Rudenstine offer a useful sketch (91–94). They note, for example, that by 1980—following the precipitous decline of fellowship support over the previous decade—even as relatively well-heeled an institution as Cornell reported that over 60 percent of students in English, history, political science, economics, mathematics, and physics held teaching assistantships "during *both* the early years of graduate study and the dissertation writing stage" (92).

2. As far as I know, there is no extended history of these labor practices, not least because it is unclear whether the materials exist from which such a history might be fashioned. Among the best and most relevant studies to date is an essay I refer to for a variety of purposes, Robert Connors's "Rhetoric in the Modern University: The Creation of an Underclass." Among other matters of relevance here, Connors notes that the use of TAs in U.S. universities first became widespread in the 1890s (72); he pieces together at least a partial portrait of the economics involved, noting, for example, that "[g]raduate teaching assistants during the first decade of the twentieth century did more composition work than any other sort, and their average yearly salaries lay in a range between $350 and $850 yearly, with the average around $650" (75).

3. The best published source of information on this range of formats is Allen's *The Ph.D. in English and American Literature,* Chapter 5.

4. As I have suggested throughout this chapter, however, it did not follow that these students had to learn to *teach* as the Magisterial "we" taught—this despite the fact that all involved knew they were, like their mentors, more than likely preparing for careers as college teachers. In keeping with the Germanic ideal, mastery of subject area was all that mattered. Indeed, Allen suggests that for this purpose, students might be wise to avoid *imitatio*: the "best argument in favor of many graduate courses," he argues, "is that they instruct the student in 'how not to teach'" (110).

5. Technically, the process involved the final step of printing the dissertation for dissemination. As far as I can tell, however, conferral of the degree was never contingent on some external body's acceptance of the manuscript for publication. Universities themselves, and usually university presses, would have handled this chore (as they still do in at least some European systems). Also, of course, print publication began to decline throughout the 1940s (no doubt partly as a function of costs). By the mid-1950s, microfilm publication had become standard practice.

Chapter Three

1. For Korean Conflict veterans, the operative legislation was the Veterans Readjustment Assistance Act of 1952 (PL 82-550). A third bill (PL 89-385), referred to as the Cold War GI Bill, was passed in 1966.

2. The mismatch between Ph.D. production and undergraduate enrollment demands is of course exacerbated considerably by the differences in time to degree between the two. On this as on so many features of doctoral education, exact numbers are hard to come by. Bowen and Rudenstine's analysis for 1962 to 1971, based on a rather selective set of institutions, finds a *median* time to degree of 7.9 years—in other words, half those enrolled finished more quickly, but half finished more slowly. I know of no study suggesting a time to degree of less than six years.

3. Indeed, Cameron Allen pursues this analogy in a more than figurative way:

Industrial production is increased by building more plants and by operating those already built more wisely. In agriculture more acres are put into cultivation and farming methods are improved. The essential product of the undergraduate institutions is the A.B. and other associated degrees; one cannot help but feel that the enormous increase in this division of the education industry is closely related to the increase in acreage and plant. Campuses piled with brick, stone, steel, and concrete to make shelters for body and mind have appeared from out of nowhere. Management and nonacademic personnel has grown formidably. Everything has seemed to grow in measure with everything else except trained faculty and the means of training them. (18)

4. Such "tier" rankings are always problematic, perhaps more so in English than in some other disciplines. Bowen and Rudenstine certainly acknowledge this (see, e.g., 63ff, including notes 8 and 9).

5. According to Bowen and Rudenstine,

> In our terminology, "new" programs are those that conferred degrees in some even-numbered year after 1958 but conferred no degrees in 1958, and "established" programs are those that conferred one or more degrees in 1958. These are imperfect definitions, since a new program might have been in operation in 1958 even though it conferred no degrees in that particular year, and an established program might have conferred degrees for the first time in 1959. However, inspection of the patterns of degrees conferred over time indicates that such aberrations were rare, and that this simple dichotomy serves reasonably well to divide the universe of programs into the two broad categories of new and established. (57–58 n. 3)

6. These undergraduate figures are taken from the "Facts and Figures" feature of the *ADE Bulletin* No. 110 (Spring 1995). They were derived from *Digest of Education Statistics*.

7. See, e.g., Bowen and Rudenstine, here working from H. Marmion's *Selective Service: Conflict and Compromise* (New York: Wiley, 1968):

> The Selective Service Act of 1967 became effective June 30, 1967, and Executive Order 11360 contained provisions that meant that "after a one-year moratorium to end at the close of the 1967–1968 academic year, no more 2-S deferments would be granted to graduate students except those specifically written into the law" [164] (essentially those for students in medicine and related fields)" (49).

8. A very small percentage of those reporting employment in postsecondary institutions list "Higher education administration" or "Postdoctoral fellowship." But their total portion of the whole has never amounted to more than 4.6 percent, and in any case Huber's other data confirm that the percentage of those accepting part-time and/or non-tenure-track employment has most often been higher than 30 percent.

9. It might also be assumed that the "great programs" supported Allen's effort as a means of protecting themselves against the market incursions of the postwar programs. That is, if all programs came to be structured in more or less the same way, the advantage in recruiting and placement would almost certainly have accrued to those institutions—the Harvards, Yales, and Columbias—with the oldest and best established reputations.

10. By contrast, in the two fields Bowen and Rudestine pair with English—history and political Science—the percentage of women receiving Ph.D.'s increased from about 10 percent to about 30 percent over the same span—a significant increase, to be sure, but nowhere near as dramatic as that in English.

11. Writing about the postwar years, Solomon notes that women who pursued careers in such "prestigious 'male' fields" as academia were at a disadvantage:

> Graduate education became more competitive, due to the vast numbers of men entering and priority given to veterans. Graduate women had to be far better qualified than men to gain admission; and married women desiring to enroll part-time found it very difficult. Women as potential graduate students . . . often found themselves rejected, due in part to the discriminatory quotas favoring veterans. (190)

Chapter Four

1. To some extent, the demographic dimension of this diversification, especially in terms of hiring Ph.D.'s who are also women and/or members of certain minorities, has been made possible by affirmative action initiatives. However, there has been nothing magical about the process. Huber's 1995 review of tenure-track hiring disparities between men and women indicates that while the majority of Ph.D. earners in each of four survey years (1979–80, 1983–84, 1991–92, 1993–94) were women (50.1 percent, 56.2 percent, 57.6 percent), it has been only in the 1990s that "the employment prospects of men and women with newly minted PhDs in English have been roughly equivalent" (51).

2. It is also worth noting that as a form of institutional leverage, the field-coverage principle in research universities, especially the midsized institutions, seems to have favored the newer specializations. That is, it would appear to have been easier to convince an administration to invest relatively scarce lines in fields that could be featured as "new" or "cutting edge," and that were not already dominated by older or larger institutions, than to argue for what were seen as replacements.

3. The eight organizations were the Modern Language Association, the National Council of Teachers of English, the Association of Departments of English, the College English Association, the Conference on English Education, the College Language Association, the Conference on College Composition and Communication, and the Conference of Secondary School English Department Chairs. In addition to support from these groups, the conference was funded by the Andrew W. Mellon and Rockefeller foundations, the Exxon Education Foundation, and the National Endowment for the Humanities.

4. This assembly also included representatives from D.A.-granting departments; Huber's Appendix to the published proceedings includes data from such programs. Editors Lunsford, Moglen, and Slevin offer no comment on their omission here.

5. For example, when the editors write that "our subject has been destabilized and that our methodologies are being radically questioned," what happens to the grammatical agent? Presumably the editors mean "*we* have destabilized our subject" or "*we* are radically questioning our methodologies." After all, the possibility that someone else has been doing so seems remote (who would it be?). But to say so is just too awkward: if some "we" does the destabilizing and the radical questioning, then it's hard to see them as identical with the "our," since the latter is, or at least was, subject- and methodology-based to begin with.

6. Huber (1989) does argue that

> linkages among various types of required courses suggest considerable agreement about what the literature curriculum should include. The courses generally favored are bibliographic methods, literary criticism, critical theory, historical scholarship, and textual criticism. The number of respondents abiding entirely by this consensus is limited, however, since only 22% of them require courses in textual criticism for the literature degree. (162)

However, her survey also makes clear that even this degree of consensus is somewhat illusory. For example, headings such as critical theory or literary criticism tend to mask further underlying differences. Huber asked respondents to identify trends in literary study they deemed "important for the teaching of doctoral students" (164). Heading the list was feminist criticism, at 86 percent, followed by critical pluralism at 82 percent, poststructuralism at 70 percent—a reasonable level of agreement, perhaps, although the categories themselves are still rather broad. After that, however, the range expands considerably: 66 percent considered canon revision an important issue; 55 percent promoted reader-response; 49 percent New Criticism; 48 percent new historicism; 48 percent Marxist criticism; 43 percent semiotics; and 43 percent structuralism.

7. The conferences were comprised of five meetings during 1966–67 and were supported by the Danforth Foundation in conjunction with the host universities: Johns Hopkins, Chicago, Stanford, Tulane, and NYU.

8. In retrospect, of course, one might wish that they had learned more or better. For example, this meeting was motivated, as were those in 1966–67, in part by what were interpreted as relatively positive economic trends, and with the related hope—expressed by the Commission on Writing and Literature—that "improvements in [the enterprise's] material conditions would be beneficial to the intellectual climate, as well" (Lunsford, Moglen, and Slevin, v). Subsequent events indicate that those trends were once again read too optimistically and that consequently the hope was unfounded; at any rate, it is quite clear that the post-1987 increase in Ph.D. production—which Wayzata certainly did nothing to discourage—has been moving the field toward a repeat of its mid-1970s debacle, with the number of new degrees granted per year edging far too sharply toward the total number of positions advertised (see, for example, Huber 1994, Figure 5, 49).

Section II

1. It is worth noting that as the result of a grievance in 1990–91 seven people represented here only under the anonymous "Adjuncts" heading would join McCaskill under the "Lecturers" heading, indicating in their case full-time, non-tenure-track status (renewable annually). As was fairly typical for this kind of situation—itself quite common—all seven were women, five with doctorates earned at Albany. The department shortly thereafter voted to grant lecturers full voting rights.

Chapter Five

1. The first Doctor of Arts, in Mathematics, was awarded at Carnegie Mellon University in 1968. In 1970 the Committee on Graduate Studies of the American Association of State Colleges and Universities published "The Doctor of Arts Degree: A Proposal for Guidelines," and the Council of Graduate Schools of the United States issued "The Doctor of Arts Degree." In the same year, the Carnegie Corporation of New York provided funds for the development of D.A. programs at ten institutions across the United States, one of which was the State University of New York at Albany (*Eastman Conference* ix–x).

2. The other required course is Gender, Race, and Class in English Studies, which "foregrounds ideology and provides the occasion for interrogating the cultural and political influences in English studies" ("Proposal" 10).

3. Writing Theory and Practice "expands and gives theoretical body to the traditional pragmatic writers' workshops, not only in 'creative' writing but also in non-fiction prose, including translation and scholarly prose" (10). Language and Language Theory "is based on the fact that language is the focal sign system for English studies," and ranges over a "wide spectrum that includes history, pragmatics, and ideology" ("Proposal" 11).

4. However, Bettina Huber's closing comments on the matter of creative writing in her Appendix essay to *The Future of Doctoral Studies in English* have some bearing here:

> The survey findings discussed earlier show that two-thirds of the Ph.D.-granting departments in the sample offer graduate courses in creative writing, while approximately one-quarter permit general examinations and dissertations. In addition, little more than one-third of the doctoral programs offering courses in creative writing also permit examinations. Departments with rhetoric programs are almost twice as likely as other departments to allow general examinations and dissertations in creative writing (34 percent vs. 20 percent)
>
> It may be important to assess these findings in light of the 1983–84 survey of English programs, which found that four-fifths of the undergraduate English programs in the United States have courses in creative writing and that close to half have degree programs. . . . Thus, there is considerable likelihood that the average college teacher of English will be expected to teach creative . . . writing. (Huber 1989, 173)

5. In his analysis of the rise of "'the New Criticism'" in *Professing Literature* (see especially pages 145–61), Graff notes that

> many of the first critics to achieve a foothold in the university did so on the strength of their poetry rather than their criticism. It is worth pondering the probability that the critical movement would not have succeeded in the university had it not been tied to creative writing, from which it was soon to part company. (153)

The group he has in mind includes Allen Tate, John Crowe Ransom, Yvor Winters, and Delmore Schwartz.

6. Huber's survey indicates that departments featuring the rhetoric Ph.D. are more likely than those without it both to offer creative writing courses *and* to allow exams and theses in this area. The differences are not so great, however, as to constitute what we would judge to be an emerging rapprochment between rhetoric and composition and creative writing. Moreover, nothing that has happened over the subsequent ten years suggests that such a connection is any more likely now.

Chapter Six

1. Ruth Ray makes a related argument for writing along these lines in Chapter 6 of *The Practice of Theory* ("Toward a Teacher-Research Approach to Graduate Studies"), although she is writing specifically about graduate education in composition and not English Studies in general. Current practices, she argues, favor too exclusively an "analytic" perspective, one from which writing by students is evaluated solely in terms of its publishability: "If a text is deemed appropriate for a national conference or a refereed journal, it is an acceptable contribution" (146). The alternative, she suggests, is a "more interpretive, process-oriented graduate program" that would focus on additional purposes for writing:

> to generate and sustain a conversation with established scholars; to connect personal knowledge with theoretical knowledge; to reflect on experience; to test the consequences of following various theoretical perspectives; to articulate hypotheses, beliefs, assumptions, and personal theories; and to express doubts, anxieties, hopes and fears about entering the scholarly community. From an interpretive perspective, graduate students write in order *to construct* the field *for themselves* and to consider the personal possibilities of researching and teaching within it. (148; Ray's emphasis)

In addition, in their case study of a first-year graduate student in Carnegie Mellon's rhetoric program, Berkenkotter, Huckin, and Ackerman indicate that "the technique of using informal, expressive writing to explore new ideas had considerable heuristic power . . . during the period that [Nate] had to make the adjustment from 'oral' to 'literate' strategies . . . in his academic papers" (27). The graduate program Nate entered is represented as favoring the perspectives—and the attendant rhetorics—of cognitive psychology and sociolinguistics, so that the direction and perhaps the means of "disciplining" his writing are not immediately relevant here. (Indeed, the invocation of the oral/ literate binary is quite problematic, and all the more so given the implication that Nate somehow outgrows the ostensibly more primitive oral mode.) Still, the study does help illustrate at least the possible potential of such alternative discursive spaces, even when they are intended to sponsor evanescent texts.

2. For one argument concerning such writing and its functions, see Elbow "Forward."

3. The metaphysical debates concerning precisely these issues of "text" and "representation" have, of course, long been the focus of scholarly attention in English, all the more so since the advent in the United States of deconstruction. Indeed, disagreements concerning them are usually high on the list of symptoms—and sometimes causes—of what we have been calling the identity crisis in English Studies. Even at their fiercest, however, those debates appear to have been carried on as though "staging a reading" were not only possible, but indeed remained central to whatever direction the disciplinary enterprise might be taking. For example, the practice known as quotation has continued to be treated as though it were not only possible but essential to represent excerpts from an extant text in ways that could be defended as "fair" or "accurate"; and the practices grouped under the rubric of "citation" have been carried on as if in aid of a paradigmatically cumulative knowledge-making system. In fact—and it is hard to know which of the possible ironies to appreciate most here—this era of upheaval has also produced the discipline's most conspicuous effort ever to police the ways in which such readings get staged: the *MLA Style Manual* (first published in 1951, revised in 1970, 1985, and again for a 1998 edition).

4. There has always been at least some oral dimension to these expectations as well, no doubt in large part as an inheritance from the era of the disputation. Thus most institutions still have an oral portion to at least the qualifying examinations, wherein candidates are expected to stage such readings in a more literal sense. Nevertheless, given the importance of the dissertation as the ultimate degree requirement, and of publication as opposed to oratory or verbal disputation for scholarly

advancement, it seems reasonable to contend that in this as in most other things, English long has been and certainly is now a writing-based discipline.

5. The program proposal describes the course as follows: "'Composition Theory' . . . focuses on the contributions of a variety of theoreticians and researchers in the field: classical rhetoricians, philosophers, ethnographers, empiricists, clinicians, cognitive psychologists, linguists, and literary theorists. It asks whether such a contentious theoretical polyglot can be harmonized and, if not, what issues from the disputation" (11).

6. John Schilb's review is representative on this point:

> Although [Phelps] wants to identify leading assumptions of composition theory and then connect them to the specific exigencies of teaching, Phelps' book is highly selective and utterly recondite, insistently echoing the terminology of hermeneutics, phenomenology, cognitive psychology, and physics. It's more likely to be read, therefore, by those engaged with such discourses already [rather than by practicing teachers and graduate students]; indeed, I suspect even they'll get bogged down at times. Yet despite the difficulties of its style and certain related problems, *Composition as a Human Science* does make valuable contributions to the field's intellectual concerns. It's alternately exasperating and exciting. (163)

7. Peter Elbow focuses on what he calls personal expressive *writing*:

> Personal expressive writing happens to be one among many registers or discourses we can use for academic duty. Because personal writing invites feeling does not mean that it leaves out thinking; and because it invites attention to the self does not mean that it leaves out other people and the social connection. ("Forward" 10)

Like Elbow, we would reject the worst of the knee-jerk reactions the personal/expressive label tends to provoke, the automatic assumption that such writing is entirely undisciplined and self-indulgent and so has no place in the academy.

At the same time, we would prefer to designate it—as he does, at least in passing—as a *register* in order to avoid some of the more extreme (and essentially parallel) claims about its ostensible virtues: that, e.g., it is writing (unproblematically) "close to the self" or "authentic" and therefore (though these terms are usually left unarticulated) somehow arhetorical, artless. In short, we want to avoid what seems to have been the problematic tendency of claims about such writing to drift toward a kind of formalist absolute: to suggest that certain texts are "personal/expressive" because they have a particular relationship with the "self" of the writer, and that this relationship essentially *resides* in certain textual features, exercising its power—its expressivity, its authenticity—regardless of context.

8. The "Audience Categories" introduced by Britton et al. in *The Development of Writing Abilities (11–18)* characterize this relationship quite well under the heading of "Pupil to teacher, particular relationship": "Writing for a specifically 'educational adult'; a personal relationship but also a professional one, based upon a shared interest and expertise, an accumulating shared context" (overleaf). In this case, the professional dimension of the relationship is not fully developed, but nevertheless it is clearly there.

9. In Berkenkotter et al.'s case study, by contrast, one key measure of Nate's programmatic progress is precisely his ability to move away from what is characterized as "his expressive-writing background" (35).

10. It is important to note, however, that Phelps invites precisely this kind of speculation, even though the invitation is not cited in the response: "We need to explore deeply, through such methods as phenomenological inquiry and protocol analysis, exactly how changing interpretations of structure come into being and what their function is in the craft of writing or careful reading" (Phelps 156).

11. The catalogue description of the rubric:

> A study of texts, authors, or groups of authors in their historical contexts, and in relation to the critical traditions that have been built around, upon, or in ignorance of them. Why have certain writings, or aspects of writings, been regarded as more important than others (for instance Shakespeare in general, *Hamlet* in particular, certain readings of the play over others)? This course will be taught in a variety of ways, with, for example, reference to "neglected" writers (Clare, Burns, Smedley, Lourde) or to groupings of writers by race, gender, class, ethnicity" (*English Graduate Study* 17).

The particular version of the course Jeff enrolled in is described as follows:

The seminar will focus on contemporary British women novelists: Muriel Spark, Iris Murdoch, Anita Brookner, Jeanette
Winterson, Eva Figes, A.S. Byatt. While the center of the course
will entail reading, discussing, and writing about the novels
themselves, attention will be paid to the critical issue of a
woman's literary tradition—what tradition can be taken to
mean, whether it can belong to one sex, what the objections
are to the ideas of "reading as a woman" or "writing as a
woman" and how such contestation can help reshape our sense
of tradition, canon, and literary discourse, itself. One critical
seminar paper will be required, but for other papers creative
papers (reimagining scenes, characters, styles, even chapters
from the novels) will be welcome. ("Graduate Courses" Spring
1993 8)

12. The passage is from the book's Prologue:

The female imagination, if one may conceive of such a thing, is
my subject and guiding principle; this study depends upon psychological and literary awarenesses more than political ones. I
am trying to find the themes that have absorbed female minds
during the past three centuries as recorded in literature written
in English. Surely the mind has a sex, minds *learn* their sex—
and it is no derogation of the female variety to say so. At any
rate, for readily discernible historical reasons women have characteristically concerned themselves with matters more or less
peripheral to male concerns, or at least slightly skewed from
them. The differences between traditional female preoccupations and roles and male ones make a difference in female writing. Even if a woman wishes to demonstrate her essential
identity with male interests and ideas, the necessity of making
the demonstration, contradicting the stereotype, allies her initially with her sisters. And the complex nature of the sister-
hood emerges in the books it has produced. (7; Spacks's
emphasis)

Chapter Seven

1. No doubt there were frequently—even always—pressures to conform ideologically as well, although the term was not likely to have
been invoked very often. We also have the sense, however, that what
might have been characterized as ideological differences were more tol-
erable as long as they did not also insist on manifesting themselves in
topical, methodological, or especially formal divergence.

2. It has always been possible for students to satisfy these formal, topical, and broader methodological requirements without following the attendant behavioral strictures. A savvy academic writer—Borges comes to mind—can certainly construct some version of a plausible "paper" both "about" and "from" entirely nonexistent textual sources. In our experience, though, nearly all students follow most such behavioral strictures most of the time. Moreover, it is far from unheard of for instructors to work at reinforcing them (much as English teachers at lower levels do) by requiring annotated bibliographies, précis, outlines, and the like.

3. To be sure, the interview—especially the published interview, which is in any case something of a hybrid oral/print form—has gradually acquired a greater authority in various areas of English Studies. Nevertheless, the overwhelming bias in literary history, if only as a function of available technologies, is in favor of the written, and even more powerfully the printed, word.

4. The *MLA Style Manual* requires that all quotations be typed—like the rest of any manuscript—double-spaced. Presumably as a function of typeset presentations, however, a good many students at all levels seem inclined to single-space block quotations unless specifically instructed otherwise.

5. The 1995 Fourth Edition of the *MLA Handbook for Writers of Research Papers,* authored by Joseph Gibaldi, preserves this distinction. However, the index to the 1986 edition of the *MLA Style Manual* (Walter S. Achtert and Gibaldi)—clearly aimed at an audience of professional scholars—does not list this term.

6. It is worth noting that the final poem, "Collage," also opens with such an image: "Symmetrical columns, the structure of/the understandable, and no room for chance/(what our blueprints allow, we build)."

7. We got an earlier glimpse of students like this one in the poem "Room, subject, view," in which their mentor urged them to move away from tradition and toward some sort of individuality: "not so much toward what was never so well/as along the fissures, our discontents."

8. Garber's essay was written for the inaugural issue of a departmental newsletter called, with a certain obvious irony, *Second Thoughts,* which was created specifically as a forum for discussing this doctoral curriculum during the years after it had been approved by the department but before its approval by the State Education Department.

Chapter Eight

1. According to Robert A. Phillips Jr., Ph.D., the author of the Introduction and Epilogue to *When Rabbit Howls,* the book constitutes "an autobiography constructed by the various personalities"—more than ninety of them—existing within the body identified legally as Truddi Chase. Ostensibly, at least, these many personalities came into being (frequently without knowledge of one another) as the result of sexual abuse committed against their shared body, as it were, between the ages of two and sixteen. When the "first-born," a two-year old who may actually have been named Truddi Chase, could not deal with the trauma of such abuse—could not name and come to terms with what was happening to her—she "lived in a small recess, 'asleep,' and her place was taken by a succession of persons" (Phillips viii).

2. "Enough already, right? I'm sure I'll be writing more about this later—how cultures have always used imagic story to create and know the self, etc. I'll also be scanning my self-help books for specific ways they do this, if they do. Your comments will be most welcome" (Chepaitis 10).

3. According to Ramjerdi, "All writing not specifically cited by author is taken from my own journals, poetry, and fiction" ("Composition" 8). It is also worth noting that "Foucault on Foucault" and "Cicero on Cicero" are texts composed in other classes by combining passages from within each author's writings according to a randomizing selection process.

Chapter Nine

1. On a few occasions, students have mounted one sort of challenge or another to the default formal and methodological limits of this first part of the exam, but it seems to be quite difficult. Claudia Ricci, for example, whose subsequent dissertation would be a novel (*Sugarbush,* 1996), addresses the following as one of two questions:

> 1. Most of the critics on your [reading] list provide analysis of the difficulties that confront women writers and suggest ways out. Some of the suggestions are fairly tame, e.g., ensure that the traditional humanist respect for all individuals is truly extended to women. Others are more radical, e.g., rediscover the pre-oedipal wells of poetic inspiration that have been overlaid by patriarchal culture. Others variously advise disruptions of genre, embracing of the avant-garde, return to myth, reviving the landscape/writing space of the female body, etc. Does a

woman writer have to choose one of these ways? Or can several be combined? What, in fact, have your most successful female fictionists done?

Her answer begins with this rather self-consciously fictive, and thematically relevant, frame:

> She is Eva and she is sitting in the English Department's graduate library which doubles as an exam room. She says "mirrors," and in good magical poetic tradition, they appear, in front of her. She is Eva and she is facing a bank of mirrors that is the patriarchal reality she lives in. Behind her is a shelf, floor to ceiling, filled with handsome blue and gold books, books that form a tradition. Books that were written by men. Books that form a tradition that is behind her, in front of her. Books she cannot escape, not easily at least. (1)

After a break in the text signaled by extra spacing, she shifts into a more familiar exam mode:

> Question three asks me to evaluate whether women have to select one "way out" in trying to escape the patriarchal tradition. Or can women writers, conversely, combine several strategies for escaping master narratives. It is my firm belief that we must rely on as many strategies as possible in working against master narratives. We must be pluralistic (and exceedingly creative, stubborn and persistent and committed) in our approach to "escape."
>
> That's not to say, of course, that feminists are in perfect agreement on what this plurality of strategies looks like, or how it is achieved. Annette Kolodny, in "Dancing Through the Minefield," suggests that we must follow a multitude of paths within feminism. There are other prominent feminists, however, who say we need to strive for a unified approach; we need to establish "the feminine" within womens' writing traditions and move ahead with some kind of agenda based on that definition. (1)

Most of the rest of her six-page, single-spaced answer is devoted to a similar review/discussion of other relevant sources: Elaine Showalter (on gynocritism), Virginia Woolf (especially *Mrs. Dalloway*), H. D. (*HERmione*), Clarice Lispector, and so on. Thus, while she does return to the Eva narrative another four times, it serves more as a kind of framing commentary than as the centerpiece of the exam-as-text.

2. So, for example, Joanne aligns her work as a poet with such writers as Chase Twichell, Amy Gerstler, Carol Muske, and Tess Gallagher ("Qualifying" 19), while respectfully but firmly distancing it from what critics such as Sandra Gilbert and Alicia Ostriker, at least, understand to be the comparable efforts of such writers as Denise Levertov, Anne Sexton, Adrienne Rich, and Muriel Rukeyser (17).

3. The key official step in this process at Albany, as at most institutions, is gaining committee approval for a formal dissertation proposal.

4. That one title appears to be at least partly a function of local influence: Judith Fetterley's *The Resisting Reader*. There was also one author who appeared on all three lists, although not for the same publications: Nina Baym.

5. This is the day on which she learns of her husband's apparent sailing accident: "We returned today from the beach/at Viareggio where Trelwany showed us/the wreckage."

Chapter Ten

1. The figures on the bachelor's degrees are taken from "Facts and Figures," *ADE Bulletin* 110, Spring 1995. According to the note, the *Bulletin*'s sources were the *Digest of Education Statistics*: for 1949 to 1968, Table 169 of the 1987 edition; for 1970 to 1992, Table 276 of the 1994 edition; and for total degrees granted, Table 234 of the 1994 edition.

2. See, for example, "Doctoral Programs Decide That Smaller Is Better," *The Chronicle of Higher Education*, 26 February 1999, Section A, 12–13.

3. It doesn't hurt that these are also sound business practices. All of these proposals seem likely to improve the relationship between teaching assistants as organized labor and faculty, or at least departmental administrators, as management.

# WORKS CITED

Achtert, Walter S., and Joseph Gibaldi. 1985. *The MLA Style Manual.* New York: Modern Language Association.

Allen, Don Cameron. 1968. *The Ph.D. in English and American Literature.* New York: Holt, Rinehart and Winston.

Allison, Alexander W. et al. 1975. *The Norton Anthology of Poetry (Revised).* New York: Norton.

*American Heritage Dictionary of the English Language.* 1979. New College Edition. Boston: Houghton Mifflin.

Anderson, Lori. 1991. "Out on the Border." Unpublished manuscript.

Applebee, Arthur. 1974. *Tradition and Reform in the Teaching of English: A History.* Urbana, IL: National Council of Teachers of English.

Beck, Jennifer. 1995. "The Poetry Workshop 'after New Criticism.'" Unpublished manuscript, SUNY–Albany.

Berelson, Bernard. 1960. *Graduate Education in the United States.* New York: McGraw-Hill.

Berkenkotter, Carol, Thomas N. Huckin, and John Ackerman. 1988. "Conventions, Conversations, and the Writer: Case Study of a Student in a Rhetoric Ph.D. Program." *Research in the Teaching of English* 22.1 (February): 9–44.

Berlin, James. 1987. *Rhetoric and Reality: Writing Instruction in American Colleges, 1900–1985.* Carbondale: Southern Illinois University Press.

———. 1996. *Rhetorics, Poetics, and Cultures: Refiguring College English Studies.* Urbana, IL: National Council of Teachers of English.

Berry, R. M. 1994. "Theory, Creative Writing, and the Impertinence of History." In *Colors of a Different Horse: Rethinking Creative Writing Theory and Pedagogy,* ed. Wendy Bishop and Hans A. Ostrom, 57–76. Urbana, IL: National Council of Teachers of English.

Birr, Kendall A. 1994. *A Tradition of Excellence: The Sesquicentennial History of the University at Albany, State University of New York, 1844 to 1994*. Virginia Beach: Donning Company.

Bizzaro, Patrick. 1994. "Reading the Creative Writing Course: The Teacher's Many Selves." In *Colors of a Different Horse: Rethinking Creative Writing Theory and Pedagogy*, ed. Wendy Bishop and Hans A. Ostrom, 234–47. Urbana, IL: National Council of Teachers of English.

Bowen, William G., and Neil L. Rudenstine. 1992. *In Pursuit of the PhD*. Princeton, NJ: Princeton University Press.

Brereton, John, ed. 1995. *The Origins of Composition Studies in the American College, 1875–1925: A Documentary History*. Pittsburgh: Pittsburgh University Press.

Britton, James, Tony Burgess, Nancy Martin, Alex McLeod, and Harold Rosen. 1975. *The Development of Writing Abilities (11–18)*. London: Macmillan/Schools Council Publications.

Campbell, Oscar James. 1939. "The Failure of Freshman English." *English Journal* 28: 177–85.

Chepaitis, Barbara. n.d. Response paper, Constructions of Self and the Teaching of Writing (academic course). Unpublished manuscript, SUNY–Albany.

Coles, William E., Jr., and James Vopat. 1985. *What Makes Writing Good: A Multiperspective*. Lexington, MA: Heath.

Connors, Robert. 1991. "Rhetoric in the Modern University: The Creation of an Underclass." In *The Politics of Writing Instruction: Postsecondary*, ed. Richard Bullock, John Trimbur, and Charles Schuster, 55–84. Portsmouth, NH: Boynton/Cook.

Dillon, Millicent. 1989. "Jane Bowles: Experiment as Character." In *Breaking the Sequence: Women's Experimental Fiction*, ed. Ellen G. Friedman and Miriam Fuchs, 140–47. Princeton, NJ: Princeton University Press.

"Doctoral Programs Decide That Smaller Is Better." 1999. *Chronicle of Higher Education* (26 February): Sec. A, 12–13.

DuPlessis, Rachel Blau. 1985. "For the Etruscans." In *The New Feminist Criticism: Essays on Women, Literature, and Theory*, ed. Elaine Showalter, 271–91. New York: Pantheon.

Eastman, Arthur, ed. 1970. *Proceedings of the Wingspread Conference on the Doctor of Arts Degree, October 25–27, 1970.* Washington, DC: Council of Graduate Schools in the United States.

Elbow, Peter. 1990. "Forward: About Personal Expressive Academic Writing." *Pre-Text* 11.1-2 (Spring/Summer): 5–20.

———. 1990. *What Is English?* New York: Modern Language Association/National Council of Teachers of English.

*English Graduate Study, Department of English, University at Albany, SUNY: Master of Arts-Doctor of Philosophy.* n.d. (Departmental information, limited release.)

"Facts and Figures." 1995. *ADE Bulletin* 110 (Spring).

Fallon, Daniel. 1980. *The German University: A Heroic Ideal in Conflict with the Modern World.* Boulder: Colorado Associated University Press.

Farnan, Christiane. 1997. "A History of Recovery: 19th Century American Women Writers." Unpublished manuscript, SUNY–Albany.

Fetterley, Judith. 1978. *The Resisting Reader: A Feminist Approach to American Fiction.* Bloomington: Indiana University Press.

Franklin, Phyllis. 1984. "English Studies: The World of Scholarship in 1883." *PMLA* 99.3 (May): 356–70.

Gallagher, Chris. 1997. Qualifying Examination. Unpublished manuscript, SUNY–Albany.

———. 1998. "Reflexive Enquiry: Rethinking Pedagogy and Literacy." Ph.D. diss., SUNY–Albany.

Garber, Eugene. 1990. "Every Classroom a Nexus of Discourses." *Second Thoughts* (Spring): n.p.

Gates, Henry Louis, and Sunday Anozie. 1984. *Black Literature and Literary Theory.* New York: Methuen.

Gayley, Charles Mills. [1885] 1989. "English at the University of California." In *English in American Universities* [1885], ed. William Morton Payne. Reprinted in *The Origins of Literary Study in America,* ed. Gerald Graff and Michael Warner, 54–60. New York: Routledge.

Gibaldi, Joseph. 1995. *MLA Handbook for Writers of Research Papers.* 4th ed. New York: Modern Language Association.

Ginsberg, Warren. 1994. "Institutional Identity at the State University of New York at Albany: The New Ph.D. in English." In *English Studies/Culture Studies: Institutionalizing Dissent,* ed. Isaiah Smithson and Nancy Ruff, 157–66. Urbana: University of Illinois Press.

"Graduate Courses in English." 1991 (Spring). Department of English, SUNY–Albany.

———. 1991 (Fall). Department of English, SUNY–Albany.

———. 1992 (Fall). Department of English, SUNY–Albany.

———. 1993 (Spring). Department of English, SUNY–Albany.

Graff, Gerald. 1987. *Professing Literature: An Institutional History.* Chicago: University of Chicago Press.

Grigg, Charles M. 1965. *Graduate Education.* New York: Center for Applied Research in Education.

Harmon, Lindsey R., and Herbert Soldz, comps. 1963. *Doctorate Production in United States Universities, 1920–1962.* Washington, DC: National Academy of Sciences/National Research Council, Publication no. 1142.

Hart, James Morgan. [1874] 1989. *German Universities: A Narrative of Personal Experience.* Excerpted in *The Origins of Literary Study in America,* ed. Gerald Graff and Michael Warner, 17–24. New York: Routledge.

Huber, Bettina J. 1989. "Appendix: A Report on the 1986 Survey of English Doctoral Programs in Writing and Literature." In *The Future of Doctoral Studies in English,* ed. Andrea Lunsford, Helene Moglen, and James Slevin, 121–76. New York: Modern Language Association.

———. 1994. "The MLA's 1991–92 Survey of PhD Placement: The Latest English Findings and Trends through Time." *ADE Bulletin* 108 (Fall): 42–51.

———. 1995. "The MLA's 1993–94 Survey of PhD Placement: The Latest English Findings and Trends through Time." *ADE Bulletin* 112 (Winter): 40–51.

———. 1996. "Undergraduate English Programs: Findings from an MLA Survey of the 1991–92 Academic Year." *ADE Bulletin* 115 (Winter): 34–73.

James, William. 1903. "The Ph.D. Octopus." *Harvard Monthly* 36 (March): 1–9.

John, Walton C. 1935. *Graduate Study in Universities and Colleges in the United States.* Washington, DC: U.S. Government Printing Office.

Jones, Howard Mumford. 1930. "Graduate Study in English: Its Rationale." *Sewanee Review* 38: 465–76.

———. 1931. "Graduate English Study: Its Rationale." *Sewanee Review* 39: 68–79, 200–208.

Kahn, Wilma. 1990. "Cogitations of Phelps." Unpublished manuscript, SUNY–Albany.

Kelsh, Deb. 1990. "Spec[ulative] Essay. Phelps: *Composition as a Human Science.*" Unpublished manuscript, SUNY–Albany.

Kitzhaber, Albert R. 1990. *Rhetoric in American Colleges, 1850–1900.* Dallas: Southern Methodist University Press.

Knoblauch, C. H. 1991. "The Albany Graduate English Curriculum." ADE Bulletin 98 (Spring): 19–21.

Lane, Laura. 1990. Response paper to *Composition as a Human Science.* Unpublished manuscript, SUNY–Albany.

Latta, John. 1993. "Reading the *Biographia Literaria.*" Unpublished manuscript, SUNY–Albany.

Lloyd-Jones, Richard, and Andrea Lunsford, eds. 1989. *The English Coalition Conference: Democracy through Language.* New York: Modern Language Association/National Council of Teachers of English.

Lunsford, Andrea, Helene Moglen, and James Slevin, eds. 1989. *The Future of Doctoral Studies in English.* New York: Modern Language Association.

Maclean, Ron. n.d. "The Source of Streets" [poem]. Unpublished manuscript, SUNY–Albany.

———. 1991. "Letter from the Kahn." Unpublished manuscript, SUNY–Albany.

———. 1991. "Structures." Unpublished manuscript, SUNY–Albany.

———. 1991. "What My Book Is About, and What That Has to Do with This Class." Unpublished manuscript, SUNY–Albany.

———. 1992. "Nexus." Unpublished manuscript, SUNY–Albany.

Miller, Susan. 1991. *Textual Carnivals: The Politics of Composition.* Carbondale: Southern Illinois University Press.

MLA Committee on Professional Employment. 1998. "Final Report" *ADE Bulletin* 119 (Spring): 27–45.

Moglen, Helene. 1989. "Crossing the Boundaries: Interdisciplinary Education at the Graduate Level." In *The Future of Doctoral Studies in English,* ed. Andrea Lunsford, Helene Moglen, and James Slevin, 84–90. New York: Modern Language Association.

Myers, D. G. 1996. *The Elephants Teach: Creative Writing Since 1880.* Englewood Cliffs, NJ: Prentice-Hall.

National Academy of Sciences/National Research Council. 1956. *The Baccalaureate Origins of Doctorates in the Arts, Humanities, and Social Sciences Awarded in the United States from 1936 to 1950 Inclusive.* Comp. by the Office of Scientific Personnel. Washington, DC: National Academy of Sciences/National Research Council.

North, Stephen M. 1987. *The Making of Knowledge in Composition: Portrait of an Emerging Field.* Upper Montclair, NJ: Boynton/Cook.

Paulsen, Friedrich. 1908. *German Education: Past and Present.* Trans. T. Lorenz. New York: Charles Scribner's Sons.

Payne, William Morton, ed. 1895. *English in American Universities.* Boston: D. C. Heath.

Perry, Bliss. 1935. *And Gladly Teach: Reminiscences.* Boston: Houghton Mifflin.

Phelps, Louise Wetherbee. 1988. *Composition as a Human Science: Contributions to the Self-Understanding of a Discipline.* New York: Oxford University Press.

Phillips, Robert A. Jr. 1987. Introduction; Epilogue. In *When Rabbit Howls* by Truddi Chase. New York: Dutton.

Post, Jonathan. 1994. "The Container of Collective Performance: Theory and Practice for Teachers and Practitioners." D.A. diss., SUNY–Albany.

"Proposal for a Ph.D. in English." 1992. The University at Albany, State University of New York. Unpublished.

Rabine, Brenda-Lee, and Lois Dellert Raskin. 1997. "Multivocalities: Writing in the Disciplines at SUNYA." Unpublished manuscript, SUNY–Albany.

Ramjerdi, Jan. 1990. "Composition." Unpublished manuscript, SUNY–Albany.

————. 1990. "Response: Jasper Neel's *Plato, Derrida, and Writing.* Unpublished manuscript, SUNY–Albany.

Rasula, Jed. 1996. *The American Poetry Wax Museum: Reality Effects, 1940–1990.* Urbana, IL: National Council of Teachers of English.

Ray, Ruth. 1993. *The Practice of Theory: Teacher Research in Composition.* Urbana, IL: National Council of Teachers of English.

*Rhetoric Review.* 1994. Special Issue on Doctoral Programs in Rhetoric and Composition 12.2 (Spring).

Ricci, Claudia. 1996. Qualifying Examination, Part I. Unpublished manuscript, SUNY–Albany.

Rice, Warner G. 1962. "Teachers of College English: Preparation: Supply and Demand." *College English* 23: 470–76.

Russell, David R. 1991. *Writing in the Academic Disciplines, 1870–1990: A Curricular History.* Carbondale: Southern Illinois University Press.

Samuel, R. H., and R. Hinton Thomas. 1949. *Education and Society in Modern Germany.* New York: Routledge.

Schilb, John. 1989. Review of *Composition as a Human Science: Contributions to the Self-Understanding of a Discipline* by Louise Wetherbee Phelps. *Rhetoric Review* 8.1 (Fall): 162–66.

Schoch, Amy. n.d. "Check-out Time Is Always Already." Unpublished manuscript, SUNY–Albany.

Sherman, Stuart P. [1913] 1989. "Professor Kittredge and the Teaching of English." In *The Origins of Literary Studies in America,* ed. Gerald Graff and Michael Warner, 147–55. New York: Routledge.

Shumway, David. 1994. *Creating American Civilization: A Genealogy of American Literature as an Academic Discipline.* American Culture series, vol. 11. Minneapolis: University of Minnesota Press.

Simpson, David. 1991. "Teaching English: What and Where Is the Cutting Edge?" *ADE Bulletin* 98 (Spring): 14–18.

Slevin, James. 1989. "Conceptual Frameworks and Curricular Arrangements: A Response." In *The Future of Doctoral Studies in English,* ed. Andrea Lunsford, Helene Moglen, and James Slevin, 30–39. New York: Modern Language Association.

Smitherman, Geneva. 1977. *Talkin and Testifyin: The Language of Black America.* Detroit: Wayne State University Press.

Solomon, Barbara Miller. 1985. *In the Company of Educated Women: A History of Women and Higher Education in America.* New Haven, CT: Yale University Press.

Sosnoski, James. 1994. *Token Professionals and Master Critics: A Critique of Orthodoxy in Literary Studies.* Albany: State University of New York Press.

Spacks, Patricia Meyer. 1975. *The Female Imagination.* New York: Knopf.

"Statement from the Conference on the Growing Use of Part-Time and Adjunct Faculty." 1998. *ADE Bulletin* 119 (Spring): 19–26.

Storr, Richard J. 1953. *The Beginnings of Graduate Education in America.* Chicago: University of Chicago Press.

Sustana, Catherine. 1996. Qualifying Examination. Unpublished manuscript, SUNY–Albany.

———. 1997. "Letters in Excess: Cross-Genre Investigations in Sentimentality, Feminist Poetics, and Counterhistory." Ph.D. diss., SUNY–Albany.

Tangorra, Joanne. 1994. Qualifying Examination. Unpublished manuscript, SUNY–Albany.

———. 1995. "Waterborne: Poems, Poetics, and Pedagogy." Ph.D. diss., SUNY–Albany.

Thwing, Charles Franklin. 1928. *The American and the German University: One Hundred Years History.* New York: Macmillan Company.

Troops for Truddi Chase, The. 1987. *When Rabbit Howls.* New York: Dutton.

Vanderbilt, Kermit. 1986. *American Literature and the Academy: The Roots, Growth, and Maturity of a Profession.* Philadelphia: University of Pennsylvania Press.

Van Schaick, Jeffery. n.d. Response paper to *Excellent Women.* Unpublished manuscript, SUNY–Albany.

Varnum, Robin. 1996. *Fencing with Words: A History of Writing Instruction at Amherst College during the Era of Theodore Baird, 1938–1966.* Urbana, IL: National Council of Teachers of English.

Vitanza, Victor. 1987. "Critical Sub/Versions of the History of Philosophical Rhetoric." *Rhetoric Review* 6.1: 41–66.

Waller, Gary. 1989. "Polylogue: Reading, Writing, and the Structure of Doctoral Study." In *The Future of Doctoral Studies in English,* ed. Andrea Lunsford, Helene Moglen, and James Slevin, 111–20. New York: Modern Language Association.

Watkins, Evan. 1989. *Work Time: English Departments and the Circulation of Cultural Value.* Stanford: Stanford University Press.

Wellek, Rene, and Austin Warren. 1942, 1947, 1949. *Theory of Literature.* New York: Harcourt, Brace.

Wilbers, Stephen. 1980. *The Iowa Writers' Workshop: Origins, Emergence & Growth.* Iowa City: University of Iowa Press.

# INDEX

*Concert of Tenses, A* (Gallagher), 196
Conference of Secondary School English Department Chairs, 272n. 3
Conference on College Composition and Communication, 272n. 3
Conference on English Education, 272n. 3
conformity, 129, 279–280nn. 1–2. *See also* formal conformity; methodological conformity; topical conformity
Connors, Robert, 5, 9, 41, 99, 101–102, 266n. 11
conservatism, 62
constraint, freedom balanced with, 159–160
Constructions of Self in the Teaching of Writing course, 167–177, 190
"Container of Collective Performance, The" (Post), 191
contemporary writers perspective project, 143–153
contracting out, 234
"Conventions, Conversations, and the Writer" (Berkenkotter), 263n. 1
convergence of constituent discourses, 164–165, 176–177, 184–185
core introductory courses, 92
Cornell University, 268n. 1, 268n. 19
corporate compassion, 68–69
corporate compromise strategy, 71–73, 77, 93–94, 96, 253–254
corporate economy. *See* College English Teaching, Inc.
corporate voice-over, 135, 138, 146
Crane, R. S., 13
*Creating American Civilization* (Shumway), 131–132

creative writing
  equality of status, 93
  graduate course offerings, 274n. 4
  perspectives, 131
  program emphases in, 54
  as qualifying examination topic, 207
  writing perspectives, 102–104
*Creative Writing in America* (Moxley), 167
Cremin, Lawrence, 145n. 1
*Criterion,* 103
critical literacy, 222–225
critical pedagogy, 210–215, 221, 222–225
critical pluralism, 272–273n. 6
"Critical Promise, A" (Ferruci), 230
"Critical Sub/Version" (Vitanza), 112–113
critical theory, 54, 65, 207, 272–273n. 6
"Crossing the Boundaries" (Moglen), 76
Cubberly, Ray Ellsworth, 213
Culler, Jonathan, 71
culling process, 30–34
cultural studies, 54
Cummins, Maria Susanna, 133, 136, 137, 141, 207
curriculum. *See also* Magisterial curriculum
  dispute over, 63–66, 68–77
  division into new specialties, 69
  fusion-based, 109, 228, 255–256

"Dancing Through the Minefield" (Kolodny), 281–282n. 1
Danforth Foundation, 47, 273n. 7
Dartmouth Seminar, National Council of Teachers of English, 138
Davidson, Lâle, 168

# AUTHOR

**Stephen M. North** is professor of English at the University at Albany, State University of New York, where he has directed both the Writing Program and the Writing Center. He is the author of *The Making of Knowledge in Composition: Portrait of an Emerging Field*, founding co-editor of *The Writing Center Journal*, and founding editor of the Refiguring English Studies series. His writings have appeared in *College English, College Composition and Communication, Writing on the Edge, Rhetoric Review, Research in the Teaching of English*, and a variety of other venues.

# CONTRIBUTORS

**Barbara A. Chepaitis** is author of the novels *The Fear Principle* and *The Fear of God* and co-author of the novel *Feeding Christine* (with Lâle Davidson, SuEllen Hamkins, and Cindy Parrish). She is a member of the performance group Archetext, which takes writing off the page and onto the stage, and of the storytelling group The Snickering Witches. She is recipient of an Associated Writing Programs Intro Award for her short fiction, and past editor of *13th Moon*. Currently she is a lecturer at the University at Albany, State University of New York, and runs workshops in storytelling, writing, creative chaos, and other forms of kinetic pedagogy.

**David Coogan** is assistant professor of English in the Department of Humanities at the Illinois Institute of Technology, where he teaches courses in composition, rhetorical theory, technical communications, and poetry. He is the author of *Electronic Writing Centers: Computing the Field of Composition* and of several essays on computers and writing centers in such publications as *Computers and Composition* and *Wiring the Writing Center*. His current work explores the intersections among rhetorical theory, technical communications, and the various discourses surrounding engineering, science, and technology.

**Lâle Davidson** is a fiction writer, professor of creative writing at Adirondack Community College, and past fiction editor of *The Little Magazine*. Her short story "The Haunting of Zelda" was turned into an opera and premiered at OperaDelaware in December 1998. She is part of two collaborative performance groups: The Snickering Witches and Archetext, and she collaborated on the novel *Feeding Christine*, co-authored with Barbara Chepaitis, SuEllen Hamkins, and Cindy Parrish. Her short stories have been published in *The North American Review*, *Phoebe*, and *Library Bound: An Anthology of Saratoga Writers*. She has recently completed her first novel, *The CIphery*, and is working on her second, about the language of trees.

Contributors

Ron MacLean's award-winning short fiction has appeared in *GQ*, *Greensboro Review, Prism International*, and elsewhere. In his alternate life as an Internet marketing consultant/information architect, he has worked on Web sites for IBM, American Express, Olympus, and others. He holds a Doctor of Arts from the University at Albany, State University of New York, and enjoys teaching occasionally as opportunity allows. He has just completed a novel, *Blue Winnetka Skies*.

Cindy L. Parrish is a faculty lecturer with Project Renaissance, a first-year, interdisciplinary live-and-learn project at the University at Albany, State University of New York. From 1994 to 1998, she taught at Simon's Rock College in Great Barrington, Massachusetts, in the English and Theatre departments, where she also founded and directed the Simon's Rock Writing Center. A writer of screenplays and novels, she recently collaborated on *Feeding Christine* (with Barbara Chepaitis, Lâle Davidson, and SuEllen Hamkins), which will be published in 2000. She lives in Cherry Plain, New York, with her husband, Jonathan Post, and daughters Emma (age 5) and Fiona (age 2), in the round cordwood house they built together by hand.

Jonathan Post grew up overseas, mainly in Africa, where he attended Waterford/Kamhlaba and where his classmates included Theresa Tutu and Zinzi Mandela. He earned his B.A. in English from Antioch College, taking a year off from that project to work on oil rigs in Wyoming. At various times, he has done office work in New York City, served as project manager for a not-for-profit construction company, and directed a Mohawk Indian not-for-profit organization called The Tree of Peace Society, founded by Chief Jake Swamp. He currently teaches full time at the University at Cobleskill, State University of New York, writes fiction and poetry, does storytelling, and continues to present at conferences on the uses of performance. He is at work on a book about performance that will be written collaboratively with members of the performance collective, Archetext. He lives in Cherry Plain, New York with his wife, Cindy Parrish, and daughters Emma (age 5) and Fiona (age 2), in the round cordwood house they built together by hand.

Beth Weatherby's first book, *Small Invasions* (Plains Press), won the 1998 Minnesota Book Award for short fiction. Also in 1998, she was selected by the McKnight Foundation for a fellowship to attend an international seminar in Salzburg, Austria, on the contemporary novel. The first chapter of her novel-in-progress, *Curved World*, won a 1997 Loft-McKnight Award. She is associate professor of English at Southwest State University in Marshall, Minnesota, and has directed the creative writing program there since 1992. She received an undergraduate degree in journalism from the Medill School of Journalism, Northwestern University, in Evanston, Illinois. Her doctorate in English is from the University at Albany, State University of New York. Her stories have been published in magazines and journals, including *The Little Magazine, 13th Moon, Short Story, The Wolf Head Quarterly, River Oak Review,* and *Eureka Literary Magazine.*

*This book was typeset in Adobe Sabon.*
*The typeface used on the cover was Trade Gothic.*
*The book was printed by Versa Press.*